THE U.S. MILITARY ONLINE

THE U.S. MILITARY ONLINE

A Directory for Internet Access
to the Department of Defense

2nd Edition

William M. Arkin

BRASSEY'S

Washington • London

A NATIONAL SECURITY ARCHIVE BOOK

Editorial Offices:	**Order Department:**
22883 Quicksilver Drive	P.O. Box 960
Dulles, VA 20166	Herndon, VA 20172

Brassey's books are available at special discounts for bulk purchases for sales promotions,
premiums, fund-raising, or educational use.

Library of Congress Cataloging-in-Publication Data

Arkin, William M.
    The U.S. military online : a directory for Internet access to the
Department of Defense / William M. Arkin. — 2nd ed.
        p.   cm.
    Includes index.
    ISBN 1-57488-178-7
    1. United States. Dept. of Defense—Computer network resources—Directories.
    2. Web sites—Directories. I. Title. II. Title: United States military online.
    UA23.3.A85   1998
    025.06'355'00973—DC21   98-22207
                                                                                    CIP

10 9 8 7 6 5 4 3 2 1
Printed in Canada.

Contents

Introduction and Overview

They say that the average Internet address lasts just 40 days before it changes or disappears, which certainly makes a written guide to sites on the Net a difficult endeavor. However, since this guide is about the ".mil" domain—that part of the Internet that is used exclusively by the U.S. military—and since the U.S. military is a disciplined and hierarchical organization, the task is not impossible. Still, the Internet has a fleeting quality and the U.S. military has its own culture of constant reorganization (and it is in the midst of a major post–Cold War downsizing, adding to the turbulence). Hence a directory needs frequent revision.

The U.S. military's embrace of the Net means that every aspect of the incredibly complex organization is represented online. Since the first edition of this guide was published in 1997, use of the World Wide Web for so-called "public affairs" and internal communications and for basic business has continued to expand. The list of commands or bases that don't have a public Internet presence is getting very small, and the scope of activity on the Net is so broad now that even a directory of this size covers only the top-level and most publicly relevant sites, ignoring much specialized material "below."

Through the Internet, gaining access to the U.S. military and its enormous storehouse of military information has become easier than it has ever been. As some online initiatives gather steam (for example, electronic commerce, electronic reading rooms, Freedom of Information access, and "paperless" publishing), the public benefits also grow enormously. Probably only a year or so ago it was remarkable to note that speeches by Defense Department and military service officials, press releases, and fact sheets were available online 24 hours a day, seven days a week. But now the novelty of online PR has waned, and it is the regulations and manuals, studies, program descriptions and documents, budget data and business solicitations, and databases and search engines that are the guts of Internet content, particularly in terms of a public service by the U.S. government.

In the first edition, I remarked that the military, having invented the Internet, was quietly leading the Internet revolution, linking virtually every base and facility, command and office, unit and major ship to the World Wide Web. Now the commercial revolution has overshadowed this effort, and the big business of the Internet has left even an organization like the Pentagon scrambling to catch up technologically. "Commercial off-the-shelf" is not just a buzz phrase, it is a matter of survival. It is in the area of information technology that the U.S. government finds itself trailing civilian developments, with the Internet being just a small public slice of the activity.

The intense competition for consumer business on the Net and the extraordinary growth of the Internet overall relegate noncommercial and specialized Web activity to secondary status. That is to say, it is no longer economical or even technically possible for the commercial search engines to index everything that is online, nor to do so in a timely and reliable manner. For a segment of the Internet such as the .mil domain, the result is that much material goes largely unindexed by the commercial businesses and is consequently more difficult to find. Couple this commercial reality with the increasing use of databases and other types of special (non-HTML) materials connected to the Web that cannot be indexed, and you have a growing cache of hidden riches, much of it unknown except to a small circle of users.

The *U.S. Military Online* is not a how-to guide to accessing or using the Internet or an exhaustive listing of resources available on it. It is instead a decoding of the U.S. military and its information assets as represented by hundreds of bases, commands, and activities, presented, it is hoped, in easily accessible form—by organization, subject matter, and geographic location. Because I believe that the Internet does not threaten the end of the printed word, a variety of means are presented for contacting military establishments, whether by good old-fashioned telephone and postal service or via E-mail. This book is thus also a general directory of the U.S. military that will be useful to any scholarly researcher, journalist, librarian, or active citizen hoping to comprehend America's most influential institution.

Below the hierarchical level of major headquarters and commands, there are hundreds upon hundreds of additional "homepages" dealing with ever more specialized and obscure matters. I hope that the basic organization and geographic guideposts can direct the user to these sites even when they are not individually listed.

Conventions Used in the Guide

The World Wide Web (WWW; "Web") is a hypertext-based communications system that links together sites and files across the Internet. With a Windows-based operating system and a Web "browser" (e.g., Netscape Navigator), hypertext allows the user to click on an underlined or highlighted link to move to another site, page, or file. It has quickly become the dominant means for sharing information, and though there are some File Transfer Protocol (FTP) and Gopher sites listed in this guide, it is clearly the dominant protocol. The only other protocol relevant at all for the .mil user is Telnet, which is a computer-to-computer protocol that allows direct connections into remote computer systems. It is particularly common for remote access to library card catalogs.

Throughout this directory, Internet addresses (called Uniform Resource Locators or URLs officially) of World Wide Web, Gopher, Telnet, and FTP sites are presented in GillSans type (e.g., http://www.dtic.mil/defenselink/). A number of other icons and conventions are used to provide information compactly:

 BASE SCHEDULED TO CLOSE $ COMMERCIAL, BUSINESS OPPORTUNITY   E-MAIL ADDRESS    INTERNAL SEARCH ENGINE

☎ Telephone number

✉ E-mail address

⧗ Base scheduled to close

NEW New listing in this edition

⌕ Internal search engine

★ Recommended site

$ Commercial or business opportunity site

📖 Publications repository or library

✎ Online fact sheet

In this edition, I've designated over 50 sites as my favorites, because of the content of the sites, the presentation of materials, and the frequency of revisions and changes.

For each organization (e.g., Air Force Materiel Command), the common identifying acronym is added in parentheses (e.g., AFMC), followed by the major command the organization or unit is subordinate to (if it is below the service or DOD level).

When multiple homepages or units are nested together because of the geographic proximity or organizational relationship, hierarchy is designated by indenting subordinate organizations and Internet sites. Thus, a typical entry designates an organization as follows:

Air Force Development Test Center (AFDTC) (AFMC)
http://www.eglin.af.mil/afdtc/afdtc.html

46th Test Wing
http://tw1.eglin.af.mil/

(The Air Force Development Test Center is subordinate to the Air Force Materiel Command, and the 46th Test Wing is subordinate to the AFDTC.)

When a login or username—the word or code needed to access a site—is required, what must be typed in is shown in Times Roman Italic type in brackets (e.g., *Username: <AFITPAC>*). Passwords are shown in the same way.

Note that multiple homepages are often listed for a single command or installation. In some cases, the addresses go to the same homepages. In others, they go to different servers (and when one is busy or down another can be used).

For convenience, I include the entire URL, including the prefix "http://" even though it is no longer necessary to type this into a modern browser. Also, there are no spaces in Internet addresses. When the address is too long to fit on one type line and has been extended onto the next line, the entire address should be typed as if it were one line. Internet addresses never end with a period (.), so addresses that appear at the ends of sentences should be typed without the period.

 NEW LISTING IN THIS EDITION    ONLINE FACT SHEET   PUBLICATION REPOSITORY OR LIBRARY   RECOMMENDED SITE   TELEPHONE NUMBER

Contents

The Directory is in three main parts, and the military establishment is presented by organization, subject, and location. The Department of Defense is made up of the three military departments (Army, Navy, and Air Force) and a number of defense agencies. The four armed services are subordinate to the military departments (the Marine Corps is subordinate to the Department of the Navy). While the military departments are responsible for recruiting, training, and equipping the armed forces, military units are assigned to one of nine unified commands during actual operations. Five of these are regional (e.g., European Command, Pacific Command) and four have global responsibilities (e.g., Transportation Command). Each of the military departments is itself organized along similar staff lines (e.g., personnel, intelligence, operations) and contains major commands and agencies, as well as operating forces.

Geographically, the Defense Department manages more than 500 major installations and properties in the United States, with an equal number of generally smaller facilities located overseas. As the department continues to shrink after the Cold War, the number of properties (and activities) also shrinks. In recent years, the DOD has closed more than 200 major bases. Because the U.S. military is undergoing such a significant drawdown, this guide takes into consideration anticipated base closings and consolidations, designating bases and/or organizations slated for closure or consolidation.

Given the ever shifting nature of the military, it is as important to know how to find something online as it is to rely on the snapshot provided in this directory. Chapter 1 provides background on general search tools of the Internet, as well as descriptions of the mega-directories that will be useful for finding Internet assets (including official Web indexes maintained by the military as well as some commercial services). Sources for understanding military acronyms and terminology are provided, as well as the means to locate military personnel, related associations, biographies, fact sheets, photos, etc.

Chapter 2 highlights the most prominent homepages ("gateways") maintained by the Defense Department (DefenseLINK) and the services (AirForceLINK, ArmyLINK, Navy-Online, MarineLINK), as well as some mega-pages of note, such as the Defense Technical Information Center (DTIC). Given the decentralized and complex nature of the military, official gateways are hardly comprehensive directories of subordinate bases and organizations. Under each entity in Chapter 2 are some of the more popular public affairs resources, such as the many military news services available online at websites and the growing number of Pentagon-published magazines and journals, the full text of which is freely available online.

Chapter 3 covers the impressive array of official think tanks, schools, libraries, and military history collections. These institutions are of the greatest value to the social science researcher or journalist, for they deal with subjects ranging from military sociology to international relations. The think tanks and academic institutions of the military tend to have excellent websites with plenty of useful information (e.g., reports, bibliographies, and analysis) online. The extensive military history establishment is far behind the think tanks

 BASE SCHEDULED TO CLOSE

 COMMERCIAL, BUSINESS OPPORTUNITY

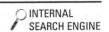 E-MAIL ADDRESS

INTERNAL SEARCH ENGINE

and schools in terms of resources online, though the day of online historical documents and finding aids is not far away. Finally, the major military libraries with publicly accessible online catalogs and other Internet materials are listed, with instructions for online access. Some of the collections are truly unique.

Chapter 4 covers defense policies, weapons information, and other high-profile war-fighting and doctrinal initiatives. Tracking current military policy is now feasible online, and the official doctrine of the military, in the form of joint publications, field manuals, and naval warfare publications, is increasingly accessible in full text. What is more, Defense Department directives and regulations, as well as an increasing array of service regulations, publications, and forms, are also being placed online.

Chapter 5, which is new with this edition, covers the business of the Defense Department. This includes resources for tracking the defense budget and the Defense Department's research, development, test, evaluation, and contracting activities.

Chapters 6, 7, 8, and 9 are thorough explanations of Defense Department organization and online access. Chapter 6 proceeds, more or less hierarchically, through the Defense Department headquarters, the Office of the Secretary of Defense, defense agencies, and DOD field activities, followed by the Joint Chiefs of Staff and unified commands. Chapters 7, 8, and 9 repeat the process for the Departments of the Air Force, Army, and Navy. For each service, the Office of the Secretary and the Chiefs are described, as are the headquarters staff, major commands, field operating agencies, and operating forces. For major commands and agencies, full descriptions of online resources are provided in these chapters.

Chapters 10 and 11 list, state by state and country by country, major military installations in the United States and overseas, including a description of the commands, activities, and units at each facility. The coverage is only of major active duty organizations and facilities. For brevity, only military units at higher echelons are included (that is, generally down to wing level in the Air Force, division and separate brigade in the Army, regiment in the Marines, wing and group level in the Navy). Many of the base or headquarters homepages listed provide links to further subordinate units and activities.

The United States maintains military bases and facilities in more than 50 overseas countries and territories. Most are minor communications, surveillance, and testing-related activities connected to the materiel commands and laboratories. They do not currently have any online connections. Others are major congregations of U.S. forces, such as in Germany, Japan, and Korea. But the hundreds of military facilities located in these countries during the Cold War are being significantly reduced.

Acknowledgments

This project began partly as a result of my departure from Washington and my subsequent curiosity about the usefulness of the Internet for serious research. I am particularly indebted to Tom Blanton, Director of the National Security Archive in Washington, for financing the

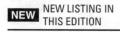 NEW LISTING IN THIS EDITION   ONLINE FACT SHEET    PUBLICATION REPOSITORY OR LIBRARY   RECOMMENDED SITE   TELEPHONE NUMBER

first edition. Special thanks as always to Stan Norris, colleague and confidant extraordinaire. Wayne Nail of Sassy Computers continued to be my systems adviser. Brassey's quickly embraced the concept of a directory in 1996, and particular thanks go to Don McKeon and Betsy Qualls for their work on the first edition, as well as to Tom Hall for the initial design of the book. Don and Kim Borchard have been enthusiastic supporters of this second edition. Special thanks to my friends at NBC, MSNBC, and *The Washington Post,* particularly Jen Belton, Leslie Walker, and Bob Windrem, and to Eliot Cohen and Andy Bacevich, all for their enthusiasm about the Internet and their support of my work. Numerous webmasters of the military have contacted me over the past year with thoughts, complaints, suggestions, etc. I appreciate all the communications. Special thanks to Jim Knotts, DOD webmaster.

On a personal note, thanks to my wife, Susan Horn, who is now online herself and thus somewhat more tolerant, though I suspect she still thinks I've lost my mind. My daughter Rikki, almost four, doesn't much care about the subject matter at hand, but has seen Arthur online, so she knows the Internet is for real.

This directory will likely be revised again. Errors in addresses and other mistakes and unintended slights to the pride of military units and organizations are, of course, all my doing. My E-mail address is warkin@igc.org

Any word about new sites or changes to sites, as well as comments about homepage content and importance, would be appreciated and welcome.

Finding the U.S. Military
on the Internet

With the Web now exceeding 300 million pages, there is no longer any comprehensive index or search engine for what's online. There is no comprehensive government or Defense Department search database of note, and the DOD itself readily admits that it does not know how many public Internet sites it maintains. What is more, military sites are themselves a mix of open pages, password-protected pages, and restricted sites. Add to this a growing "hidden Internet"—databases and a vast array of information that is not in the form of hypertext markup language (HTML) documents and therefore is largely inaccessible to automated search engines—and more than ever it is difficult to find information.

The big commercial search engines, themselves locked in fierce competition for users, also focus more and more on consumer services (e.g., delivery of news, entertainment, and E-mail) rather than scouring all of the nooks and crannies of the Web to build ever larger indexes. This is understandable on another count, for the major complaint of most Internet users is too much information, not too little. "Popular" sites are indexed completely and with great frequency to keep the search engines "fresh," but many—perhaps hundreds—of sites in the .mil domain are increasingly left behind.

Still, search engines remain the essential tools to find material on the Internet. The big five—AltaVista, Excite, HotBot, Infoseek, and Lycos—dominate the field and are central to research in the .mil domain. But a host of other services are also needed: specialized search engines, general and specialized directories and catalogs of websites (specialized link bibliographies), and, increasingly, the internal search engines of individual websites. One of the biggest innovations in the .mil domain over the past year has been the introduction of these internal search engines (throughout the Directory the sites with these search engines are designated with a $\wp$). As websites themselves become bigger and more complex, and also serve as gateways to databases, such as publications repositories, search engines are needed to find materials. The internal engines are invariably more inclusive and up-to-date than any Web-wide resource, and in the .mil domain, they often index material that is otherwise not cataloged at all.

Search Fundamentals

Internet-wide search services can be categorized in four basic groups: the big five large search engines, Web-wide directories, "metasearch" sites that aggregate the results of many search engines, and specialized search sites for specific tasks.

The big five Web-wide search engines are huge automated systems that rely on "spiders" or "bots" to troll the Internet, compiling databases that are then searchable by keyword. Though they vary in size, in the protocols for use, and in their freshness, they all exceed 50 million pages of material (the largest are well over 100 million), and each has attributes that distinguish it from the others.

Directories differ from search engines in that they are subject catalogs of web resources, created manually by people. The largest of these indexes (Yahoo! and Infoseek) are beyond the size for much selectivity. Smaller catalogs (e.g., Magellan and Lycos) can be more selective and also often offer in-depth reviews.

Metasearch sites parse out searches to more than one search engine or directory at the same time. A profusion of these sites—All-in-One, Mamma, MetaCrawler, Savvy Search—are attempting to tap the combined wisdom of the individual search services. They are good for very precise searches and when other search tools fail, particularly to check whether some nugget of information is available anywhere.

The various search services not only index the Web, but also include access to information in Gopher, File Transfer Protocol (FTP), Telnet, and newsgroup (USENET) sites.

Web-wide Search Engines

Alta Vista Search Engine
   http://altavista.digital.com/

Excite Search
   http://www.excite.com/

HotBot
   http://www.hotbot.com/

Infoseek Guide
   http://www.infoseek.com/

Lycos
   http://www.lycos.com/

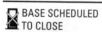 

Web Directories

Magellan
http://www.mckinley.com

Yahoo!
http://www.yahoo.com/

Metasearch Engines

All in One Search Page
http://www.albany.net/allinone/

Dogpile
http://www.dogpile.com/

Inference Find
http://www.inference.com/ifind/

Mamma
http://www.mamma.com/

MetaCrawler Searching
http://www.metacrawler.com/

Metafind
http://www.metafind.com/

SavvySearch
http://savvy.cs.colostate.edu:2000/form

Though the major search engines all have conventions to limit searches by domain, allowing retrieval only of official information—i.e., in the .gov (U.S. government), .mil (U.S. military), and .int (international governmental organization) domains—the GovBot Database of Government Web Sites (http://cobar.cs.umass.edu/ciirdemo/Govbot/) is a search engine exclusively of U.S. government sites. Its depth is not as great as that of AltaVista or HotBot, but it does have the advantage of specialization, particularly as the big search engines increasingly are unable to index everything on the Web, or uninterested in doing so.

The Defense Department itself does not maintain anything close to a .mil-wide search engine, but the DefenseLink site (http://www.defenselink.mil) offers a frequently updated internal search engine that includes press releases, transcripts, statements, and contract announcements. The Defense Technical Information Center (DTIC) Catalog Search (http://www-cat.dtic.mil:8883/cgi-bin/search.cgi/x-catalog:/www-cat.dtic.mil:8883/

catalog-o) searches the extensive collection of the military's main server. The Center for Army Lessons Learned (CALL) Broad Catalog Search engine (http://call.army.mil:1180/cgi-bin/search.cgi/x-catalog:/call.army.mil:1180/CALL) pulls together the web resources of numerous Army sites, including the main academic institutions.

Military-Oriented Web Directories

The main Web-wide directories mentioned above, including directories of the search engines such as Infoseek and Lycos, provide already prepared net directories or "subject trees" of websites organized by categories and retrievable via keyword searching. The military aptitude of these sites is not particularly high, but they are useful for browsing, and they include references to nonofficial military resources, which are not the focus of this directory. There are also a number of more specialized military-related directories. These tend to be more inclusive, and often have comments and authoritative descriptions of Web resources.

NEW AFDA Library Military and Strategic Studies
http://www.lib.adfa.oz.au/web/military/mil.htm

> *Compiled at the Australian Forces Defence Academy.*

AJAX: United States and International Government Military and Intelligence Agency Access
http://www.sagal.com/ajax/

Bulletin Board for Libraries (BUBL) Information Service
http://bubl.ac.uk/link/subjects/BUBL_by-subject_listings

> *UK-based index to resources in Aerospace Engineering, Development Studies, Geography, Government and Public Administration, History, Military Science, Politics and Social Sciences, and Russia.*

NEW CARL's Gateway to the Internet
http://www-cgsc.army.mil/carl/gateway.htm

> *Compiled by the Combined Arms Research Library (CARL) at Ft. Leavenworth, KS, links to topical areas of military interest.*

Electronic Headquarters for the Acquisition of War Knowledge (E-HAWK)
http://www.e-hawk.com/

> *Includes the Catalog of Military Internet Resources (Mil-Cat) and World Wide Web Site for Scholars of Military History (Mil-Hist).*

 BASE SCHEDULED TO CLOSE $ COMMERCIAL, BUSINESS OPPORTUNITY   E-MAIL ADDRESS   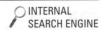 INTERNAL SEARCH ENGINE

NEW International Affairs Network (IAN)
http://www.pitt.edu/~ian/

> *Comprehensive academic-oriented directory of international relations resources on the web.*

NEW International Relations and Security Network (ISN) (Switzerland)
http://www.isn.ethz.ch/

> *Swiss directory of international security resources on the web, including many non–U.S. sites.*

National Defense University Library's Defense Nexus
http://www.ndu.edu/ndu/library/military.html

> *Guide to U.S. and international military links, official and private.*

★ **NEW** War, Peace and Security WWW Server
http://www.cfcsc.dnd.ca/

> *An excellent and comprehensive site of military resources worldwide, compiled by the Canadian Forces Command and Staff College.*

Official Military Internet Listings

Given the propensity of the U.S. military to endlessly change organizational structure and names—and given the transitory nature of the Internet—familiarity with the various official listings of websites compiled by the Defense Department and the various services is essential to find organizations and resources. Some of these listings and search engines are also interfaces for the Government Information Locator Service (GILS), an initiative mandated by the Office of Management and Budget by which government agencies are to use electronic means for providing information to the public.

Defense Department and DOD-wide

Guide to GILS Records
http://www.defenselink.mil/locator/

Defense Technical Information Web (DTIW) Locator
http://www.dtic.mil/dtiwl/

Air Force

Alphabetical listing
http://www.af.mil/sites/alphabetical

 NEW LISTING IN THIS EDITION   ✎ ONLINE FACT SHEET    PUBLICATION REPOSITORY OR LIBRARY   ★ RECOMMENDED SITE   ☎ TELEPHONE NUMBER

Starting Points

Military Starting Points

Defense Department/DefenseLINK	http://www.defenselink.mil/
Joint Chiefs of Staff	http://www.dtic.mil/jcs
AirForceLINK	http://www.af.mil/
ArmyLINK	http://www.army.mil/
NavyOnLine	http://www.navy.mil/
Marine Corps/MarineLINK	http://www.usmc.mil/
Air Force Reserve	http://www.afres.af.mil/
Air National Guard	http://www.ang.af.mil/
Army National Guard	http://132.80.130.121/
Army Reserve	http://www.army.mil/usar/
National Guard	http://www.ngb.dtic.mil/
Navy Reserve	http://www.navy.mil/homepages/ navresfor/navres.html
Marine Corps Reserve	http://www.marforres.usmc.mil/

Other National Security Starting Points

Central Intelligence Agency	http://www.odci.gov/cia/
Coast Guard	http://www.dot.gov/dotinfo/uscg/
Department of Energy	http://www.doe.gov
Department of State	http://www.state.gov
Federal Bureau of Investigation	http://www.fbi.gov
Federal Emergency Management Agency	http://www.fema.gov/
National Aeronautics and Space Administration	http://www.nasa.gov
North Atlantic Treaty Organization	http://www.nato.int/
Veteran Affairs	http://www.va.gov/
White House	http://www.whitehouse.gov

Organizationally by major command
　http://www.af.mil/sites/sites_com.html

Army

Search engine by organization and keyword
　http://www.army.mil/

Alphabetical listing
　http://www.army.mil/alphabetical_official.htm

Chronological listing, with newer sites listed on top
　http://www.army.mil/date_official.htm

| BASE SCHEDULED TO CLOSE | $ COMMERCIAL, BUSINESS OPPORTUNITY | ✉ E-MAIL ADDRESS | 🔍 INTERNAL SEARCH ENGINE |

Navy

Navy Online Homepage
http://www.ncts.navy.mil/nol

Search engine by title
http://www.navy.mil/cgi-bin/sites.pl

Alphabetical listing
http://www.navy.mil/cgi-bin/sites.pl?-alpha

By category
http://www.navy.mil/cgi-bin/sites.pl?-cat

Marine Corps

MarineLink websites
http://www.usmc.mil/websites.nsf

Military Locators

Military Bases, Units, Ships

★ The Armed Forces Communications, Inc. Homebase http://www.armedforces.com/thomebase/index.htm is a privately maintained worldwide installations and units list and directory of note.

Standard Installation Topic Exchange Service (SITES)
http://www.dmdc.osd.mil/sites/

> *Maintained by the Defense Manpower Data Center, provides information on major installations organized for military personnel transferring duty stations (e.g., education, employment, medical services). The graphics-intensive and slow site includes detailed descriptions of bases with listings of major units.*

DOD Worldwide List of Military Installations
http://www.defenselink.mil/pubs/installations

> *Somewhat outdated but still useful.*

★ Distribution of Personnel by State and by Selected Locations and Atlas/Data Abstract for the United States and Selected Areas
http://web1.whs.osd.mil/mmid/pubs.htm

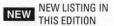 

Navy Bases and Air Stations—U.S.
http://www.chinfo.navy.mil/navpalib/bases/navbases.html

NEW Naval Vessel Register
http://www.nvr.navy.mil

> *The official U.S. Navy register of commissioned ships and craft.*

Navy Ships
http://www.ncts.navy.mil/navpalib/ships/

> *Listings of ship home ports, ship mailing addresses, and ships by type and hull number, all in separate files.*

Directories of Units and People

The Defense Switched Network (DSN) Directory online at a number of websites, including at http://dsnbbs.ncr.disa.mil/. A searchable online version of the somewhat dated *Air Force Address Directory* (AFDIR 37-135) (March 1995) is located at afdir.hq.af.mil/afdir/index.cfm and at http://www.afmc.wpafb.af.mil/lib/AFADDR.html. The Army's Aerodrome Directory at http://leav-www.army.mil/usaasa/FIB/AD2qtr.htm profiles descriptions of airfields in the United States.

Biographies

The biographies of most active duty general officers (generals and admirals) are contained either at central repositories or at the commands and organizations where they are assigned. The regularly updated "General/Flag Officer Worldwide Roster" is also located at http://web1.whs.osd.mil/mmid/m13/fobtop.htm.

The DOD Network Information Center (NIC) Whois Database Lookup at http://nic.ddn.mil/cgi-bin/whois provides a search capability for DOD E-mail users. The **NEW** Navy X.500 Directory Service at http://www.public-navydirectory. newnet.navy.mil:9090/ has more comprehensive coverage for Navy activities.

Defense Department and Service Officials
http://www.defenselink.mil/bios/biographies.html

Air Force Leaders 🔎
http://www.af.mil/lib/bio

NEW Air Force General Officer Roster Page
http://www.hq.af.mil/DP/afgomo/ROSTERS.HTM

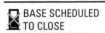 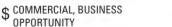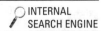

Navy Leaders
   http://www.chinfo.navy.mil/navpalib/people/bio-top.html
   http://www.chinfo.navy.mil/navpalib/people/flags

Marine Corps General Officers and Senior Executive Service Biographies
   http://www.usmc.mil/generalo.nsf/

Personnel Locators

Each of the services provides locators for active duty and former military personnel (military regulations and the Privacy Act of 1974 protect the home addresses of service personnel).

Air Force Worldwide Locator
   http://www.afpc.af.mil/afwwloc.htm

Army Worldwide Locator
   http://www.army.mil/vetinfo/persloc.htm

Navy World Wide Locator
   http://www.chinfo.navy.mil/navpalib/people/faq/.www/locate.html

Marine Corps Locator
   http://www.usmc.mil/wwwusmc.nsf/finding+Marines

Veterans and Veterans' Organizations

The National Personnel Records Center of the National Archives http://www.nara.gov/regional/stlouis.html is the repository of military personnel records of veterans during the 20th century.

NEW DOD Alumni Database
   http://www.army.mil/vetinfo/default.htm

Army Alumni Organizations/Associations ⌀
   http://www.army.mil/vetinfo/vetloc.htm

   Database of Army unit and branch alumni organizations and associations, including links to private homepages.

Military Acronyms and Terminology

As one browses through the military on the electronic highway, it is hard not to be confused by the acronyms and special language. Each military service and each military disci-

pline (e.g., artillery or aviation or intelligence) has its own language, and very few provide much assistance in deciphering their official-speak for the uninitiated. The authoritative *Department of Defense (DOD) Dictionary of Military and Associated Terms* (Joint Pub 1-02) is itself available in Adobe Acrobat format online via the Joint Electronic Library at http://www.dtic.mil/doctrine/jel/new_pubs/jp1_02.pdf A searchable dictionary database including the *DOD Dictionary* and the Joint Acronyms and Abbreviations master data file is located at http://www.dtic.mil/doctrine/jel/doddict/

Army Acronym and Abbreviation Glossary Search
   www.pica.army.mil/apps/a+a_search/bin/a+a_search.cgi?

Army Training Digital Library's Acronym Database
   http://www.atsc-army.org/atdl/search/acronym.htm

★ Center for Army Lessons Learned (CALL) Dictionary and Thesaurus
   http://call.army.mil/call/thesaur/index.htm

   Continually updated database of terminology, acronyms, geographic codes, and operations.

Program and System or Equipment Codes Query
   http://web1.whs.osd.mil./peidhome/guide/mn02/sysquery.htm

U.S. Military Abbreviation and Acronym List
   http://sierra.nosc.mil/seymour/FoG/acronym6.html

Weapons Facts Sheets and Characteristics

Air Force Fact Sheets
   http:/www.dtic.mil/airforcelink/pa/indexpages/fs_index.html

   Includes combat and combat support aircraft and helicopters, space launch vehicles, and missiles.

Army Weapon Systems Handbook
   http:/www.dtic.mil/armylink/factfile

   Searchable database including helicopters, artillery and missiles, air defense systems, armored vehicles, trucks and logistical equipment, ammunition and ordnance, communications and intelligence collection (including satellites), and small arms.

Defense Fact File
   http:/www.defenselink.mil/factfile/

   Gateway database to DOD and service fact sheets dealing with aircraft, ammunition, armor, communications, artillery and fire support radar, missiles, ships and submarines, vehicles and weapons.

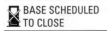  

Marine Corps Fact File
http:/www.hqmc.usmc.mil/factfile.nsf

> *Includes aircraft and helicopters, amphibious raid equipment, anti-armor weapons, armored and tracked vehicles, uniforms and personal supplies, communications, artillery and missiles, infantry weapons, and land-mine-related equipment.*

Navy Fact File
http:/www.chinfo.navy.mil/navpalib/factfile/ffiletop.html

> *Includes aircraft and helicopters, shipboard guns and torpedoes, missiles, surface ship, and submarine types.*

Sources of Photographs

In addition to a number of specialized homepages providing images online, virtually every command and base also has a photo gallery. Two NASA image archives—the **NEW** NASA Image Exchange ⌕ (http://nix.nasa.gov) and the Dryden Flight Research Center Photo Server http://www.dfrc.nasa.gov/PhotoServer/—contain thousands of online photographs, many relevant to the military.

The DOD Visual Information Center (1363 Z Street, March AFB, CA 92518; ☎ 909-413-2522) is the public archive for images and photos from 1982 to the present.

NEW ★ Joint Combat Camera Center ⌕
http://dodimagery.afis.osd.mil

> *Online searchable database of publicly released and restricted photos by military specialists, accessible with username and password of "public."*

DefenseLINK photos
http://www.defenselink.mil/photos/index.html

> *Comprehensive official photo library, including portraits, all services, weapons, and special operations or announcements such as Bosnia or Taiwan straits operations.*

American Forces Press Service photos
http://www.dtic.mil/afps/photos/

Air Force people, operations, weapons ⌕
http://www.af.mil/photos/

NEW ACC Image Bank
http://www.acc.af.mil/imagebank

AFIT Gallery
http://www.afit.af.mil/Schools/PA/gall4.htm

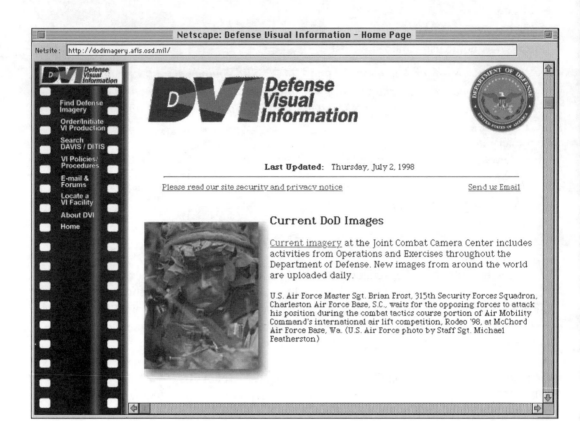

Air Force Museum
http://www.wpafb.af.mil/museum/

Aviation images
http://www.au.af.mil/au/aul/image/image.htm

NEW Army photos
http://www.dtic.mil/armylink/photos

Army Equipment Photo Gallery
http://www.jmu.edu/rotc/gallery.html

Navy Digital Imagery
http://www.navy.mil/navpalib/.www/digital.html

NEW Marine Corps Image Archive
http://www.usmc.mil/images.nsf

 BASE SCHEDULED
TO CLOSE

 COMMERCIAL, BUSINESS
OPPORTUNITY

E-MAIL
ADDRESS

 INTERNAL
SEARCH ENGINE

Basic Information Resources

Defense Department

★ **DefenseLINK** 🔍
http://www.defenselink.mil/

Department of Defense online homepage and official World Wide Web service, officially inaugurated 10 November 1994 and hosted by DTIC on behalf of the DOD office of public affairs. DefenseLINK provides a single starting point for information about DOD and its organizations and functions. It contains numerous DOD publications, frequently asked questions (FAQs) about the military, press statements and advisories, and Congressional testimony, as well as links to the armed services. DefenseLINK fact sheets provide the latest military strength figures, active duty military personnel by region/country, and base closure information, as well as other major announcements. There is also access to contract award announcements (for awards of $5 million or more), daily public schedules of the Secretary and Deputy Secretary of Defense, and selected speeches. The Publications Section links to online copies of major publications, speeches, and Department of Defense directives and instructions.

DOD Organizations and Functions Guidebook
http://www.defenselink.mil/pubs/ofg.html

Online guide (September 1996) to the missions and functions of the Office of the Secretary of Defense (OSD), defense agencies, and DOD field activities, unified commands, and military departments.

DOD Fact File
http://www.defenselink.mil/factfile/

Fact sheets on DOD organizations and equipment.

NEW **ReserveLINK**
http://raweb.osd.mil/Reservelink.htm

Gateway to information about service reserve opportunities and forces and to the resources of the Army, Air Force, Naval, Marine Corps, and Coast Guard reserves, as well as the National Guard.

`NEW` **GuardLINK**
  http://www.defenselink.mil/guardlink/
  http://www.ngb.dtic.mil

  Gateway to information about and the guard units of the Air and Army National Guards.

Department of Defense Public Affairs Office
Office of the Assistant to the Secretary of Defense (Public Affairs)
The Pentagon
Washington, DC 20301-1400
☎ 703-697-5737
  http://www.defenselink.mil/osd/asdpa.html

  The Directorate for Public Communications has a series of fact sheets dealing with commonly asked questions (e.g., recruitment, service academies, military records requests, finding military people, UFOs, base closures).

  `NEW` DOD Freedom of Information Act (FOIA) Office
    http://www.defenselink.mil/pubs/foi

Defense Department News Services
`NEW` DefenseLINK News 🔎
  http://www.defenselink.mil/news

  Feed from the American Forces Press Service, as well as news releases, transcripts of DOD press and background briefings, and other public affairs documents. Postings are normally made within 20 minutes of official release. Anyone can register to receive announcements via E-mail.

American Forces Press Service
  http://www.dtic.mil/afps/

`NEW` National Guard News
  http://www.ngb.dtic.mil/newsctr.htm

Joint Chiefs of Staff

JCSLink
  http://www.dtic.mil/jcs

  An ever-improving site with access to JCS organizations, joint publications and doctrine, and materials on military future vision.

 BASE SCHEDULED TO CLOSE $ COMMERCIAL, BUSINESS OPPORTUNITY   E-MAIL ADDRESS    INTERNAL SEARCH ENGINE

Office of the Chairman of the Joint Chiefs of Staff
Special Assistant for Public Affairs
The Pentagon, Room 2E857
Washington, DC 20318-9999
☎ 703-697-4272

Joint Force Quarterly (Joint Chiefs of Staff)
   http://www.dtic.mil/doctrine/jel/jfq_pubs/index.htm

   Joint Staff-sponsored journal of thought and opinion.

Air Force

AirForceLINK 🔍
   http://www.af.mil/

   *Department of the Air Force homepage created by Secretary of the Air Force Office of
   Public Affairs and the Defense Technical Information Center and inaugurated in April
   1995. Contains the Air Force FAQ, news, fact sheets and photographs of weapon systems, biographies of senior civilian leaders and general officers, the latest popular
   publications about the Air Force, and photographs of current operations around the
   world. Links are provided to Air Force activities worldwide. The search gateway
   (http://www.af.mil/search/search.html) allows keyword searches of news, people,
   features, fact sheets, and speeches.*

   The AirForceLINK Publications and Resources Section
      http://www.af.mil/lib/pubs.html/ *includes popular publications and information
      resources published by the Air Force.*

Air Force Public Affairs
Office of the Director of Public Affairs
Department of the Air Force
1670 Air Force Pentagon
Washington, DC 20330-1670
☎ 703-697-6061; ☎ 703-697-1128
   http://www.af.mil/

   Air Force Awards and Decorations
      http://www.afpc.af.mil/awards

   Air Force Recruiting
      http://www.airforce.com/

   Air Force Demographics
      http://www.afpc.af.mil/demographics/

 NEW NEW LISTING IN THIS EDITION    ✎ ONLINE FACT SHEET   📖 PUBLICATION REPOSITORY OR LIBRARY   ★ RECOMMENDED SITE   ☎ TELEPHONE NUMBER

NEW Air Force Freedom of Information (FOIA) Office
http://www.foia.af.mil

NEW USAF Air Demonstration Squadron ("Thunderbirds")
http://www.nellis.af.mil/thunderbirds

Air Force News Services

The Air Force maintains a search engine for the major news services at http://www.af.mil/news/index.html and a gateway to base newspapers at www.af.mil/lib/pubs.html

Air Force News Service
http://www.af.mil/news

Air Combat Command News
http://acc.af.mil/public/news

Air Education and Training Command News
http:/www.aetc.af.mil/news.html

Air Force Materiel Command News
http://www.afmc.wpafb.af.mil/organizations/HQ-AFMC/PA/

Air Force Reserves News
http://www.afres.af.mil/news/default.htm

NEW Air Force Space Command News
http://www.spacecom.af.mil/hqafspc/news/Default2.htm

Air Mobility Command News
http://www.safb.af.mil/hqamc/pa/news/news.htm

Pacific Air Forces News
http://www.hqpacaf.af.mil/news

US Air Forces in Europe News
http://www.usafe.af.mil/news

Public Affairs Management Network (PAMNET)
http://tecnet2.jcte.jcs.mil:8000/

PAMNET, managed by the Air Force Reserve (AFRES), includes reserve and active duty news (including a huge selection of major command news services; see below), biographies, fact sheets, and speeches.

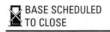 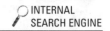

Air Force Magazines and Journals

Air Chronicles (expanded online edition of *Airpower Journal*)
http://www.cdsar.af.mil/air-chronicles.html

Air Force Journal of Logistics
http://www.il.hq.af.mil/AFLMA/lgj/afjlhome.html

Airman Magazine (the flagship U.S. Air Force magazine)
http://www.af.mil/news/airman

Airpower Journal (the professional journal of the U.S. Air Force)
http://www.cdsar.af.mil/apje.html

ASTRO News (Air Force Space and Missile Systems Center)
http://www.laafb.af.mil/SMC/PA/Astro_News/index.html

NEW *Citizen Airman* (AF Reserves)
http://www.afres.af.mil/hq/citamn/default.htm

Civil Engineer (Air Force)
http://www.afcesa.af.mil/library.html

Guardian (Air Force Space Command)
http://www.spacecom.af.mil/hqafspc/index.htm

Intercom (Air Force C4I newspaper)
http://infosphere.safb.af.mil/~rmip/intercom.htm

Leading Edge (Air Force Materiel Command)
http://www.afmc.wpafb.af.mil/organizations/HQ-AFMC/PA/leading_edge/

Mobility Forum (Air Mobility Command)
http://www.safb.af.mil/hqamc/pa/tmf/themobil.htm

Program Manager Magazine (Defense Systems Management College)
http://www.dsmc.dsm.mil/pubs/pdf/pmtoc97.htm

Spokesman On-line (official online magazine of the Air Intelligence Agency)
http://www.aia.af.mil/aialink/homepages/pa/cyberspokesman/index.html

TIG Brief (the Inspector General of the Air Force online magazine)
http://www-afia.saia.af.mil/tig/tig_index.html

USAF Medical Service Digest (Air Force Surgeon General)
http://usafsg.satx.disa.mil/

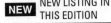 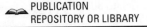

Army

ArmyLINK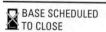
http://www.army.mil/

Army homepage inaugurated in February 1995 and maintained for the Army Office of Public Affairs by the Director of Information Systems for Command, Control, Communications and Computers. ArmyLINK is a gateway to the central index for all Army sites, listed alphabetically, chronologically, and by subject area. It also has an organization and keyword search engine.

Army Public Affairs Office
Office of the Chief of Public Affairs
Department of the Army
Washington, DC 20310-1508
☎ 703-697-5662
http://www.dtic.mil/armylink

> **NEW** Army Freedom of Information Act (FOIA) Office
> http://www.rmd.belvoir.army.mil/err.htm
>
> Army Recruiting
> http://www.goarmy.com/
>
> Civilian Marksmanship Program
> http://www.army.mil/marks.htm
>
> Directory of Army Museums
> http://www.army.mil/cmh-pg/musdir.htm

Army News Service
http://www.army.mil

Army Magazines and Journals

Armor Magazine
http://www.know.army.mil/dtdd/armormag

Army Communicator (Army Signal Corps professional magazine)
http://www.gordon.army.mil/OCOS/BMdiv/AC/default.htm

Army Echoes (Army Retirement Services)
http://www.army.mil/retire-p/echos.htm

Army Logistician
http://www.almc.army.mil/orgnzatn/alog/alog.htm

 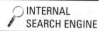

Army RD&A: Research Development Acquisition (professional publication of the Army RD&A community)
http://www.army.mil/aac-pg/pub/rda/rda.htm

Engineer (the professional bulletin for Army engineers)
http://www.wood.army.mil/engrmag/emag%5hp.html

Field Artillery
http://sill-www.army.mil/

NEW *INSCOM Journal* (Army Intelligence and Security Command)
http://www.vulcan.belvoir.army.mil/journal/backissues.htm

Military Intelligence Professional Bulletin
http://huachuca-usaic.army.mil/contlearning/infrastructure/media/MIPB/index.htm

Military Review (Army Command and General Staff)
http://www-cgsc.army.mil/milrev/index.htm

Parameters (Army War College)
http://carlisle-www.army.mil/usawc/Parameters/

PS Magazine (Army Preventive Maintenance Monthly)
http://wwwlogsa.army.mil/psmag/pshome.html

Soldier's (the official U.S. Army magazine)
http://www.dtic.mil/soldiers

Special Warfare Professional Bulletin
http://www.usasoc.soc.mil/swcs/dotd/sw-mag/sw-mag.htm

Navy

NavyOnline

✉ navyonline@ncts.navy.mil
http://www.navy.mil/

> *Navy homepage and Internet gateway to Navy organizations and commands, first set up in November 1993 and operated by the NavyOnline Working Group in Pensacola, FL, for the Chief of Naval Information (CHINFO). The homepage includes access to a variety of fact sheets, background information, biographies, and photographs via the extensive Navy Public Affairs Library.*

Navy Public Affairs Office
Office of Information (CHINFO)
1200 Pentagon
Washington, DC 20350-1200
☎ 703-697-5342; ✉ chinfo-pubinq@opnav-emh.navy.mil
http://www.chinfo.navy.mil/navpalib/chinfo/chinfo.html 🔎

> **NEW** Blue Angels (Navy aerial demonstration squadron)
> www.BlueAngels.navy.mil

> **NEW** Department of the Navy Organization
> http://www.chinfo.navy.mil/navpalib/organization/org-top.html

> **NEW** Navy Freedom of Information Act (FOIA) Online Resource Guide
> http://www.ogc.secnav.hq.navy.mil/foia/index.html

> Navy Public Affairs Directory 🔎
> http://www.chinfo.navy.mil/navpalib/chinfo/paodir/

> Navy Recruiting
> http://www.navyjobs.com/

> ★ Navy Public Affairs Library (NavPALib)
> ✉ navpalib@opnav-emh.navy.mil
> http://www.chinfo.navy.mil/navpalib/.www/subject.html

> Current status of the Navy
> http://www.chinfo.navy.mil/navpalib/news/.www/status.html
>
> > *Weekly summary of Navy activities, ship movements, and major exercises.*

Navy News Services

A gateway page to the latest Navy news from a variety of commands is located at
http://www.chinfo.navy.mil/navpalib/.www/latest.html

NavPALib News
http://www.chinfo.navy.mil/navpalib/news/.www/news.html

> *The NavPALib contains links to various news services and a list of Navy external and internal wires.*

> Navy Europe News Service (USNAVEUR News Service)
> http://www.chinfo.navy.mil/navpalib/news/eurnews/.www/eurnews.html

> Navy News Service
> http://www.chinfo.navy.mil/navpalib/news/navnews/.www/navnews.html

---

Naval Service Medical News
http://www.chinfo.navy.mil/navpalib/news/mednews/.www/mednews.html

Navy Wire Service
http://www.chinfo.navy.mil/navpalib/news/navywire/.www/navywire.html

Navy Magazines and Journals

Chips (Navy telecommunications)
http://www.norfolk.navy.mil/chips/

Naval Aviation News
http://www.history.navy.mil/branches/nhcorg5.htm

Naval Reservist News
http://www.ncts.navy.mil/navresfor/nrn/

`NEW` *Naval War College Review*
http://www.usnwc.edu/nwc/press.htm

Marine Corps

MarineLINK
http://www.usmc.mil/

The Marine Corps homepage, initially set up in November 1994 and now operated by the Division of Public Affairs. MarineLINK contains news, history, organizational information, Marine FAQs, directives, policies, and links to other Marine websites.

Marine Corps Public Affairs
Director of Public Affairs
Headquarters, U.S. Marine Corps
Washington, DC 20380
☎ 703-614-1492
http://www.hqmc.usmc.mil/pashops.nsf/PA+shops

Includes a directory of Marine Corps Public Affairs Offices worldwide.

Marines Almanac
http://www.usmc.mil/marines/almnac96.htm

Detailed organizational guide and background information dealing with Marine Corps heritage, history, and weapons.

Marine Corps Marathon
http://issb-www1.quantico.usmc.mil/marathon

Marine Corps Recruiting
http://www.Marines.com

NEW Marine Freedom of Information Act Electronic Reading Room
http://www.hqmc.usmc.mil/foia.nsf

NEW "The President's Own" U.S. Marine Band
http://www.marineband.hqmc.usmc.mil

Marine Corps News ⌀
http://www.usmc.mil/new98.nsf/approved

Marines (monthly magazine)
http://www.usmc.mil/marines/marines.nsf

Military Mega-Homepages

★ **Defense Technical Information Center (DTIC)**
8725 John J. Kingman Road, Suite 0944
Fort Belvoir, VA 22060-6218
http://www.dtic.mil/
ftp://ftp.dtic.mil/pub/

> *Though DTIC was not created to serve the general public—and most of its activities are oriented toward government contractors and defense industry—as the Defense Department has increased its online presence and made information available over the Internet, DTIC has made much of its technical information freely available. It compiles publicly accessible online bibliographies on subjects of high public interest (e.g., mine warfare and peacekeeping), maintains scientific and technical-related homepages, and produces publications and budgetary databases.*

Defense Technical Information Web
http://www.dtic.mil/dtiw/

> *Bibliographic listings of Internet sites by military subjects, including acquisition reform, computer security, defense conversion, defense operations, environment, high-performance computing, information technology, modeling and simulation, science and technology, and testing and evaluation.*

Manpower and Training Research Information System (MATRIS)
http://dticam.dtic.mil/

Directory of Researchers in Manpower, Personnel, Training and Human Factors

http://dticam.dtic.mil/resdir/

Searchable directory of DOD and non–DOD specialists in personnel and human factors research.

Scientific and Technical Information Network (STINET)

http://www.dtic.mil/stinet/

The public side of an otherwise restricted and fee-based site, home to the DTIC "How to Get It" database, DOD directives and instructions, the DTIC unclassified scientific and technical reports database, the Air University Library Index of Military Periodicals, and links to the Department of Energy and NASA scientific reports databases.

The Defense Technical Information Center's *How to Get It: A Guide to Defense Related Resources,* available online at http://www.dtic.mil/gils-input/htgi/, identifies and lists government-published or -sponsored documents, maps, patents, specifications, or standards by type of document, with information on the purpose, currency, and originator of the record. The guide was first created to assist military librarians and information specialists to locate documents not necessarily indexed, announced, or distributed by government information services or traditional depository methods.

★ Directorate for Information Operations and Reports (DIOR)

http://web1.whs.osd.mil/diorhome.htm

The Directorate of the Office of the Secretary of Defense is the source of statistical information on the Department of Defense, including personnel, research and development, and procurement. Its homepage, created in October 1995, includes access to a full electronic catalog of publicly available reports (http://web1.whs.osd.mil/ DIORCAT.HTM) dealing with manpower and prime contracts, procurement and geographic data, casualty information, and full listings of Defense Department reports required by legislation or directive (List of Recurring and One-time DOD Public-Use Reports and List of Recurring and One-time DOD Internal Reports) http://web1.whs.osd.mil/ICDHOME/REPORTS.HTM. The DIOR homepage also includes online statistical data on DOD contracts, payroll, casualties, and manpower, either as separate fact sheets or as full online reports.

Bosnia Information

BosniaLINK

http://www.dtic.mil/bosnia/

DOD website, including operation maps, fact sheets, briefing transcripts, speeches and congressional testimony, news releases, and biographies of key commanders

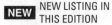 

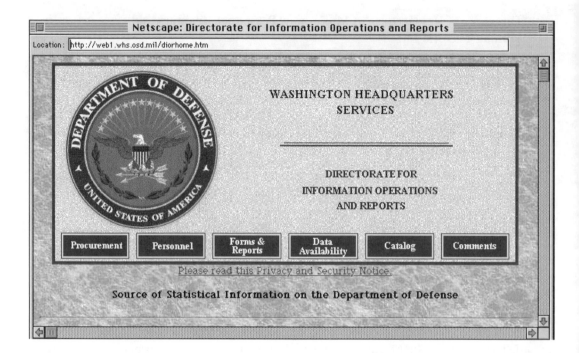

involved in Operation Joint Endeavor, the NATO peacekeeping mission. When BosniaLINK was inaugurated, there was a fourfold increase in traffic on DefenseLINK, the "parent" homepage.

Air Force Bosnia News
   http://www.af.mil/bosnia/

Army Bosnia News
   http://www.dtic.mil/bosnia/army/

Navy Bosnia News
   http://www.chinfo.navy.mil/navpalib/bosnia/bosnia1.html

European Command (EUCOM) Bosnia Homepage
   http://www.eucom.mil/europe/bosnia/index.htm

NEW Task Force Eagle (1st Armored Division)
   http://www.tfeagle.1ad.army.mil

NEW NATO/SFOR
   http://www.nato.int/ifor/ifor.htm

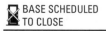 BASE SCHEDULED TO CLOSE    $ COMMERCIAL, BUSINESS OPPORTUNITY   E-MAIL ADDRESS   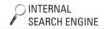 INTERNAL SEARCH ENGINE

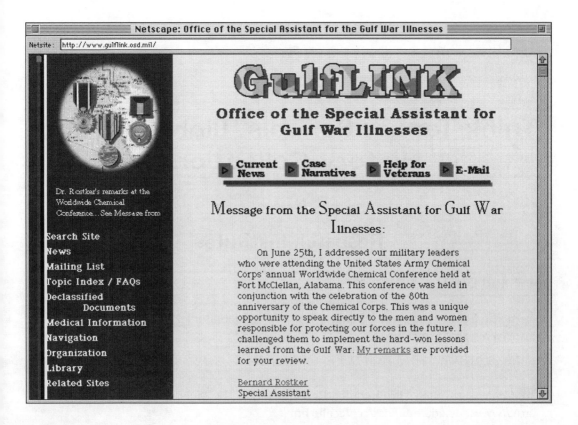

Netscape: Office of the Special Assistant for the Gulf War Illnesses

Netsite: http://www.gulflink.osd.mil/

GulfLINK

Office of the Special Assistant for Gulf War Illnesses

▷ Current News   ▷ Case Narratives   ▷ Help for Veterans   ▷ E-Mail

Dr. Rostker's remarks at the Worldwide Chemical Conference... See Message from

Search Site
News
Mailing List
Topic Index / FAQs
Declassified
    Documents
Medical Information
Navigation
Organization
Library
Related Sites

Message from the Special Assistant for Gulf War Illnesses:

On June 25th, I addressed our military leaders who were attending the United States Army Chemical Corps' annual Worldwide Chemical Conference held at Fort McClellan, Alabama. This conference was held in conjunction with the celebration of the 80th anniversary of the Chemical Corps. This was a unique opportunity to speak directly to the men and women responsible for protecting our forces in the future. I challenged them to implement the hard-won lessons learned from the Gulf War. My remarks are provided for your review.

Bernard Rostker
Special Assistant

Gulf War Illness

★ GulfLINK 🔍
www.gulflink.osd.mil

Established in 1995 as a clearinghouse of the Persian Gulf War Veterans Illness Task Force, GulfLINK contains declassified Gulf War–related documents, links, and reports dealing with the Gulf War illnesses and subjects primarily relating to chemical and biological weapons, medical issues, and environmental health.

DOD Office of Health Affairs Gulf War Illness page
http://www.ha.osd.mil/

Comprehensive Clinical Evaluation Program for Persian Gulf War Veterans
http://www.ha.osd.mil/cs/pgulf/18k_toc.html

NEW Gulf War Health Center
http://www.wramc.amedd.army.mil/departments/gulfwar

Think Tanks, Schools, Libraries, and History Collections

Research Institutes

Joint and DOD

Asia-Pacific Center for Security Studies (PACOM) (Honolulu, HI)
http://www.pacom.mil/apc

Established by Secretary of Defense William Perry on 4 September 1995.

`NEW` Center for Counter Proliferation Research (NDU, Ft. McNair, Washington DC)
http://www.ndu.edu/ndu/inss/ccp/ccphp.html

`NEW` ★ Center of Excellence in Disaster Management and Humanitarian Assistance (Tripler Army Medical Center, Hawaii)
http://coe.tamc.amedd.army.mil/

`NEW` Center for Hemispheric Defense Studies (NDU, Ft. McNair, Washington DC)
http://www.ndu.edu/ndu/chds/index.html

Defense Equal Opportunity Management Institute (OSD) (Patrick AFB, FL)
http://www.pafb.af.mil/deomi/deomi.htm

Maintains race, gender, and ethnic group statistics for DOD, and includes reports online.

Defense Resources Management Institute (Monterey, CA)
http://vislab-www.nps.navy.mil/~drmi/

Responsible for economic analysis and cost estimating methodology.

DOD Security Institute (DIS)
http://www.dtic.mil/dodsi/

Focusing on security classification and industrial security, with the "Security Awareness Bulletin" online.

George C. Marshall European Center for Security Studies (Garmisch, Germany) (EUCOM)
http://www.marshall.adsn.int/marshall.html

> *Established in 1993; includes the College of Strategic Studies and Defense Economics, the Research and Conference Center, and the Institute for Eurasian Studies.*

Institute for National Strategic Studies (NDU, Ft. McNair, Washington, DC) ♅
http://www.ndu.edu/ndu/inss/insshp.html

> *Access to "McNair Papers," Strategic Forum special reports, other reports and studies, and the annual "Strategic Assessment."*

NEW Joint C4ISR Battle Center (JBC) (ACOM) (Suffolk, VA)
http://www.jbc.js.mil

Joint Warfighting Center (ACOM) (Ft. Monroe, VA)
http://www.jwfc.js.mil/

> *Created from the combination of the Joint Doctrine Center and the Joint Warfare Center, and formerly a JCS agency.*

Air Force

Air Force Doctrine Center (Maxwell AFB, AL)
http://www.hqafdc.maxwell.af.mil

> *New direct reporting unit created in May 1997 to focus Air Force doctrinal development. Moved from Langley AFB, VA, to incorporate elements of Air University.*

Air Force Studies and Analyses Agency (The Pentagon)
http://www.afsaa.hq.af.mil/

College of Aerospace Doctrine, Research and Education (CADRE)
(AU, Maxwell AFB, AL)
http://www.cdsar.af.mil/home.html

> *Includes the Airpower Research Institute and the Air Force Wargaming Institute. To be incorporated into the enlarged Air Force Doctrine Center.*

Institute for National Security Studies (Air Force Academy, Colorado Springs, CO)
http://www.usafa.af.mil/inss/

Army

Army Research Institute for Behavioral and Social Sciences (Alexandria, VA)
http://www.ari.army.mil

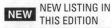 

Deputy Chief of Staff for Personnel institute on cognitive sciences, artificial intelligence, and synthetic environments.

Infantry Forces Research Unit (Ft. Benning, GA)
http://www.ari.army.mil/ifru.htm

Center for Army Leadership (CGSC, Ft. Leavenworth, KS)
http://www-cgsc.army.mil/cal/index.htm

★ Center for Army Lessons Learned (CALL) (Ft. Leavenworth, KS) 🔎
http://call.army.mil:1100/call.html

Searchable website of CALL products including newsletters and reports providing observations and lessons learned from Army operations and training exercises.

Center for Strategic Leadership (Army War College, Carlisle Barracks, PA)
http://carlisle-www.army.mil/usacsl/csl.htm
http://144.99.192.240/usacsl/csl.htm

The Army Peacekeeping Institute, founded in 1993 to study peace operations "at the strategic and high operational levels," is a part of the Center.

Foreign Military Studies Office (FMSO) (Ft. Leavenworth, KS)
http://leav-www.army.mil/fmso

Online resources include publications relating to geostrategic issues, foreign special operations forces, a Low Intensity Conflict/Operations Other Than War homepage, and translations from Russian and Polish.

Strategic Studies Institute (Army War College, Carlisle Barracks, PA)
http://carlisle-www.army.mil/usassi/

Includes the publication "World View," a strategic assessment compiled by SSI scholars.

Navy and Marine Corps

Center for Naval Warfare Studies (Naval War College, Newport, RI)
http://www.usnwc.edu/nwc/cnws.htm

Includes the CNO's Strategic Studies Group.

Commandant's Warfighting Laboratory (Quantico, VA)
http://www.mcwl.org
http://208.198.29.7

Established in 1995 to serve as the test bed for development and enhancement of future Marine Corps operational concepts.

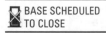 BASE SCHEDULED TO CLOSE    $ COMMERCIAL, BUSINESS OPPORTUNITY   E-MAIL ADDRESS    INTERNAL SEARCH ENGINE

Institute for Joint Warfare Analysis (NPS, Monterey, CA)
http://www.nps.navy.mil/~opnsrsch/ijwa.html

Marine Corps Research Center (Quantico, VA)
http://www.mcu.quantico.usmc.mil/www/mcrc.htm

> *Housing the James Carson Breckinridge Professional Library, the Research Library, the Marine Corps University Archives, and the Marine Corps Lessons Learned Library.*

NEW Naval Doctrine Command (Norfolk, VA)
http://www.ndc.navy.mil

Higher Education Institutions

Joint and DOD

Armed Forces Staff College (7800 Hampton Boulevard, Norfolk, VA 23511-1702)
☎ 804-444-5302
http://www.afsc.edu/

> *Includes the Joint Command, Control, and Information Warfare School, the Joint and Combined Staff Officers School, and the Joint and Combined Warfighting School.*

Defense Acquisition University (2001 North Beauregard Street,
Alexandria, VA 22311-1772)
☎ 703-845-6766
http://www.acq.osd.mil/dau/dau.html

> *Established in 1990 to integrate DOD acquisition education and training; includes the Acquisition Education, Training and Career Development Publications Repository.*

Defense Systems Management College (Ft. Belvoir, VA)
http://www.dsmc.dsm.mil/

> *Includes the* Program Manager's Notebook, Acquisition Review Quarterly, *and* Program Manager Magazine *author indices, the DSMC catalog, and DSMC Press guidebooks.*

National Defense University (NDU) (Ft. McNair, Washington DC)
http://www.ndu.edu/

> NDU Research and Publications 🔍
> http://www.ndu.edu/search/query.htm

>> *Searchable database and full text of NDU Press studies and books,* Strategic Forum, McNair Papers, *miscellaneous faculty and student studies, and the journal* Joint Force Quarterly.

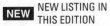 

Industrial College of the Armed Forces
http://www.ndu.edu/ndu/icaf/homepage.html
http://198.80.36.91/ndu/icaf/icafhp.html

Information Resources Management College
http://www.ndu.edu/ndu/irmc/homepage.html
http://198.80.36.91/ndu/irmc/62_hopg.html

School of Information Warfare and Strategy
http://www.ndu.edu/ndu/inss/act/iwscvr.html

Formerly part of the Institute for National Security Studies.

National War College
http://www.ndu.edu/ndu/nwc/nwchp.html

Air Force

Air Force Institute of Technology (AFIT) (Wright-Patterson AFB, OH)
http://www.afit.af.mil/

Includes the graduate schools of engineering, logistics, and acquisition management.

Air University (AU) (Maxwell AFB, AL)
http://www.au.af.mil/

Air University Education Digest
http://www.au.af.mil/au/digest/

Official guidebook and statistical information.

Air University Press
http://tuvok.au.af.mil/au/oas/aupress/aubanner.htm

★ Air University Research Database
http://www.au.af.mil/au/database/research.html

Searchable database of ongoing research projects, papers, and reports at Air University schools and institutes. Includes the full text of reports from 1995 to the present.

Air Command and Staff College (ACSC)
http://wwwacsc.au.af.mil/

ACSC Knowledge Warrior Homepage
http://wwwacsc.au.af.mil/knwldgwr.htm

 BASE SCHEDULED TO CLOSE $ COMMERCIAL, BUSINESS OPPORTUNITY   ✉ E-MAIL ADDRESS   ⌕ INTERNAL SEARCH ENGINE

Air War College (AWC)
http://www.au.af.mil/au/awc/awchome.htm

> *Includes excellent links to other sites categorized to include space and its uses, weapons, science and technology, leadership, terrorism and special operations, politics, and law.*

School of Advanced Airpower Studies (SAAS) (ACSC)
http://www.au.af.mil/au/saas/

Squadron Officer School
http://www.au.af.mil/au/sos/

Air Force Officer Accession and Training Schools
http://www.afoats.mil

★ College of Aerospace Doctrine, Research and Education (CADRE)
http://www.cdsar.af.mil/home.html

Ira C. Eaker College for Professional Development
http://www.au.af.mil/au/cpd/

Air Force Judge Advocate General School
http://www.au.af.mil/au/cpd/jagschool/

Community College of the Air Force
http://www.au.af.mil/au/ccaf/

Army

Command and General Staff College (CGSC) (Ft. Leavenworth, KS)
http://www-cgsc.army.mil/

> *Links to schools (Command and General Staff School, Combined Arms and Services Staff School, School for Command Preparation, School of Corresponding Studies), centers, doctrinal development, and* Military Review, *the Army's professional journal.*

NEW School of Advanced Military Studies (SAMS)
http://www-cgsc.army.mil/sams/index.htm

Army Logistics Management College (Ft. Lee, VA)
http://www.almc.army.mil

> *Includes the Schools of Acquisition Management, Logistics Science, Management Science, and Packaging Technology.*

Army Management Staff College (Ft. Belvoir, VA) 🔎
http://www.amsc.belvoir.army.mil

Army War College (Carlisle Barracks, PA)
http://carlisle-www.army.mil

Navy

★ Naval Postgraduate School (Monterey, CA) 🔎
http://www.nps.navy.mil/
gopher://peacock.nps.navy.mil/

> Joint C4I Systems Homepage
> http://www.stl.nps.navy.mil/c4i
>
> > *Including the C4I Professionals Mailing List, an open forum (discussion group) dealing with command, control, communications, computers, and intelligence matters.*
>
> Space Systems Academic Group
> http://www.sp.nps.navy.mil/

Naval War College (Newport, RI)
http://www.usnwc.edu/nwc/

> College of Continuing Education
> http://www.usnwc.edu/nwc/cce/index.htm
>
> College of Naval Command and Staff
> http://www.usnwc.edu/nwc/cnc&s.htm
>
> College of Naval Warfare
> http://www.usnwc.edu/nwc/cnw.htm
>
> Naval Command College
> http://www.usnwc.edu/nwc/ncc.htm
>
> **NEW** Naval Justice School
> http://www.njs.jag.navy.mil
>
> Naval Staff College
> http://users.ids.net/nwc/nsc.htm
>
> Surface Warfare Officers School Command
> http://www.swos.navy.mil

 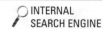

Marine Corps

Marine Corps University (Marine Corps Base Quantico, VA)
http://www.mcu.quantico.usmc.mil

Amphibious Warfare School
http://www.mcu.quantico.usmc.mil/aws/index.htm

Marine Command and Staff College
http://138.156.204.100/

Marine Corps War College
http://www.mcu.quantico.usmc.mil/mcwar/mcwar.htm

Military Libraries

More than 900 libraries, large and small, are located at different military organizations and local bases. Most are just post libraries no different from small public libraries, but quite a few are major academic resources with significant collections. They are mostly at the service war colleges and academies, but some are attached to research and development organizations, and specialized medical and legal libraries also exist.

The DOD *Libraries Directory,* compiled by the Defense Technical Information Center (DTIC) Scientific and Technical Information Network Management Division (STINET), provides information about the military libraries approved for public access. The complete version of the directory is accessible via the STINET homepage at http://www.dtic.mil/gils-input/lib/ The searchable directory includes name, address, and telephone and fax numbers, and information on collection size, special collections and special subjects, and availability of library resources and services. The Canadian Forces Defence College also maintains a worldwide directory of military libraries on the Internet at
NEW http://www.cfcsc.dnd.ca/links/index.html

The ★ **NEW** Military Education Research Library Network (MERLN) at http://www.inf.pims.org:8000/ is the combined online catalogs of eight of the largest Defense Department libraries.

Air Force Academy Library (Colorado Springs, CO)

Online Catalog
telnet://library.usafa.af.mil

Login: <library>

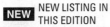 

Air Force Institute of Technology (AFIT) Academic Library
(Wright-Patterson AFB, Dayton, OH)
　　http://library.afit.af.mil

　　　　Online Catalog
　　　　http://sabre.afit.af.mil/
　　　　http://129.92.1.10
　　　　telnet://sabre.afit.af.mil

　　　　Username: <afitpac>

Air University Library/Fairchild Library (Maxwell AFB, AL)
☎ 334-953-5074
　　http://www.au.af.mil/au/aul/

　　　　*Largest library in the Defense Department and the largest federal library outside
　　　　Washington, DC. The AUL produces excellent bibliographies dealing with current
　　　　military-related subjects, a list of which is available online at*
　　　　http://www.au.af.mil/au/aul/bibs/bib97.htm

　　　　Online Catalog
　　　　http://130.60.136.133:8002/

　　　　*Includes the Air University Index of Military Periodicals (AULIMP) from 1990 to the
　　　　present.*

Armed Forces Staff College Library (Norfolk, VA)
☎ 757-444-5321
　　http://www.afsc.edu/libindx.htm

　　　　*Bibliographies on military topics (e.g., arms control, joint task forces, peacekeeping,
　　　　space warfare).*

Army War College Library (Carlisle Barracks, PA)
　　http://carlisle-www.army.mil/library/

　　　　*Bibliographies on military topics (e.g., operations other than war, peacekeeping,
　　　　special operations, and war-gaming) and a monthly periodical review of the military
　　　　literature.*

　　　　Online Catalog (Carlisle library catalog system)
　　　　http://carlisle-www.army.mil/library/cats.htm
　　　　telnet://144.99.67.128

　　　　Login and password: <cats>

China Lake (Naval Air Weapons Center) Technical Library
　　http://www.nawcwpns.navy.mil/~teclib/tec-home.htm/

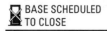 BASE SCHEDULED
　　　　　　　　　TO CLOSE

 COMMERCIAL, BUSINESS
　　　　　　　　　OPPORTUNITY

 E-MAIL
　　　　　　ADDRESS

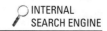 INTERNAL
　　　　　　SEARCH ENGINE

Combined Arms Research Library (CARL) (CGSC, Ft. Leavenworth, KS)
☎ 913-758-3001
http://www-cgsc.army.mil/carl/index.htm

> *Army archival and special collections relating to doctrine and operations. CARL publications include bibliographies, the* Guide to Readings in American Military History, *and* Named Operations 1989–1993. *"CARL's Bookmarks" is an excellent resource.*

> Online Catalog
> telnet://160.149.102.62

David D. Acker Library (Defense Systems Management College, Ft. Belvoir, VA)

> Online Catalog
> http://www.library.dsmc.dsm.mil/

Dudley Knox Library (Naval Postgraduate School, Monterey, CA)

> *Specializing in operations research.*

> Online Catalog (BOSUN Online)
> http://web.nps.navy.mil/~library/

Marine Corps University Libraries (Quantico, VA)
http://www.mcu.quantico.usmc.mil/www/library/library.htm

> Online Catalog ("Chesty Online")
> telnet://138.156.201.109

> *Login and password: <chui>*

National Defense University (NDU) Library (Ft. McNair, Washington, DC)
http://www.ndu.edu/ndu/library/home01.html

> *NDU Information Quest (NDU IQ), the library's online catalog systems, includes the NDU Library and the Armed Forces Staff College Library. Other online resources include "Current Journal Articles," citations and abstracts of military-related periodical literature, and a number of excellent Internet military resources guides ("Defense Nexus") (see Chapter 1).*

> Online Catalog
> http://www.ndu.edu/ndu/library/liq.html
> telnet://198.76.88.253

> *Password: <nduiq>*

Naval Research Laboratory Ruth H. Hooker Research Library (Washington, DC)
http://infoweb.nrl.navy.mil

Online Catalog
http://infoweb.nrl.navy.mil/htbin/webcat

Naval War College Library (Newport, RI)
http://user.id.net/nwc/lib.htm

★ Navy Department Library (Washington Navy Yard, Washington, DC)
☎ 202-433-4132
http://tlc.library.net/ndl/
http://www.history.navy.mil/branches/nhcorg7.htm

Pentagon Library (Room 1A518, The Pentagon)
☎ 703-697-4301
http://www.hqda.army.mil/penlibweb/

Online Catalog
telnet://134.11.24.2

Login: <guest>; type <P>; press Enter

Phillips Laboratory/Phillips Research Site Technical Library (Kirtland AFB, NM)
http://library.plk.af.mil

Online Catalog
http://library.plk.af.mil/
telnet://library.plk.af.mil
telnet://129.238.35.181

Login: <mosaic>

★ Redstone Scientific Information Center (Redstone Arsenal, Huntsville, AL)
http://library.redstone.army.mil/

Comprehensive scientific and technical library with abstracts of over 300,000 books and technical reports.

Online Catalog
http://library.redstone.army.mil/RSIC/

Uniformed Services University of the Health Sciences Library (Bethesda, MD)
http://lrcgwf.usuf2.usuhs.mil

Online Catalog
http://lrcgwf.usuf2.usuhs.mil

U.S. Naval Academy Nimitz Library (Annapolis, MD)
http://www.nadn.navy.mil/Library/

Online Catalog
telnet://131.121.188.001
telnet://library.nadn.navy.mil

Login: <library>

Virtual Information to All (VITAL) Walter Reed Library Homepage
http://wrair-www.army.mil/research/RECENT.htm

Waterways Experimental Station (WES) Research Library (Vicksburg, MS)
http://libweb.wes.army.mil/

Online Catalog
http://libweb.wes.army.mil/lib/libcat.htm
telnet://134.164.84.4

Login: <guest>; password: <weslib>

Wright Research Site Technical Library
http://www.wrs.afrl.af.mil/infores/library/

Online Catalog
http://b022-libl.wpafb.af.mil/webpac-bin/wgbroker?new+-access+top.wright

Military History Collections

Department of Defense History Office
http://web2.whs.osd.mil/histhome.htm

Includes the public statements of the Secretary of Defense online from 1994.

NEW Joint Chiefs of Staff History Publications
http://www.dtic.mil/doctrine/jel/hist_pubs.htm

Air Force Historical Research Agency (Maxwell AFB, AL)
http://www.au.af.mil/au/afhra/

Includes online bibliographies relating to historical holdings of the Air Force.

NEW Air Force History Support Office (Bolling AFB, MD)
http://www.airforcehistory.hq.af.mil

Army Center of Military History (1099 14th Street NW, Washington DC 20005-3402)
http://www.army.mil/cmh-pg/

Contains the master index of Army records depositories, microfilm library holdings related to military history, guide to military record groups at the National Archives, index of historical Army operations, campaigns and code names, guide to Army museums, and links to military history sites.

Army Military History Institute (Carlisle Barracks, PA)
http://carlisle-www.army.mil/usamhi

Depository for Army unit histories, personal papers, diaries, and photographs. The online searchable catalogs include reference bibliographies and the Army archives database.

NEW Marine Corps History
http://www.usmc.mil/history.nsf/table+of+contents

Naval Historical Center (Washington Navy Yard, Washington DC)
http://www.history.navy.mil

Online topics range from the evolution of naval aircraft markings to a UFO Research Guide, including biographies, bibliographies, active ship levels from 1917 to the present, aviation squadron lineages, and fact sheets on the current aircraft inventory, as well as photographic sources. The Historical Center is the umbrella organization for the Navy Museum, the Navy Art Collection, the Department of the Navy Library, and the USS Constitution display ship.

★ Redstone Arsenal Historical Information
http://wwwsun.redstone.army.mil/history/welcome.html

Excellent collection of historical documents, photographs, and video on Cold War missile developments.

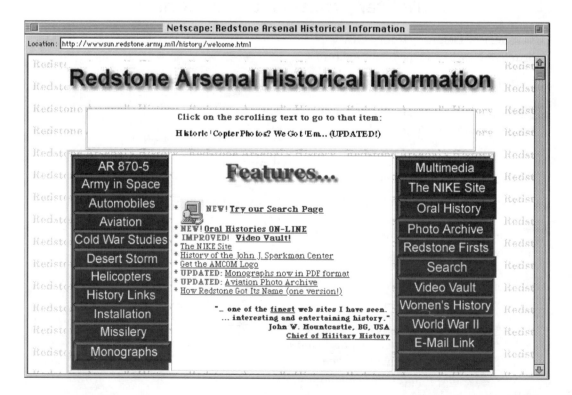

Defense Policies, Weapons, and Systems

Virtually every aspect of U.S. defense policy, from basic statements of national security and military policy, to speeches and public statements of the Secretary of Defense and other high-level officials, to extensive libraries of science and technology plans, doctrine, and policy regulations, is online. Much of the material can be found through DefenseLINK and other main homepages, but there are also extensive specialized pages down to the service level that deal with policy. Three overarching reports on national security strategy are:

National Security Strategy (White House)
http://www.whitehouse.gov/WH/EOP/NSC/strategy

National Military Strategy of the United States of America (DOD)
http://www.dtic.mil/jcs/nms.html

United States Security Strategy for Europe and NATO
http://www.dtic.mil/defenselink/pubs/europe/

The Secretary of Defense's *Annual Report to the President and Congress,* a fundamental statement of DOD policy, is online at http://www.dtic.mil/execsec/adr_intro.html 🔍 in the form of a fully searchable database starting with the 1995 report. The Chairman of the Joint Chiefs of Staff also delivers a biennial *Posture Statement* which is online at http://www.dtic.mil/jcs/chairman/shelton/98posture.pdf

Three influential panels and initiatives that have an impact on DOD activities have homepages:

NEW National Defense Panel
http://www.dtic.mil/ndp

Defense Reform Initiative
http://www.dtic.mil/defenselink/pubs/dodreform/

Quadrennial Defense Review
http://www.dtic.mil/defenselink/pubs/qdr/

Policy Directives and Regulations

The DOD has also made its directives and instructions available online, and each organization within the DOD and each military service, command, and facility (down to the lowest level) is increasingly placing directives, instructions, and regulations online. The Department of Defense Directives, Instructions and Publications website (http://web7.whs.osd.mil/corres.htm) maintained by the Washington Headquarters Services is a searchable repository of DOD directives and instructions. The DOD and DOD Agencies Libraries page (http://www.afmc.wpafb.af.mil/pdl/otherdod.htm), maintained by the Air Force Materiel Command, has links to the main policy libraries of other defense agencies and activities.

The Air Force Departmental Publishing Directorate (http://afpubs.hq.af.mil/elec-products/) manages the Air Force online policy publishing effort, posting Air Force Doctrine Documents (AFDDs), Air Force Mission Directives (AFMDs), Air Force Policy Directives (AFPDs), Air Force Instructions (AFIs), Air Force Manuals (AFMs), interim changes, publishing bulletins, recurring periodicals, unnumbered publications, and indexes. Other major Air Force commands and bases are also posting their regulations and administrative publications online, and a gateway to Air Force major command and field operating agency repositories is maintained by the Air Force Materiel Command at http://www.afmc.wpafb.af.mil/mil/pdl/majfoa.htm

The ★ Air Force Materiel Command (AFMC) Publishing Distribution Library (http://www.afmc.wpafb.af.mil/pdl) contains Air Force and AFMC directives of all types, as well as the gateways to other DOD activities and activities. Air Force Technical Orders (TOs) are also online at http://www.pdsm.wpafb.af.mil/to-system.html

The new NEW Army Publications Bookshelf (http://books.hoffman.army.mil/cgi-bin/bookmgr/Shelves), maintained by the Army Publishing Agency, replaces the original repository of IBM "Bookmaster" Army and multiservice regulations, indexes, and general orders with Web-compatible documents. Army technical and equipment publications are online at http://www.logsa.army.mil

Another new website is the NEW Navy Electronic Directives System at http://www.dodssp.daps.mil/usndirs.htm, which has Secretary of the Navy (SECNAV) and Chief of Naval Operations (OPNAV) instructions and notices online in Adobe (.pdf) format.

Marine Corps orders and directives are online at http://www.usmc.mil/directiv.nsf/web+orders The Automated ALMAR's Library (of "All Marine" policy messages from the Commandant) is also online at www.usmc.mil/almar98.nsf/98almars

BASE SCHEDULED TO CLOSE $ COMMERCIAL, BUSINESS OPPORTUNITY   E-MAIL ADDRESS   INTERNAL SEARCH ENGINE

Military Doctrine and Future Vision

Joint Doctrine

The Chairman of the Joint Chiefs of Staff 1996 statement of concepts for future military operations—Joint Vision 2010—is located at http://www.dtic.mil/doctrine/jv2010/index.html and numerous other doctrine-related sites. Joint Vision 2010 is, according to the JCS, the "conceptual template for how we will channel the vitality of our people and leverage technological opportunities to achieve new levels of effectiveness in joint warfighting." DTIC's Hot Topics Bibliography on Joint Vision 2010 (http://www.dtic.mil/dtic/bibtopics/joint_vision_2010.html) has hyperlinks to supplementary materials.

The single most useful source of official doctrinal information is the ★ Joint Electronic Library (JEL), an online (http://www.dtic.mil/doctrine/jel/ 📖) and CD-ROM compilation prepared by the Joint Staff. The JEL contains the text of unclassified joint publications, selected service publications dealing with operations and joint doctrine, related papers produced at the war colleges and military schools, and military indexes of articles in periodicals. The *Compendium of Joint Doctrine Publications* (JP 1-01.1) contains abstracts—and some executive summaries—of both unclassified and classified publications, including those in production. The Joint Warfighting Center (http://www.jwfc.js.mil) is the joint doctrine center responsible for the creation of joint doctrine.

The Joint Warrior Interoperability Demonstration (JWID), a worldwide annual exercise held since 1995, is designed to foster improvements in unified operations and information technology. Each year, a different service takes the lead. The exercise has a significant online presence, and its activities and products provide insight into current military thinking.

Army JWID 96 Homepage
http://www.army.mil/jwid96.htm

Navy JWID 97 Homepage
http://www.jwid97.bmpcoe.org

Shaw Air Force Base (CENTAF) JWID96 Homepage
http://www.jwid.centaf.af.mil/

Air Force Doctrine and Vision

The annual Air Force Posture Statement by the Secretary and Chief of Staff of the Air Force to Congress (http://www.af.mil/lib/afissues/1998/posture) reports on the current state of the service and its budget. A number of statements of Air Force vision, both to supplement Joint Vision 2010, and to promote airpower, include:

Our Nation's Air Force
  http://www.af.mil/lib/nations/

> *A paper with information about the nation's Air Force and its contributions to national security, update of the 1992 Global Reach—Global Power.*

Global Engagement—A Vision for the 21st Century Air Force
  http://www.xp.hq.af.mil/xpx/21/nuvis.htm

Cornerstones of Information Warfare (1995)
  http://www.dtic.mil/airforcelink/pubs/corner.html

> *Secretary and Chief of Staff of the Air Force White Paper on information warfare.*

Air Force Congressional Issue Papers
  http://www.af.mil/lib/afissues/1998/issue98.html

> *Executive summaries of key issues facing the Air Force as provided to Congress.*

Air Force Issue Book
  http://www.af.mil/lib/afissues/1997/index.html

> *A yearly blueprint to explain how the Air Force will reach its goals and initiatives.*

Air Force Policy Letter Digest
  http://www.af.mil/lib/policy/

> *A monthly digest of "leadership messages from senior officials on issues affecting the Air Force and its members."*

The Air Force Strategic Planning Directorate (AF/XPX) (http://www.af-future.hq.af.mil/) maintains an online reading list of these and other doctrinal and planning documents bearing upon current and future policy.

A series of research projects and studies to define the long-term future of the Air Force began with the *Spacecast 2020* study conducted at the Air University at Maxwell AFB, AL, and continued with the *Air Force 2025* Study. In 1995, the Air Force Scientific Advisory Board also completed a major study of the state of technology and the future of the service—*New World Vistas: Air and Space Power for the 21st Century,* the first comprehensive evaluation of aerospace technology in decades.

Air Force 2025 Final Report Homepage
  http://www.au.af.mil/au/2025/

New World Vistas Study Page
  http://web.fie.com/fedix/vista.html

 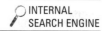

Spacecast 2020
http://www.au.af.mil/Spacecast/Spacecast.html

The newly created Air Force Doctrine Center (http://hqafdc.maxwell.af.mil) is responsible for doctrine, while the Air Force Battle Laboratories (http://www.hq.af.mil/xo/afbattlelab) test operational concepts in different disciplines. The laboratories are Air Expeditionary Force Battlelab (AEFB), Information Warfare Battlelab (IWB), Unmanned Air Vehicle Battlelab (UAVB), Space Battlelab (SB), Force Protection Battlelab (FPB), and Command and Control, Battle Management Battlelab (C2BMB). The Air Force Expeditionary Experiment (EFX) (http://www.efx.acc.af.mil) has a particularly extensive collection of materials.

Army Doctrine and Vision

The text of the latest Army Posture Statement as presented to Congress by the Secretary and Chief of Staff is online at http://www.army.mil/aps/default.htm Army Vision 2010— ". . . the blueprint for the operational concepts identified in Joint Vision 2010. It is the conceptual template for how the United States Army will channel the vitality and innovation of its soldiers and civilians and leverage technological opportunities to achieve new levels of effectiveness as the land component member of the joint warfighting team. The blueprint following on Joint Vision 2010 . . ."—is online at http://www.army.mil/2010 "America's Army . . . Projecting Decisive Power Into the 21st Century," the basic future Army White Paper, is online at http://www.asafm.army.mil/army/sep95/intro.htm Further elaborations of Army vision are contained in the *Force of Decision* White Paper at http://www.hqda.army.mil/ocsa/

The Army has an extensive futuristic warfare development program, derived from the *Report on the Army After Next* (1996) and myriad "Force XXI" activities. They are coordinated by TRADOC and are articulated in *Force XXI Operations: A Concept for the Evolution of Full-Dimensional Operations for the Strategic Army of the Early Twenty-first Century* (TRADOC PAM 525-5), the text of which is contained at the Force XXI homepage.

NEW Army After Next
http://www-tradoc.monroe.army.mil/dcsdoc/aan.htm

Including access to Army Vision 2010, Land Combat in the 21st Century, Force XXI Operations, integrated concept teams, future operational capabilities (FOCs), and various workshops and conference papers.

Force XXI Homepage
http://204.7.227.75:433

Background, history, and status of the program, including a calendar, minutes of meetings, the Force XXI Campaign Plan, briefings, articles, acronyms, and links to other XXI initiatives and demonstrations (e.g., Infantry Force XXI, Leader XXI, Engineering XXI).

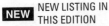 

Force XXI Intranet
http://199.221.105.201/digitize

Warfighter XXI/Battle Command Training Program
http://leav-www.army.mil/bctp

Army Battle Labs Homepage
http://battlelabs.monroe.army.mil/

> *Includes the Air Defense Battle Lab (Ft. Bliss, TX), Battle Command (Ft. Huachuca, AZ; Ft. Gordon, GA; and Ft. Leavenworth, KS), Battle Command Training Program (Ft. Leavenworth, KS), Brigade Command and Battle Staff Training Program (Ft. Leavenworth, KS), Combat Service Support Battle Lab (Ft. Lee, VA), Depth and Simultaneous Attack Battle Lab (Ft. Sill, OK), Dismounted Battlespace Battle Lab (Ft. Benning, GA), Early Entry Lethality and Survivability Battle Lab (Ft. Monroe, VA), Military Police School—Battle Laboratory Support (Ft. McClellan, AL), and Mounted Battlespace Battle Lab (Ft. Knox, KY).*

NEW Army Technologies and Concepts—Network (ARTAC-Net)
http://tiu-arl.mil/artac

Act II Program
http://www.aro.ncren.net/arowash/rt/actii.htm

Army Materiel Command (AMC) Science & Technology Objectives
http://www2.brtrc.com/stos/

Army Digitization Office 🔎
http://www.ado.army.mil

Both the Army Training and Doctrine Command (TRADOC) (http://www-tradoc.army.mil/dcsdoc/index.html) and the Command and General Staff College Doctrine Digital Library (http://www-cgsc.army.mil/cgsc/cdd/doc-lib.htm) maintain doctrine homepages with links to reports and Army manuals. The Army budget office also maintains a library of policy publications at http://134.11.192.15/pubs/pubs.html Formal Army doctrine is generally developed by the various doctrinal centers associated with the different branches of the service (e.g., infantry, air defense, etc.). In addition to the TRADOC and Leavenworth homepages, each of these schools and centers maintains doctrinal homepages.

The ★ Army Training Digital Library (http://www.atsc-army.org/atdls.html 🔎 📖), the "electronic library without walls," contains a growing online library of Field Manuals (FMs), training plans, training circulars, soldiers' manuals, and other documents containing instructional, informational, and reference material relating to military training and operations. It has an excellent search engine that covers JCS publications as well.

Navy Doctrine and Vision

Forward . . . From the Sea: Anytime, Anywhere, the 1998 posture statement of the Navy (http://www.chinfo.navy.mil/navpalib/policy/fromsea/pos98/pos-top.html), amplifies the Joint Vision 2010 strategy and highlights the status of the Navy. Other White Papers that articulate Navy vision include:

Forward Presence (December 1996)
http://www.chinfo.navy.mil/navpalib/policy/fromsea/fwdpresn.html

> *Written by the Chief of Naval Operations and the Commandant of the Marine Corps.*

Enduring Impact . . . From the Sea (1997 Posture Statement)
http://www.chinfo.navy.mil/navpalib/policy/fromsea/pos97/pos-top.html

Forward . . . From the Sea, the Navy Operational Concept (March 1997)
http://www.chinfo.navy.mil/navpalib/policy/fromsea/ffseanoc.html
http://www.dtic.mil/doctrine/jv2010/navy/b014.pdf

Copernicus . . . Forward (1995)
http://www.chinfo.navy.mil/navpalib/policy/coperfwd.txt

> *Navy White Paper on the C4I information management architecture for supporting the fleet.*

Forward . . . From the Sea (November 1994)
http://www.chinfo.navy.mil/navpalib/policy/fromsea/forward.txt

> *Update to the original 1992 White Paper.*

Carriers for Force 2001 (May 1993)
http://www.chinfo.navy.mil/navpalib/policy/fromsea/ftsucf2.txt

Force Sustainment (May 1993)
http://www.chinfo.navy.mil/navpalib/policy/fromsea/ftsufs.txt

Joint Operations . . . From the Sea (May 1993)
http://www.chinfo.navy.mil/navpalib/policy/fromsea/ftsujo.txt

Naval Forward Presence . . . Essential for a Changing World (May 1993)
http://www.chinfo.navy.mil/navpalib/policy/fromsea/ftsunfp.txt

. . . From the Sea (September 1992)
http://www.chinfo.navy.mil/navpalib/policy/fromsea/fromsea.txt

The **NEW** Naval Doctrine Command (http://ndc.navy.mil) is responsible for the development and publication of naval doctrine, much of which is available at this website or via the Joint Electronic Library. The **NEW** Navy Acquisition Research and Development Center

(NARDIC) Publications and Regulations Site (http://nardic.nrl.navy.mil/pubs.htm ✉) is an online library of policy and budget-related materials. The Naval Warfighting Innovation homepage (http://ssginnov.cna.org/) is intended to be the concept generation process formed around the Strategic Studies Group located at the Naval War College.

Marine Corps Doctrine and Vision

Operational Maneuver from the Sea (http://www.dtic.mil/doctrine/jv2010/usmc/omfts.pdf) is the current Marine Corps vision statement supplementing Joint Vision 2010. The central statement of Marine Corps vision is the *Commandant's Planning Guidance,* found online at http://www.usmc.mil A searchable database of Marine Corps concepts and issues relating to ongoing programs and policies is accessible at http://www.ismo-www1.mqg.usmc.mil/concepts/concepts.htm ⌕

The Marine Corps Combat Development Command (MCCDC) Doctrine Division (http://ismo-www1.mqg.usmc.mil/docdiv/index.html) maintains the central online repository of Marine Corps Doctrinal Publications (MCDPs), Warfighting Publications (MCWPs), and Reference Publications (MRPs), new types of documents replacing older Fleet Marine Force Manuals (FMFMs). Marine Corps Doctrine Manuals are also online at http://138.156.107.3/docdiv/manuals.htm The MCCDC Concepts Branch (http://ismo-www1.mqg.usmc.mil/concepts) deals with broader concepts and publishes White Papers dealing with operational challenges facing the Marines.

Marine Corps Science and Technology Program Plan
   http://www.usmc-awt.brtrc.com/FY98PP/pp_toc.htm

Marine Corps Warfighting Lab
   http://ismo-www1.mqg.usmc.mil/cwl-main

Weapons and Systems

Research, Development, and Testing

The Office of the ★ Under Secretary of Defense for Acquisition and Technology (http://www.acq.osd.mil/) website is the main weapons and systems starting point for DOD-wide programs and includes extensive links to a variety of specialized sites dealing with all aspects of defense research, development, and acquisition.

The basic documents of defense science and technology planning are fully available online at http://www.dtic.mil/dstp/index.html ⌕, including the *Defense Science and Technology Strategy,* the *Basic Research Plan,* the *Defense Technology Objective,* the *Defense Technology Area Plan,* and the *Joint Warfighting Science and Technology Plan,* as well as selected service and defense agency planning documents.

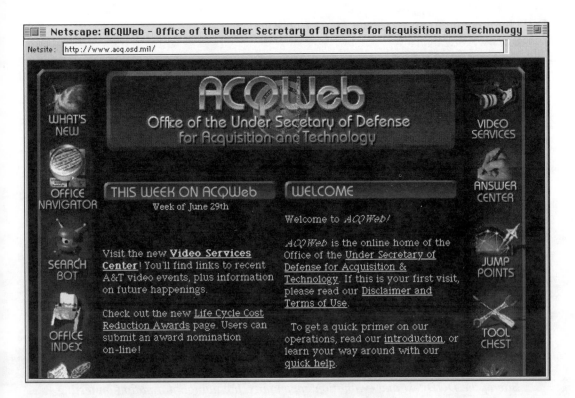

The Science and Technology Planning Information Website (http://www.afmc.wpafb.af.mil/STBBS) maintained by the Air Force Materiel Command has many of the same documents, as well as the *Technology Area Plans* of the Air Force. The Army Science & Technology Master Plan is online at http://www.sarda.army.mil/sard-zt/ASTMP/index.htm, and the Army Air and Missile Defense Master Plan is online at http://147.71.152.73/amd/ The 1997 Navy Science and Technology Requirements Guide (STRG) is also online at http://www.hq.navy.mil/strg97/

Defense Research and Engineering LabLINK Homepage
    http://www.dtic.mil/lablink/

Defense Research and Engineering Laboratory Management (Labman) and Technology Transition
    http://www.dtic.mil/labman/

> *Includes the "DOD In-house RDT&E Activities: Management Analysis Reports" for fiscal years 1993 to the present and documents related to laboratory management.*

Defense Research and Engineering Network (DREN)
    http://info.arl.army.mil/ACIS/ACD/DREN/index.html

> *The networking component of the DOD High Performance Computing Modernization Program.*

DOD Information Analysis Center (IAC) Hub Page
http://www.dtic.mil/iac/

DOD Laboratories Activities List
http://www.dtic.mil/labman/projects/list.html

Federal Laboratory Consortium for Technology Transfer
http://www.fedlabs.org/

Live Fire Test and Evaluation Homepage
http://www.dote.osd.mil/lfte/index.html

TechTRANSIT
http://www.dtic.mil/techtransit/index.html

> *Technology transfer issues including Federal Defense Laboratory Diversification (FDLD), Small Business Innovation Research (SBIR), and Independent Research and Development (IR&D).*

★ Test and Evaluation (T&E) Community Network (TECNET) Homepage
http://tecnet0.jcte.jcs.mil:9000/

> *Site of the DOD test and evaluation community, including information on testing facilities and projects, the Major Range Test Facility Base (MRTFB) Database, various bulletin boards, news, and references.*

DOD Weapons Programs and Information

C4ISR Cooperative Research Program
http://www.dodccrp.org

Chemical Warfare/Chemical & Biological Defense IAC (CBIAC)
http://www.cbiac.apgea.army.mil

Chemical Weapons
http://www.cbdcom.apgea.army.mil/RDA/erdec/risk/safety/msds/

Cooperative Threat Reduction Homepage
http://www.ctr.osd.mil

NEW Counterproliferation Homepage
http://www.acq.osd.mil/cp

Department of Defense Explosives Safety Board
http://www.acq.osd.mil/ens/esb/

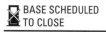 

Department of Defense Homepage for Space
http://www.acq.osd.mil/space/

Global Command and Control System (GCCS)
http://spider.osfl.disa.mil/index.html
http://204.34.175.79

NEW Humanitarian Demining Homepage 🔎
http://www.demining.brtrc.com

> *Includes an interactive mine database developed by the former Office of Humanitarian and Refugee Affairs in the Secretary of Defense's office, and other information.*

Survivability/Vulnerability Information Analysis Center (SURVIAC)
http://surviac.flight.wpafb.af.mil/

Joint Weapons and Systems Programs and Information

Defense Meteorological Satellite Program (DMSP)
http://www.laafb.af.mil/SMC/CI

NEW Joint Non-lethal Weapons Program
http://www.hqmc.usmc.mil/nlw/nlw.nsf

Joint Modeling and Simulation System (J-MASS) (Wright-Patterson AFB, OH)
http://www.jmass.wpafb.af.mil/

Joint Service Small Arms Program (JSSAP) (Picatinny Arsenal, Dover, NJ)
http://www.pica.army.mil/orgs/ccac/ccj.html

Joint Simulation System (JSIMS)
http://www.jsims.mil/

Joint Standoff Weapons (JSOW) Program Office (Eglin AFB, FL)
http://www.acq-ref.navy.mil/jsow.html

Joint Strike Fighter (JSF) Program Office
http://www.jast.mil/

> *Formerly called Joint Advanced Strike Technology (JAST).*

Joint Surveillance Target Attack Radar System (JSTARS) Joint Program Office
(Robins AFB, GA)
http://www.jstars.af.mil

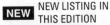 

Joint Tactical Unmanned Aerial Vehicles (UAVs) Project Office (Redstone Arsenal, Huntsville, AL)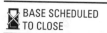
http://wwwjtuav.redstone.army.mil/

Joint Warfare System (JWARS)
http://www.dtic.mil/jwars

Military Satellite Communications Joint Program Office
http://www.laafb.af.mil/smc/mc

> *Links to Defense Satellite Communications System (DSCS), Orion Global Broadcast Satellite (GBS), Military Strategic and Tactical Relay (Milstar), and Advanced Programs.*

★ Navstar Global Positioning System (GPS) Joint Program Office (Los Angeles AFB, CA)
http://www.laafb.af.mil/SMC/CZ/homepage/

Small Arms Program Manager (Picatinny Arsenal, NJ)
http://www.pica.army.mil/orgs/pmsa/

Air Force Programs

Air Force Global Command and Control System
http://www.afgccs.hanscom.af.mil

Air Force Space Page
http://ax.laafb.af.mil/frame3.html

NEW Airborne Laser Program
http://prs.plk.af.mil/ABL/tm.html

B-1B "Lancer" System Program Office (ASC, Wright-Patterson AFB, OH)
http://www.b1b.wpafb.af.mil

B-52 System Program Office
http://bncc.tinker.af.mil/alclhl/

Combat Air Forces System Program Office
http://tbmcs.af.mil

> *Formerly the Theater Battle Management Core Systems.*

Evolved Expendable Launch Vehicle (EELV) Program Office
http://www.laafb.af.mil/SMC/MV/eelvhome.htm

F-15 Eagle System Program Office (Robins AFB, GA)
http://eaglenet.robins.af.mil

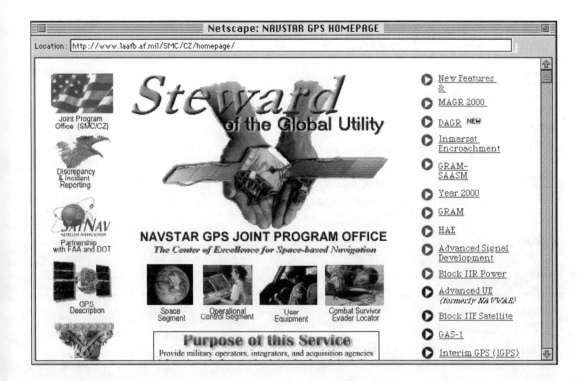

F-16 System Program Office (Wright-Patterson AFB, OH)
http://f16.wpafb.af.mil

NEW Theater Battle Arena
http://www.tba.hq.af.mil

Army Programs

★ Command, Control, Communications, Computers, Intelligence and Electronic Warfare
Project Book (CECOM)
http://cecom5.monmouth.army.mil/intranet/projbk98.nsf

*Alphabetical, nomenclature, and system/equipment name index and descriptions of
over 100 Army C4I-related projects and programs.*

Crusader (Project Manager, Picatinny Arsenal, NJ)
http://www.pica.army.mil/orgs/crusader/top.html

Enhanced Fiber-Optic Guided Missile System
http://efogm.redstone.army.mil

Paladin/Field Artillery Ammunition Support Vehicle (Program Manager,
Picatinny Arsenal, NJ)
http://www.pica.army.mil/orgs/paladin

 NEW LISTING IN THIS EDITION   ONLINE FACT SHEET   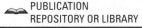 PUBLICATION REPOSITORY OR LIBRARY   ★ RECOMMENDED SITE   TELEPHONE NUMBER

NEW Program Executive Office Intelligence, Electronic Warfare and Sensors (PEO IEWS)
http://www.monmouth.army.mil/peoiw/peoiw.html

NEW Program Executive Office C3 Systems
http://www.monmouth.army.mil/peoc3s

NEW Program Executive Office Ground Combat and Support Systems
http://www.pica.army.mil/orgs/peogcss/

NEW Project Manager for Mines, Countermine, and Demolitions (ARDEC)
http://www.pica.army.mil/orgs/pm-mcd/1mcdhome.htm

Navy and Marine Corps Programs

CVX (Future Aircraft Carrier Information Site, NAVSEA)
http://www.navsea.navy.mil/cvx/teamcvx.html

NEW Naval Arms Control
http://www.nawcwpns.navy.mil/~treaty/arms_control.html

NEW New Attack Submarine (NSSN)
http://www.nssn.navy.mil

LPD-17 Program
http://lpd17.nswc.navy.mil/

Surface Combatant for the 21st Century (Project Office, NAVSEA)
http://sc21.crane.navy.mil

Modeling and Simulation Initiatives

Defense Modeling and Simulation Office (DMSO)
http://www.dmso.mil/

Includes links and the modeling and simulation resource repository.

Defense Modeling, Simulation, and Tactical Technology Information Analysis Center
(DMSTTIAC)
http://dmsttiac.hq.iitri.com/

Information Technology Service Center
http://www.sc.ist.ucf.edu/

Modeling and Simulation Operational Support Activity
http://www.msosa.mil.inter.net

BASE SCHEDULED
TO CLOSE

 $ COMMERCIAL, BUSINESS
OPPORTUNITY

 E-MAIL
ADDRESS

 INTERNAL
SEARCH ENGINE

Air Force Agency for Modeling and Simulation
http://www.afams.af.mil

NEW Air Force Center for Modeling, Simulation and Analysis (AFIT)
http://www.afit.af.mil/Schools/EN/ENS/CMS&A.html

Air Force Modeling and Simulation Resource Repository
http://afmsrr.afams.af.mil

Army Model and Simulation Office
http://www.amso.army.mil

NEW Army Model and Simulation Resource Repository
http://www.msrr.army.mil

Army Simulation, Training and Instrumentation Command (STRICOM)
http://www.stricom.army.mil/

Chief of Naval Operations Office of Training Technology
http://www.ott.navy.mil

NEW Department of the Navy Modeling and Simulation Management Office
http://navmsmo.nosc.mil/default.htm

Navy Test and Evaluation Modeling and Simulation
http://www.nawcad.navy.mil/tems

NEW Marine Air Ground Task Force Staff Training Program
http://www.mstp.quantico.usmc.mil/mstp

5

The Business of the Department of Defense

The Internet is central to the federal government's commitment to electronic commerce and business "reengineering." In order to transition to a paperless way of doing business, hundreds of acquisition, budget, and contracting homepages are maintained by the DOD, the agencies, and the services, as well as individual commands and bases. All military commands, particularly the main materiel commands (e.g., Defense Logistics Agency, Air Force Materiel Command, Army Materiel Command, Navy systems commands), laboratories, and research and development centers, are increasingly making use of the Internet for posting announcements and solicitations (which appear or are announced in *Commerce Business Daily*), regulations and policy documents, program documents and background information, and award notices. The main pages are listed in this chapter, though business-related sites are also designated with the $ icon throughout the Directory.

The breadth and scope of DOD activities is such, nonetheless, that there is nowhere near any single index or database of contracting information or business opportunities, nor even a complete overview of the budget, operating systems, contracts, and procurements.

The Defense Budget

The White House Office of Management and Budget (OMB) also places a completely searchable version of the less detailed budget of the United States government on the Internet.

NEW ★ Office of the Under Secretary of Defense (Comptroller)
http://www.dtic.mil/comptroller/99budget/

> *Overview of FY 1999 defense budget request, to include economic assumptions, pay/inflation assumptions, and historical data series. Full online access to FY 1999 budget materials, National Defense Budget Estimates for FY 1999 (the "Green Book"), Program Acquisition Costs by Weapon System, Procurement Programs (P-1) (also available as Microsoft Excel 5.0 file), Procurement Programs (P-1R) (programs to support National Guard and Reserve Forces), Research, Development, Test & Evaluation Programs (R-1) (also available as Microsoft Excel 5.0 file), Military Construction Programs (C-1) (also available as Microsoft Excel 5.0 file), Operation and Maintenance Programs (O-1), and Military Personnel Programs (M-1).*

 BASE SCHEDULED TO CLOSE    $ COMMERCIAL, BUSINESS OPPORTUNITY   ✉ E-MAIL ADDRESS    INTERNAL SEARCH ENGINE

★ Research and Development Descriptive Summaries 🔎
   http://www.dtic.mil/rdds/

>   *Also known as Program Element Descriptive Summaries, this is the same data that goes to Congress to support the President's budget request, providing detailed justification and background on DOD research, development, and test and evaluation programs for fiscal years 1995 to the present.*

DOD Contract Award Announcements 🔎
   http://www.defenselink.mil/news/#CONTRACTS

Procurement History and Trends
   http://web1.whs.osd.mil/PEIDHOME/PROTREND/PROTREND.Htm

>   *DOD statistical data from FY 1951 to the present.*

Service Budgets

Assistant Secretary of the Air Force (Financial Management & Comptroller) 📖
   http://www.saffm.hq.af.mil/SAFFM/

Air Force Statistical Digest
   http://www.saffm.hq.af.mil/SAFFM/FMC/digest/digest95.html

>   *Comprehensive DOD and Air Force historical budget, equipment, personnel, and acquisition data.*

NEW Air Force Cost Analysis Agency (AFCAA)
   http://www.saffm.hq.af.mil/SAFFM/afcaa/afcaa.html

Air Force Visibility and Management of Operating and Support Costs (VAMOSC)
   http://www.saffm.hq.af.mil/SAFFM/FMC/vamosc.html

>   *Includes Air Force Cost and Planning Factors (AFI 65-503).*

★ Assistant Secretary of the Army, Financial Management and Comptroller 📖
   http://www.asafm.army.mil
   http://134.11.192.15/

Army Budget ("Green Book")
   http://134.11.192.15/pubs/greenbk/

>   *The President's budget as submitted to Congress, including budget overview, prior year actual spending and supplemental spending. Fiscal years 1995 to the present are online.*

Army Cost and Economic Analysis Center
   http://134.11.192.15/ceac.htm

NEW Assistant Secretary of the Navy, Financial Management and Comptroller
http://navweb.secnav.navy.mil/

★ Navy Budget Page
http://navweb.secnav.navy.mil/budget

Includes the full budget justification materials of the Navy and Marine Corps.

Navy Budget Documents Archive
http://www.chinfo.navy.mil/navpalib/budget/.www/budget.html

Naval Center for Cost Analysis (NCCA) Homepage
http://www.ncca.navy.mil/

Base Closures and Realignment

The Defense Base Closure and Realignment Commission closed its doors on 29 December 1995, after completing four rounds—1988, 1991, 1993, and 1995—of military base closure recommendations. In all, 243 installations were recommended for closure. The recommendations, laws, and notices in the *Federal Register* are located at http://fedbbs.access.gpo.gov/libs/fr_base.htm A number of base closures homepages detail ongoing efforts to implement the decisions and close more bases.

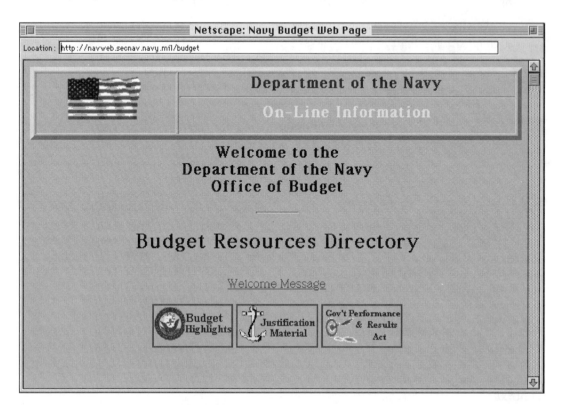

 BASE SCHEDULED TO CLOSE   COMMERCIAL, BUSINESS OPPORTUNITY E-MAIL ADDRESS  INTERNAL SEARCH ENGINE

DOD Policy on Base Closures
   http://www.defenselink.mil/other_info/brac.html

★ DOD Base Closure and Community Reinvestment (OSD)
   http://www.acq.osd.mil/iai/bccr.htm

Department of Defense Installations Homepage 🔎
   http://www.acq.osd.mil/inst/

Air Force Base Conversion Agency
   http://www.afbca.hq.mil

Army Base Realignment and Closure Web Site
   http://www.hqda.army.mil/acsimweb/brac/braco.htm

★ Navy Base Closures Staff
   http://www.n4.hq.navy.mil/n44/n44main.htm

Navy Base Closures and Realignment
   http://www.chinfo.navy.mil/navpalib/baseclos/

Doing Business with the Defense Department

The Defense Department and each of the services maintain a "Doing Business" homepage, with information about acquisitions, acquisition reform, and the various special contracting programs such as the Small Business Innovative Research (SBIR) program, as well as access to the popular publications *Selling to the Military* (http://www.acq.osd.mil/sadbu/guides.html), *Doing Business with the Department of Defense* (http://www.defenselink.mil/other_info/business.html), *Your Introduction to Electronic Commerce, Subcontracting Opportunities with DoD Major Prime Contractors, Defense Contracting Regulations: A Guide for Small Business, Small Disadvantaged Business, and Women-Owned Business, SBIR/STTR Program, Procurement Technical Assistance Program, Guide to DOD Environmental Procurement*, and *Defense Contracting Regulations*. Each of the better contracting homepages includes Announcements (synopses of upcoming solicitations, special notices, contract awards, Broad Agency Announcements), Solicitations (open solicitations, announcements as published in *Commerce Business Daily*, statements of work, personnel qualification sheets), Information Documents (draft solicitations and other advance planning information), and Points of Contact.

ACQWeb—OUSD (A&T) Homepage
   http://www.acq.osd.mil/

> *The DOD central acquisition homepage of the Office of the Under Secretary of Defense for Acquisition and Technology.*

Central Contractor Registration
http://ccr.edi.disa.mil

> *Electronic home for registration of companies as "trading partners" of the federal government.*

Defense Acquisition Board
http://www.acq.osd.mil/api/asm/dabschdl.html

Defense Acquisition Deskbook
http://www.deskbook.osd.mil
http://deskbook.osd.mil/deskbook.html

> *Online (and CD-ROM) system to help the DOD acquisition community ask and review questions dealing with policy interpretation and resource guidance. Includes a Software Tools Catalog of government-owned and -used programs, including descriptions, type, assessment, requirements, and points of contact; an Acquisition Management Bulletin Board; a Calendar of Events; and Customer and Technical Support.*

Defense Electronic Commerce Office
http://www.acq.osd.mil/ec

Defense Procurement Home Page
http://www.acq.osd.mil/dp/

The DTIC Acquisition Information Home Page
http://www.dtic.mil/hovlane/

Acquisition Reform

DOD Acquisition Reform Homepage
http://www.acq.osd.mil/ar

Air Force Acquisition Reform Homepage
http://www.safaq.hq.af.mil/SAFAQ/acq_ref/

Army Acquisition Corps Homepage
http://www.sarda.army.mil/dacm/

Navy Acquisition Reform Office
http://www.acq-ref.navy.mil/

DTIC Acquisition Reform Links
http://www.dtic.mil/dtiwl/toc_acq.q.html

TECNET Acquisition Reform Links
http://tecnet0.jcte.jcs.mil:9000/htdocs/teinfo/acqreform.html

Acquisition Regulations, Specifications, and Standards

DOD Acquisition Systems Management Publications
http://www.acq.osd.mil/api/asm/product.html

DOD Contracting Regulations
http://www.dtic.mil/contracts/

Information about the DAR (Defense Acquisition Regulations) system, including a statement on its organization and mission, as well as the 25 DAR committees. In addition, it provides information on the status of the open FAR (Federal Acquisition Regulation) and DFARS (Defense Federal Acquisition Regulations Supplement) cases, a matrix of FAR contract clauses, full text of departmental letters, and other sources of information on the FAR and DFARS.

Air Force FAR Site (AFMC Contracting Laboratory, Hill AFB, UT) 🔍
http://farsite.hill.af.mil/

Another gateway to federal acquisition regulations, DFARS, AFARS, and other acquisition regulations.

Defense Standardization Program Office Homepage
http://www.acq.osd.mil/es/std/stdhome.html

Background information, the standardization library, and reports on changes in contracting and standards.

DOD Index of Specifications and Standards
http://www.dtic.mil/stinet/htgi/dodiss

DOD Single Stock Point for Military Specifications & Standards (DODSSP) Homepage
http://www.dodssp.daps.mil

Specifications and standards homepage with ordering access to a complete collection of military and federal standardization documents and related publications.

Air Force Specifications and Standards Homepage
http://www.afmc.wpafb.af.mil/organizations/HQ-AFMC/EN/spec_std/spec_std.htm

Army Milspecs and Standards
http://acqnet.sarda.army.mil/amc/amcspec.htm

Navy Specs and Standards
http://www.acq-ref.navy.mil/specs.html

DOD Financial Management Regulations
http://www.dtic.mil/comptroller/fmr

Small Business Innovative Research (SBIR)/Small Business Technology Transfer (STTR) Program

The DOD Small Business Innovation Research (SBIR) program and the related Small Business Technology Transfer (STTR) program foster participation by small firms in high-tech research and development. A three-phased system of competitive research awards on a regular award cycle enables small business to develop (and commercialize) new ideas of military interest. The program makes available regulations, solicitations, and awards online, either through consolidated homepages or the contracting pages of major commands and laboratories.

National Technology Transfer Center (NTTC) Solicitations Homepage
(Wheeling, WV) $ ⌕
　　http://www.nttc.edu/solicitations.html

　　Federal-government-sponsored clearinghouse of SBIR/STTR solicitations, abstracts, and awards.

DOD Small Business Innovation Research (SBIR)/Small Business Technology Transfer (STTR) Program $
　　http://www.acq.osd.mil/sadbu/sbir/

DOD Director of Small and Disadvantaged Business Utilization
　　http://www.acq.osd.mil/sadbu

DTIC SBIR & STTR Homepage
　　http://www.dtic.mil/dtic/sbir/

SBIR Interactive Technical Information System (SITIS)
　　http://dticam.dtic.mil/sbir/

　　Moderated messaging system providing for anonymous dialog between potential SBIR contractors and the DOD SBIR solicitation topic authors. Using SITIS, small businesses can submit technical questions and receive answers to clarify ambiguities and/or possible omissions within the solicitation topic descriptions.

Air Force Office of Small and Disadvantaged Business Utilization (SAF/SB) $
　　http://www.safsb.hq.af.mil

　　AFMC SBIR $
　　　　http://www.afmc.wpafb.af.mil/tto/sbir/

Navy Small Business Innovative Research Program $ ⌕
　　http://www.navysbir.brtrc.com/

　　Office of Naval Research SBIR Bulletin Board $
　　　　http://www.onr.navy.mil/sci_tech/industrial/sbir_bbs/

Defense Agencies and Unified Command Business Opportunities

Ballistic Missile Defense Organization Acquisition Reporting Bulletin Board (BARBB) $
http://www.acq.osd.mil/bmdo/barbb/barbb.htm

Defense Advanced Research Projects Agency (DARPA) Business Page $
http://www.darpa.mil/info/index.htm

    DARPA Solicitations $
    http://www.darpa.mil/baa/

Defense Intelligence Agency (DIA): Doing Business with DIA $
http://www.dia.mil/vaca/prbus.html

Defense Logistics Agency $
http://www.supply.dla.mil/business.htm
http://www.dla.mil/ddas/doing.htm

National Imagery and Mapping Agency (NIMA) Procurement and Contracts $
http://164.214.2.59/poc/contracts/contracts.html

Special Operations Acquisitions and Logistics Center (SOAC) $
http://www.soac.hqsocom.mil

Strategic Command (STRATCOM) Contracting (55th Contracting Squadron, Offutt AFB) $
http://www.offutt.af.mil/55cons

Air Force Business Opportunities

The Air Force Acquisition Homepage (http://www.safaq.hq.af.mil) is the central website for
the Assistant Secretary of the Air Force for Acquisition (SAF/AQ), containing information
about acquisition reform, contracting, acquisition policy, business opportunities, acquisition
workforce development, and engineering, industrial, and environmental policy.

Deputy Assistant Secretary of the Air Force, Contracting (SAF/AQC)
http://www.safaq.hq.af.mil/contracting/

Air Force Business Opportunities $
http://www.safaq.hq.af.mil/contracting/biz_opty.html

Bases and Commands

Air Education and Training Command (AETC) Contracting $
http://www-contracting.aetc.af.mil/

Air Force Materiel Command Contracting $ 🔎
http://www.afmc.wpafb.af.mil/HQ-AFMC/PK/

> Aeronautical Systems Center (ASC) Acquisition Bulletin Board $
> http://www.wpafb.af.mil/az

> ASC Business Opportunities and Contracting Directorate $
> http://www.wpafb.af.mil/pk/

> Aeronautical Systems Center (ASC) Pre-award Information Exchange System
> (PIXS) $
> http://www.pixs.wpafb.af.mil/

Air Force Country Store, Hanscom AFB, MA
http://www.hanscom.af.mil/orgs/spo/AVC/Cstore

Air Force Development Test Center (AFDTC)/Eglin AFB Contracting Homepage $
http://EGLINPK.EGLIN.AF.mil/index.htm

Air Force Flight Test Center (AFFTC)/Edwards AFB Business Opportunities $
http://afftc_pk.elan.af.mil/

Air Force Research Laboratory (AFRL) Information Directorate/Rome Business
Opportunities $
http://www.if.afrl.af.mil/div/IFK/IFK_home.html

AFRL Materials and Manufacturing Directorate/Wright Research Site Contracting
Homepage $
http://www.wrs.afrl.af.mil/contract/

AFRL Philips Research Site Contracting $
http://prs.plk.af.mil/PK/mainmenu.htm

Air Force Special Operations Command (AFSOC) Business Opportunities $
http://www.hurlburt.af.mil/cgi-bin/afbop

Bolling AFB (11th Contracting Squadron) Washington DC Contracting $
http://www.bolling.af.mil/lg/cont/cons/default.htm

★ Hanscom Electronic RFP Bulletin Board (HERBB) $
http://herbb.hanscom.af.mil/

| ⧗ BASE SCHEDULED TO CLOSE | $ COMMERCIAL, BUSINESS OPPORTUNITY | ✉ E-MAIL ADDRESS | 🔎 INTERNAL SEARCH ENGINE |

Human Systems Center (HSC)/Brooks AFB Contracting $
http://www.brooks.af.mil/HSC/PK/master.html

Munitions Directorate/Wright Lab Business Opportunities $
http://www.munitions.eglin.af.mil/public/contract/contract.html

Ogden Air Logistics Center Contracting Directorate $
http://contracting.hill.af.mil/ktrhomepage.htm

Oklahoma City Air Logistics Center Contracting Directorate $
http://137.240.57.209

Sacramento Air Logistics Center Contracting Directorate $
http://www.mcclellan.af.mil/PK/pkhome.htm

San Antonio RFP and Acquisition Highway (SARAH) $
http://www.brooks.af.mil/HSC/PK/sarah.htm

San Antonio Air Logistics Center (SA-ALC) Business Opportunities $ 🔎
http://www.kelly-afb.org/links/procur/index.htm

The Space Page $
http://ax.laafb.af.mil/frame3.html

Space & Missile Systems Center (SMC) Business Opportunities
(Los Angeles Air Force Base, CA) $
   http://www.laafb.af.mil/SMC/PK/PKHOME/pkhome.htm

Standard Systems Group (SSG) Contracting Homepage $
   http://www.ssg.gunter.af.mil/PK/pkhome.html

Warner Robins Air Logistics Center Business Opportunities/Contracting $
   http://contracting.robins.af.mil/
   http://pkec.robins.af.mil

U.S. Air Forces in Europe (USAFE) Contracting Squadron $
   http://www.usafe.af.mil/joint/cons/cons.html

Army Business Opportunities

The Army Acquisition Website (http://acqnet.sarda.army.mil/) is the central website for
Army procurement information, business opportunities, contracting information, and acquisition reform.

Army Business Opportunities Main Page $
   http://acqnet.sarda.army.mil/busopp/default.htm

Army Electronic Commerce Website
   http://www.army.mil/ec

Army Contracting Organizations and Websites
   http://acqnet.sarda.army.mil/procorg/zpdt.htm
   Includes the Army Contracting Organization and Management Data Book.

Bases and Commands

Aberdeen Test Center Business Opportunities $
   http://www.atc.army.mil/business.html

Army C3I Business Opportunities $
   http://www.dtic.mil:80/c3i/c3ibusop.html

Armaments Research, Development and Engineering Center (ARDEC)
Procurement Information Network (ProcNet) $
   http://procnet.pica.army.mil/

      ARDEC Business Opportunities $
         http://www.pica.army.mil/pica/busops.html

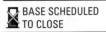 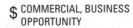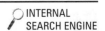

Army Aviation and Missile Command Team Redstone Acquisition Center $
   http://www.redstone.army.mil/acq_ctr
   http://michp753.redstone.army.mil/procbbs/

Army Materiel Command (AMC) Business Opportunities/Acquisition Bulletin Board System $
   http://www.amc.army.mil/business_opportuities/

     Army Materiel Command Acquisition Center $
       http://www.cbdcom.apgea.army.mil/Staff/parc/AMCAC/

     CECOM Business Opportunities Homepage $
       http://134.80.11.9/

     CECOM Business Opportunities $
       http://acbop.monmouth.army.mil/

     CECOM Fort Huachuca Acquisition Web Page $
       http://cissb.hqusec.army.mil/

     Industrial Operations Command (IOC) Acquisition Center $
       http://www-ioc.army.mil/ac/aais/ioc/

     STRICOM Business Opportunities $
       http://www.stricom.army.mil/STRICOM/A-Dir/

Army Research Laboratory (ARL) Business Opportunities $
   http://www.arl.mil/EA/busops-index.html

     ARL Contracting Homepage $
       http://w3.arl.mil/contracts/

     ARL Technology Transfer Homepage $
       http://www.arl.mil/tto/index.html

Army Research Office Business Opportunities $
   http://www.aro.army.mil/research/index.htm/

Army Space and Missile Defense Acquisition Center $
   www.smdc.army.mil/AcqCtr.html

     Army Space and Missile Defense Command Business Opportunities $
       http://www.smdc.army.mil/contract.html

Army Special Operations Command $
   http://www.usasoc.soc.mil/dcsac/

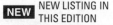 

Army Tank-Automotive and Armaments Command (TACOM) Acquisition Center $
http://www.tacom.army.mil/acq_ctr/index.htm

Army Test and Evaluation Command Business $
http://www.tecom.army.mil/frames/business.html

Army Training and Doctrine Command (TRADOC) Acquisitions $
http://www.tradoc-acq.army.mil/

Ft. Campbell Contracting $
http://150.152.51.5/

Ft. Leavenworth/Army Combined Arms Center Business Opportunities/Directorate of
Contracting $
http://www-leav.army.mil/doc

Ft. Stewart Procurement Actions $
http://www.stewart.army.mil/doc/intro.htm

Team Redstone Acquisition Center $
http://michp753.redstone.army.mil/procbbs/

Watervliet Arsenal Procurement $
http://www.wva.army.mil/PROC.Htm

Waterways Experimental Station (WES) Tri-Service Contract Solicitation Network $
http://tsn.wes.army.mil/

White Sands Missile Range (WSMR) Procurement $
http://www-wsmr.army.mil/DOCPAGE/DOCPAGE.Htm

Navy and Marine Corps Business Opportunities

The Navy Acquisition and Business Management Web (http://www.abm.rda.hq.navy.mil)
provides central access to Navy Procurement policies and procedures as well as acquisition
environmental policy, FAR/DFAR status, business practices guides, Long Range Acquisition Estimates, Congressional budgetary impact reports, and Suspension and Debarment
information.

Project Executive Officer Acquisition Related Business Systems
http://www.peoarbs.navy.mil/

Navy Acquisition Turbo Streamliner
http://www.acq-ref.navy.mil/turbo/

 BASE SCHEDULED
TO CLOSE

$ COMMERCIAL, BUSINESS
OPPORTUNITY

 E-MAIL
ADDRESS

 INTERNAL
SEARCH ENGINE

★ Navy Long-Range Acquisition Estimates $
http://lrae.abm.rda.hq.navy.mil/

Navy Online Procurement Information System
http://neelix.nosc.mil:80/contract/

Navy Online Solicitations $
http://www.abm.rda.hq.navy.mil/solicit.html

Bases and Commands

Camp Pendleton Contracting $
http://members.aol.com/contdiv/index.html

Marine Corps Systems Command Contracting $
http://www.marcorsyscom.usmc.mil/mcscctq/default.htm

Military Sealift Command (MSC) Contracting and Procurement $
http://www.msc.navy.mil/N10/CONTHP.htm

Naval Air Systems Command (NAVAIR) Business and Solicitations $
http://www.navair.navy.mil/general_info/bus_ops.html

    Naval Air Systems Command Contracts $
    http://www.navair.navy.mil/air20/air214/conthome.htm

Naval Air Warfare Center (NAWC WPNS) Public Contract Page $
http://www.nawcwpns.navy.mil/~contract/homepubl.htm

    NAWC Training Systems Division Business Opportunities $
    http://www.ntsc.navy.mil/contract.procure.htm

Naval Research Laboratory (NRL) Business Opportunities/Contracting Division $
http://heron.nrl.navy.mil/contracts/home.htm

    NRL Technology Transfer Office
    http://infonext.nrl.navy.mil/~techtran/

Naval Sea Systems Command Contracts and Solicitations $
http://www.contracts.hq.navsea.navy.mil/acq/

    NAVSEA Business Page $
    http://www.navsea.navy.mil/navsea/acquisition.html

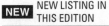 

Naval Sea Systems Command Solicitations $
http://sea02www.navsea.navy.mil/solg.html

Naval Surface Warfare Center (NSWC DD) Procurement Division $
http://www.nswc.navy.mil/supply

NSWC Crane Division Acquisition Department $
http://www.crane.navy.mil/supply/fs_acq.htm

NSWC Port Hueneme Division Doing Business Page $
http://www.nswses.navy.mil/business.htm

Naval Undersea Warfare Center (NUWC) Division Newport Contract Homepage $
http://www.npt.nuwc.navy.mil/contracts/

Office of Naval Research (ONR) Business Opportunities $
http://www.onr.navy.mil/02/bus_op.htm

ONR Funding Opportunities $
http://www.onr.navy.mil/02/baa/

Space and Naval Warfare Systems Command (SPAWAR) Headquarters Solicitations $
http://raven.spawar.navy.mil/

SPAWAR San Diego Business Opportunities/Online Procurement Information
System $
http://www.nosc.mil/nrad/html/business.html

6

Defense Department, Joint Chiefs of Staff, and Unified Commands

The Department of Defense (DOD) is composed of the Office of the Secretary of Defense, the military departments and the military services within those departments, the Chairman of the Joint Chiefs of Staff and the Joint Staff, the unified combatant commands, the defense agencies, DOD field activities, and various specialized and ad hoc offices, agencies, and activities.

The Office of the Secretary of Defense (OSD) is a vast bureaucracy, including the offices of the Deputy Secretary of Defense; the Under Secretaries for Acquisition and Technology; Policy; Comptroller/Chief Financial Officer; Personnel and Readiness; the Director of Defense Research and Engineering; and Assistant Secretaries of Defense; the General Counsel; the Inspector General; and the Director of Operational Test and Evaluation, as well as other ad hoc staff offices.

Each military department is separately organized under its own Secretary and functions under the authority, direction, and control of the Secretary of Defense (the Department of the Navy includes naval aviation and the United States Marine Corps). The Secretary of each military department is responsible to the Secretary of Defense for the operation and efficiency of the department. The Chief of each service (and the Commandant of the Marine Corps) is the ranking military officer and a member of the Joint Chiefs of Staff.

The Secretary of Defense is the principal defense policy adviser to the President and is responsible for the formulation of defense policy and for the execution of policy. The Secretary exercises authority, direction, and control over the DOD. The Deputy Secretary is delegated full power and authority to act for the Secretary of Defense.

Office of the Secretary of Defense

Office of the Secretary of Defense Homepage
http://www.defenselin.mil/osd/

> *The immediate office of the Secretary of Defense and Deputy Secretary of Defense includes executive support, military assistants, and aides and advisers.*

OSD Organization Chart
http://www.defenselink.mil/pubs/ofg/ofsecdf.pdf

Under Secretary of Defense for Policy

The office of the USD (Policy) is one of the few DOD entities that have no website. This includes the offices of the Assistant Secretaries for International Security Affairs, Strategy and Requirements, and Special Operations and Low-Intensity Conflict, and the Director, Net Assessment.

Emergency Preparedness Policy Homepage
http://www.dtic.mil/defenselink/emerg/

Searchable database of laws and regulations relating to civil and military emergency policy planning.

NEW ★ Under Secretary of Defense (Comptroller and Chief Financial Officer)
www.dtic.mil/comptroller

The website includes access to the full documentation of the DOD budget (see description in Chapter 5).

Under Secretary of Defense for Personnel and Readiness 🔍
http://dticaw.dtic.mil/prhome/

NEW Deputy Under Secretary of Defense for Program Integration
http://dticaw.dtic.mil/prhome/dusdpi.html

Deputy Under Secretary of Defense for Readiness
http://dticaw.dtic.mil/prhome/dusdr.html

Deputy Under Secretary of Defense for Requirements and Resources
http://dticaw.dtic.mil/prhome/dusdrr.html

Assistant Secretary of Defense for Reserve Affairs
http://raweb.osd.mil/

Assistant Secretary of Defense for Force Management Policy
http://dticaw.dtic.mil/prhome/asd_fmp.html

Assistant Secretary of Defense for Health Affairs
http://www.ha.osd.mil/

★ Under Secretary of Defense for Acquisition and Technology (USD (A&T)) 🔍
http://www.acq.osd.mil/

Deputy Under Secretary of Defense for Advanced Technology
http://www.acq.osd.mil/at/

Deputy Under Secretary of Defense for Acquisition Reform
http://www.acq.osd.mil/ar

NEW Deputy Under Secretary of Defense for Logistics
http://www.acq.osd.mil/log

   NEW Logistics Mosaic
http://www.acq.osd.mil/log/mosaic/

Deputy Under Secretary of Defense for Environmental Security
http://www.acq.osd.mil/ens/

   National Defense Center for Environmental Excellence
http://www.ndcee.ctc.com

   DOD Environmental Cleanup Homepage
http://www.dtic.mil/envirodod

   Assistant Deputy Under Secretary of Defense for Safety and Occupational Health
http://www.acq.osd.mil/ens/sh/

   Comprehensive homepage dealing with safety, prevention of accidents, occupational injuries/illnesses, noise pollution, radiation and electromagnetic hazards, and laser safety.

Deputy Under Secretary of Defense for Space
http://www.acq.osd.mil/space/

Director of Defense Research and Engineering (DDR&E)
http://www.dtic.mil/ddre/

Defense Acquisition Board (DAB) Executive Secretary/Acquisition Systems Management
http://www.acq.osd.mil/api/asm/

   Includes DAB schedule and Major Defense Acquisition Programs list.

Defense Airborne Reconnaissance Office
http://www.acq.osd.mil/daro/

Assistant Secretary of Defense for Command, Control, Communications and Intelligence (ASD C3I)
http://www.dtic.mil/c3i/

   Newly reorganized in 1998, including all of the communications, intelligence, and information technology issues of the Defense Department.

Assistant Secretary of Defense for Legislative Affairs
http://www.la.osd.mil/

Assistant Secretary of Defense for Public Affairs (see Chapter 2)
http://www.dtic.mil/defenselink/osd/asdpa.html

Director, Operational Test and Evaluation
http://www.dote.osd.mil/

Department of Defense General Counsel
http://www.dtic.mil/defenselink/dodgc/

> Defense Office of Hearings and Appeals
> http://www.defenselink.mil/dodgc/doha/index.html
>
> EthicsLink: Standards of Conduct Office
> http://www.defenselink.mil/dodgc/defense_ethics/index.html

★ Inspector General (400 Army-Navy Drive, Arlington, VA 22202-2884)
http://www.dodig.osd.mil/

> *Newly refurbished site with full access to IG Reports and investigations.*
> *Abstracts of DOD Audit Reports are also located at* http://www.sbaonline.sba.gov/
> ignet/internal/dod/dod.html.

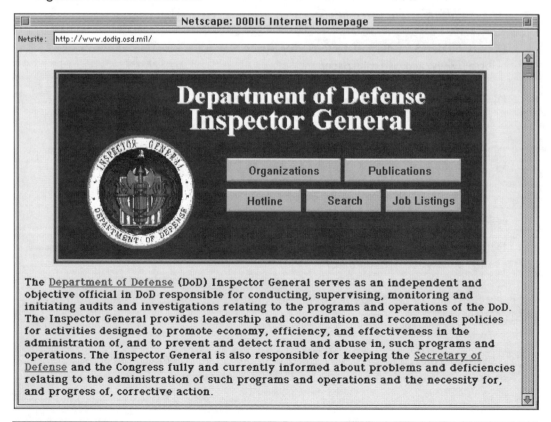

BASE SCHEDULED TO CLOSE $ COMMERCIAL, BUSINESS OPPORTUNITY   E-MAIL ADDRESS   INTERNAL SEARCH ENGINE

Defense Agencies

Ballistic Missile Defense Organization (BMDO)

The Pentagon, Room 1E1081
Washington, DC 20301-7100
☎ 703-697-4040

BMDOLink ➷ $
http://www.acq.osd.mil/bmdo/

Formerly the Strategic Defense Initiative Organization, BMDO is Presidentially chartered and mandated by Congress, and reports to the Under Secretary of Defense (Acquisition & Technology).

Defense Advanced Research Projects Agency (DARPA)

3701 North Fairfax Drive
Arlington, VA 22203
☎ 703-696-2400/2444

DARPA Homepage $
http://www.darpa.mil/

The central advanced research and development organization for the DOD. DARPA manages basic and applied research and development projects and pursues research and technology where risk and payoff are both very high and where success may provide dramatic military advances. DARPA operates under the authority, direction, and control of the Director of Defense Research and Engineering (DDR&E).

DARPA Technical Offices

Defense Sciences Office
http://www.darpa.mil/DSO

Electronics Technology Office
http://www.darpa.mil/ETOD

Information Systems Office
http://www.iso.darpa.mil/

Information Technology Office
http://www.darpa.mil/ito

Sensor Technology Office
http://www.darpa.mil/sto/

Tactical Technology Office
http://www.darpa.mil/tto/tto.html

 NEW NEW LISTING IN THIS EDITION   ✎ ONLINE FACT SHEET    PUBLICATION REPOSITORY OR LIBRARY   ★ RECOMMENDED SITE   ☎ TELEPHONE NUMBER

Defense Commissary Agency (DeCA)
Fort Lee, VA 23801-6300
☎ 804-734-8721

> NEW DeCA Homepage $
> http://www.deca.mil/default.htm

> *Established in 1990 and reporting to the Under Secretary of Defense (Personnel and Readiness).*

Defense Contract Audit Agency (DCAA)
8725 John J. Kingman Road, Suite 2135
Fort Belvoir, VA 22060-6219
☎ 703-767-3200

> DCAA Homepage
> http://www.dtic.mil/dcaa/

> *Established in 1965 and formerly located at Cameron Station, reporting to the Under Secretary of Defense (Comptroller).*

Defense Finance and Accounting Service (DFAS)
CM 3, Room 425
Arlington, VA 22240-5291
☎ 703-607-2616; ✉ dfaslane@cleveland.dfas.mil

> DFAS Lane ⬛
> http://www.dfas.mil/

> *Established in 1990 and reporting to the Under Secretary of Defense (Comptroller).*

> Military Pay Homepage
> http://www.dfas.mil/money/milpay/index.htm

Defense Information Systems Agency (DISA)
701 South Court House Road
Arlington, VA 22204-2199
☎ 703-607-6900

> DISA Home 🔍 ⬛ $
> http://www.disa.mil/disahome.html

> *Combat Support Agency of the DOD, formerly the Defense Communications Agency, and reporting to the Assistant Secretary of Defense (C3I). Includes the White House Communications Agency; the Joint Tactical Command, Control, and Communications Agency; the Defense Commercial Communications Office; and Defense Megacenters worldwide.*

Center for Computer Systems Engineering
http://sw-eng.falls-church.va.us/

ADA Information Clearinghouse.

Center for Information Systems Security
http://www.disa.mil/ciss/

DISA focal point for the DOD-wide information security and information warfare program.

Joint Interoperability Engineering Organization
http://www.disa.mil/line/jieo.html

JIEO Center for Standards
http://www.itsi.disa.mil/

National Communications System
http://164.117.147.223

Defense Intelligence Agency (DIA)
Washington, DC 20340-2033
☎ 703-695-0071

DIA $
http://www.dia.mil/
http://www.dia.osis.gov/

Combat Support Agency of the DOD established in 1961 and reporting to the Assistant Secretary of Defense (C3I). The Defense Intelligence Analysis Center (DIAC) is located at Bolling AFB, Washington, DC. The website includes "Global Threats to the United States and Its Interest Abroad," "North Korea: The Foundations for Military Strength," and other reports.

Threat Systems Office
http://ns.msic.dia.mil/to/index.htm

Defense Legal Services Agency (DLSA)
The Pentagon
Washington, DC 20301-1600
☎ 703-695-3341

Established in 1981 and under the authority, direction, and control of the General Counsel of the Department of Defense, who also serves as its director.

Defense Logistics Agency (DLA)
8725 John J. Kingman Road, Suite 0119
Fort Belvoir, VA 22060-6221
☎ 703-767-3100

DLA 🔍 $
http://www.dla.mil/

Formerly located at Cameron Station. Combat Support Agency of the DOD reporting to the Under Secretary of Defense (Acquisition & Technology).

Defense Security Assistance Agency (DSAA)
1111 Jefferson Davis Highway, Suite 303
Arlington, VA 22202
☎ 703-604-6513

Established in 1971 and reporting to the Under Secretary of Defense for Policy.

Defense Security Service (DSS)
881 Elkridge Landing Road
Linthicum, MD 21090

DSS 🔍
http://www.dis.mil/

Established in 1972 as the Defense Investigative Service (DIS) and redesignated the Defense Security Service in 1998. DSS reports to the Assistant Secretary of Defense (C3I).

Defense Special Weapons Agency (DSWA)
6801 Telegraph Road
Alexandria, VA 22310-2298
☎ 703-325-7095

DSWA $
http://www.dswa.mil/

Established in 1947 as the Armed Forces Special Weapons Project and renamed the Defense Nuclear Agency in 1971, DSWA was renamed in July 1996. DSWA is being consolidated into the new Defense Threat Reduction Agency (DTRA), established in 1998.

NEW Defense Threat Reduction Agency (DTRA)

Created as part of the Defense Reform Initiative and to activate 1 October 1998. The new agency will consolidate the On-Site Inspection Agency, the Defense Special Weapons Agency, the Defense Technology Security Administration, and some activities of the Office of the Secretary of Defense. DTRA is under the Under Secretary of Defense for Acquisitions and Technology.

| ☒ BASE SCHEDULED TO CLOSE | $ COMMERCIAL, BUSINESS OPPORTUNITY | ✉ E-MAIL ADDRESS | 🔍 INTERNAL SEARCH ENGINE |

National Imagery and Mapping Agency (NIMA)
8613 Lee Highway
Fairfax, VA 22031-2137
☎ 703-275-5864

> NIMA Home 🔍 $
> http://www.nima.mil
>
> > *Established in 1996 and incorporating the Defense Mapping Agency, the Central Imagery Office, and elements of the DIA and CIA.*

National Security Agency/Central Security Service (NSA/CSS)
Fort George G. Meade, MD 20755-6000
☎ 301-688-6311

> NSA
> http://www.nsa.gov:8080/
>
> > *Signals intelligence combat support agency of the DOD, established originally in 1952.*

On-Site Inspection Agency (OSIA)
Washington, DC 20041-0498
☎ 703-810-4449

> OSIA Homepage 🔍
> http://www.osia.mil/
>
> > *Established in 1988 and located at Dulles Airport in Virginia. OSIA is being consolidated into the new Defense Threat Reduction Agency (DTRA), established in 1998.*

DOD Field Activities

American Forces Information Service (AFIS)
601 North Fairfax Street, Suite 311
Alexandria, VA 22314-2007
☎ 703-274-4839

> AFIS
> http://www.defenselink.mil/afis/
>
> > *Established in 1977 and under the supervision of the Assistant to the Secretary of Defense (Public Affairs); responsible for the DOD's internal information program.*

> American Forces Press Service
> http://www.dtic.mil/afps/

Army and Air Force Exchange Service (AAFES)

3911 Walton Walker Road
Dallas, TX 75266
☎ 214-312-3821

> **NEW** AAFES Home $
> http://www.aafes.com

Defense Medical Program Activity (DMPA)

5109 Leesburg Pike (Skyline 6), Suite 502
Falls Church, VA 22041-3201
☎ 703-681-8717

> *Under the Assistant Secretary of Defense (Health Affairs).*

Defense Technology Security Administration (DTSA)

400 Army Navy Drive, Suite 300
Arlington, VA 22202
☎ 703-604-5215

> DTSA
> http://www.dtsa.osd.mil/index.html
>
> > *Established in 1985 and under the policy and overall management of the Under Secretary of Defense for Policy. DTSA is being consolidated into the new Defense Threat Reduction Agency (DTRA), established in 1998.*

Department of Defense Civilian Personnel Management Service (DCPMS)

1400 Key Boulevard, Suite B200
Arlington, VA 22209-5144
☎ 703-696-2788

> CPMS
> http://www.cpms.osd.mil/
>
> > *Established in 1993 and under the authority, direction, and control of the Under Secretary of Defense for Personnel and Readiness.*
>
> **NEW** Defense Manpower Data Center
> http://www.dmdc.osd.mil

Department of Defense Education Activity (DODEA)

4040 North Fairfax Drive
Arlington, VA 22203-1635
☎ 703-696-4413

⌛ BASE SCHEDULED $ COMMERCIAL, BUSINESS   ✉ E-MAIL   🔍 INTERNAL
   TO CLOSE   OPPORTUNITY   ADDRESS   SEARCH ENGINE

DODEA
http://www.odedodea.edu

> *Established in 1992 and under the authority, direction, and control of the Under Secretary of Defense for Personnel and Readiness. Operates one of the nation's largest school systems comprising overseas schools operated for dependents of military personnel.*

Office of Civilian Health and Medical Program of the Uniformed Services (OCHAMPUS)
Aurora, CO 80045
☎ 303-361-1313

TRICARE Activity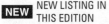
http://www.ochampus.mil/

> *Established in 1974 and reporting to the Assistant Secretary of Defense (Health Affairs).*

TRICARE Management Activity
http://www.tso.osd.mil/

Office of Economic Adjustment
400 Army Navy Drive, Suite 200
Arlington, VA 22202-2884
☎ 703-604-6020

Economic Adjustment Homepage
http://emissary.acq.osd.mil/bccr/oea/oeahome.nsf

Office of Economic Conversion Information Page
http://netsite.esa.doc.gov/occi/

> *Joint Defense–Department of Commerce retraining and retooling defense conversion program.*

Washington Headquarters Services (WHS)
The Pentagon, Room 3D972
Washington, DC 20301-1155
☎ 703-695-4436

WHS Homepage
http://odam.whs.osd.mil/whs.htm

> *Reporting to the Director of Administration and Management in the Office of the Secretary. Includes the Directorate of Information Operations and Reports (DIOR) (see Chapter 2).*

Joint Chiefs of Staff

The Joint Chiefs of Staff consist of the Chairman; the Vice Chairman; the Chief of Staff, U.S. Army; the Chief of Naval Operations; the Chief of Staff, U.S. Air Force; and the Commandant of the Marine Corps. Supported by the Joint Staff, they constitute the immediate military staff of the Secretary of Defense. The Chairman is the principal military adviser to the President, the National Security Council, and the Secretary of Defense. The other members of the Joint Chiefs of Staff are the senior military officers of their respective services and are military advisers to the President, the National Security Council, and the Secretary of Defense. The Vice Chairman of the Joint Chiefs acts as Chairman in the absence of the Chairman.

The Joint Staff under the Chairman of the Joint Chiefs of Staff assists the Chairman and, subject to the authority of the Chairman, the other members of the Joint Chiefs of Staff, in carrying out their responsibilities. It is headed by a director and consists of officers in approximately equal numbers from the Army, Navy, Marine Corps, and Air Force.

★ Joint Chiefs of Staff (JCS) Homepage
http://www.dtic.mil/jcs

> *A much-improved site; contains background information on the Joint Chiefs, the Joint Staff, history and an overview of national security structure, biographies of the Chairman and Vice Chairman, the Chiefs, and directors, links to various directorates, JCS history (see Chapter 3), reports, speeches, periodicals, the joint doctrine homepage, and the Joint Electronic Library (see Chapter 4).*

Chairman of the Joint Chiefs of Staff

Vice Chairman of the Joint Chiefs of Staff

Joint Staff Directorates

NEW Manpower and Personnel (J-1)
http://www.dtic.mil/jcs/j1

NEW Intelligence (J-2)
http://www.dtic.mil/jcs/j2

NEW Operations (J-3)
http://www.dtic.mil/jcs/j3

NEW Logistics (J-4)
http://www.dtic.mil/jcs/j4

NEW Strategic Plans and Policy (J-5)
http://www.dtic.mil/jcs/j5

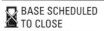 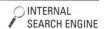

NEW Command, Control, Communications and Computers (J-6)
http://www.dtic.mil/jcs/j6/index.html

NEW Joint Spectrum Center
http://www.jsc.mil

Operational Plans and Interoperability (J-7)
http://www.dtic.mil/jcs/j7

NEW Military Education Division Homepage
http://www.dtic.mil:80/mil-ed/index.html

NEW Force Structure, Resources and Assessment (J-8)
http://www.dtic.mil/jcs/j8

Unified Commands

The unified combatant commands are the operational military forces of the United States. The commanders (called commanders-in-chief or CINCs) are responsible to the President and the Secretary of Defense for accomplishing the military missions assigned to them and exercising command authority over forces assigned to them. The operational chain of command runs from the President to the Secretary of Defense to the commanders of the unified combatant commands. The Chairman of the Joint Chiefs of Staff functions within the chain of command by transmitting the orders of the President or the Secretary of Defense to the commanders of the unified combatant commands.

Unified Commands Homepage
http://www.defenselink.mil/unified.html

U.S. Atlantic Command (ACOM)
1562 Mitscher Avenue, Suite 200
Norfolk, VA 22134
☎ 804-322-6555; ✉ acompao@jtasc.acom.mil

ACOM Homepage 🔍
http://www.acom.mil/

ACOM component commands are Air Combat Command, Langley AFB, VA; Army Forces Command, Fort Monroe, VA; Marine Forces Atlantic, Norfolk, VA; U.S. Atlantic Fleet, Norfolk, VA; and Special Operations Command Atlantic, Norfolk, VA. Subunified commands include Iceland Defense Force, Keflavik, Iceland; and U.S. Forces Azores, Lajes, Azores, Portugal.

NEW NEW LISTING IN THIS EDITION   ONLINE FACT SHEET    PUBLICATION REPOSITORY OR LIBRARY   ★ RECOMMENDED SITE   ☎ TELEPHONE NUMBER

Supreme Allied Commander Atlantic (SACLANT)
http://www.saclant.nato.int/

> The Commander-in-Chief ACOM is also the NATO SACLANT commander. SACLANT headquarters is collocated with ACOM headquarters in Norfolk, VA.

U.S. Central Command (CENTCOM)
MacDill AFB, FL 33608-7001

CENTCOM Homepage
http://www.centcom.mil

> CENTCOM component commands include U.S. Central Air Forces, Shaw AFB, SC; Army Forces, U.S. Central Command, Ft. McPherson, GA; Naval Forces, U.S. Central Command, Bahrain; Marine Forces Central Command, Camp H. M. Smith, HI; and Special Operations Command Central, MacDill AFB, FL (http://ccfs.centcom.mil/soccent.htm).

U.S. European Command (EUCOM)
(Stuttgart, Germany)
APO New York 09128-4029
✉ ecpa@hq.eucom.mil

★ EUCOM Home 🔍 📖
http://www.eucom.mil/

> EUCOM component commands include U.S. Air Forces in Europe, Ramstein AB, Germany; U.S. Army Europe, Heidelberg, Germany; U.S. Naval Forces, U.S. European Command, London, UK; and Special Operations Command Europe, Stuttgart-Vaihingen, Germany.

U.S. Pacific Command (PACOM)
Camp H. M. Smith, HI 96861-5025
☎ 808-477-1341

PACOM Home
http://www.pacom.mil/homepage.htm

> PACOM component commands include Marine Forces Pacific, Camp H. M. Smith, HI; Pacific Air Forces, Hickam AB, HI; U.S. Army Pacific, Fort Shafter, HI; U.S. Pacific Fleet, Pearl Harbor, HI; and Special Operations Command Pacific, Camp H. M. Smith, HI. Subunified commands include Alaska Command, Elmendorf AFB, AK; U.S. Forces Japan, Yokota AB, Japan; U.S. Forces Korea, Seoul, South Korea; and Joint Task Force Full Accounting.

U.S. Southern Command (SOUTHCOM)
3511 NW 91st Avenue
Miami, FL 33172
☎ 1-888-547-4025

⧗ BASE SCHEDULED TO CLOSE $ COMMERCIAL, BUSINESS OPPORTUNITY   ✉ E-MAIL ADDRESS   🔍 INTERNAL SEARCH ENGINE

Netscape: United States European Command

Location: http://www.eucom.mil/

United States European Command

Contents FAQ Feedback Search About This Site

- Dependent education pages expanded; FAQ added (3 July)
- Departure ceremony held for Gen Jamerson (2 July)
- Baltic Challenge 98 announced (30 June)
- Exercise Cornerstone 98 begins (30 June)
- More News, What's New, and New Files

Who
- Headquarters
- Newcomers
- Organization
- People

What
- Events
- Exercises NEW!
- Operations NEW!
- Programs NEW!
- Publications
- Staff Info

When

Where
- Africa
- Europe
- Middle East

Why
- Our Mission
- Posture NEW!
- Strategy

Web
- About This Site
- Contents
- Cover Photos
- FAQ
- Feedback

President Bill Clinton shakes hands with soldiers at the

NEW SOUTHCOM Homepage
http://www.ussouthcom.mil/southcom/

The headquarters relocated to Florida from Quarry Heights, Panama, in 1998. SOUTHCOM component commands include U.S. Army South, Ft. Clayton, Panama; U.S. Atlantic Fleet, Norfolk, VA; U.S. Southern Air Force, Davis-Monthan AFB, AZ; and Special Operations Command South, Albrook AFS, Panama.

U.S. Space Command (SPACECOM)
Peterson AFB, CO 80914-5001

Space Command Home
http://www.spacecom.af.mil/usspace/

The Commander-in-Chief U.S. Space Command is also the commander of North American Aerospace Defense Command (NORAD), a joint U.S.-Canadian command, and commander of the Air Force Space Command. SPACECOM component commands include Air Force Space Command, Peterson AFB, CO; Army Space Command (Forward) (Army Space and Missile Defense Command), Peterson AFB, CO; and Naval Space Command, Dahlgren, VA.

U.S. Special Operations Command (SOCOM)
MacDill AFB, FL 33621-5323
☎ 813-830-2011

> **NEW** SOCOM Home $
> http://www.dtic.mil/socom
>
> *SOCOM component commands include Air Force Special Operations Command, Hurlburt Field, FL; Army Special Operations Command, Ft. Bragg, NC; Joint Special Operations Command, Ft. Bragg, NC; and Naval Special Warfare Command, NAB, Coronado, CA.*

U.S. Strategic Command (STRATCOM)
Offutt AFB, NE 68113-6030

> STRATCOM Home $
> http://www.stratcom.af.mil/
>
> *STRATCOM component commands include Air Combat Command, Langley AFB, VA; Air Force Space Command, Peterson AFB, CO; U.S. Atlantic Fleet, Norfolk, VA; and U.S. Pacific Fleet, Pearl Harbor, HI.*

U.S. Transportation Command (TRANSCOM)
Scott AFB, IL 62225-5000

> TRANSCOM Home
> http://ustcweb.safb.af.mil/
>
> *TRANSCOM component commands include Air Mobility Command, Scott AFB, IL; Military Sealift Command, Washington, DC; and Military Traffic Management Command, Falls Church, VA.*

 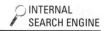

Department of the Air Force

The Department of the Air Force is headed by the Secretary of the Air Force, who is responsible for and has the authority to conduct all affairs of the department. The Secretary's responsibilities include matters pertaining to organization, training, logistical support, maintenance, welfare of personnel, administration, recruiting, and research and development. The Secretary is supported by a staff called the Secretariat.

The Chief of Staff of the Air Force is directly responsible to the Secretary of the Air Force for the efficiency and operational readiness of the Air Force and is a member of the Joint Chiefs of Staff. The Chief heads the Air Staff, which furnishes professional assistance to the Secretary. The heads of the military commands report to the Chief of Staff. Major commands have broad functional or geographic responsibility and consist of subordinate numbered air forces and wings. Numerous other organizations—field operating agencies, direct reporting units, and centers—report to major commands and to the Air Staff.

Headquarters United States Air Force
1670 Air Force Pentagon
Washington, DC 20330-1670

Air Force Homepage
http://www.af.mil/

Secretary of the Air Force

Air Force Command Section Homepage
http://www.hq.af.mil/

Support to the Secretary and Under Secretary of the Air Force.

Assistant Secretary of the Air Force (Financial Management & Comptroller)
http://www.saffm.hq.af.mil/SAFFM/

Complete access to Air Force budget materials (see Chapter 5 for more information).

Assistant Secretary of the Air Force (Space)

★ Assistant Secretary of the Air Force (Acquisition)
http://www.safaq.hq.af.mil/

Searchable and interactive site dealing with acquisition policy and reform, contracting, and program management.

Assistant Secretary of the Air Force (Manpower, Reserve Affairs, Installations, and Environment)
http://www.safmi.hq.af.mil

Air Force Environment Page
http://www.af.mil/environment

Chief Information Officer of the Air Force
http://www.cio.hq.af.mil/

Air Force Scientific Advisory Board (SAB)
http://web.fie.com/fedix/sab.html
http://stbbs.wpafb.af.mil/STBBS/sab.htm

Includes the summary volume of the New World Vistas study, a 14-volume examination of aerospace technologies.

Air Staff

The Chief of Staff of the Air Force (CSAF) is the ranking Air Force officer, a member of the Joint Chiefs, and head of the Air Staff. The Air Staff is supplemented by the Special Staff, an adjunct to the Chief of Staff, independent of the basic staff structure, providing advisory and support services to both the Chief of Staff and the Air Staff. The Special Staff consists of the Civil Engineer; the Chief of Safety; the Chief of Security Police; the Air Force Historian; the USAF Scientist; the Chief of Air Force Reserve; the Scientific Advisory Board; the Judge Advocate General; the Director, Test and Evaluation; the Surgeon General; the Chief of Chaplains; Services; and the Chief Master Sergeant of the Air Force.

A 1996 reorganization of the Air Staff incorporated intelligence functions into the Deputy Chief of Staff for Operations and created a new Deputy Chief of Staff for Plans and Programs, Deputy Chief of Staff for Communications and Information, and Deputy Chief of Staff for Installations and Logistics, as well as two new direct reporting units: the Air Force Communications and Information Center and the Air Force Doctrine Center.

Deputy Chief of Staff for Operations

NEW Deputy Chief of Staff for Plans and Programs
http://www.xp.hq.af.mil

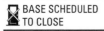 BASE SCHEDULED TO CLOSE $ COMMERCIAL, BUSINESS OPPORTUNITY   E-MAIL ADDRESS    INTERNAL SEARCH ENGINE

NEW Strategic Planning Directorate
http://www.xp.hq.af.mil/xpx

NEW Director for Command and Control (XOC)
http://www.hq.af.mil/xoctop.html
http://204.34.204.77

Deputy Chief of Staff for Personnel
http://www.dp.hq.af.mil/DP

Deputy Chief of Staff for Installations and Logistics
http://www.hq.af.mil/AFLG

Deputy Chief of Staff for Communications and Information

Judge Advocate General of the Air Force
http://www.ja.hq.af.mil
http://www.jagusaf.hq.af.mil

Air Force Legal Information Services (FLITE)
http://www.au.af.mil/maxwell/legal/

Surgeon General of the Air Force (Brooks AFB, TX)
http://usafsg.satx.disa.mil/

Chief of the Chaplain Service
http://wwwafhc.au.af.mil/

Chief, National Guard Bureau ("GuardLink")
http://www.ngb.dtic.mil/

Made up of the Army and Air National Guards.

Air National Guard (ANG) 🔎
http://www.ang.af.mil/

Air Force Major Commands

Air Combat Command (ACC)
Langley AFB, VA 23665-5583

ACC Homepage 🔎 $
http://www.acc.af.mil/

ACC provides aircraft for all five geographic unified commands, air defense forces for NORAD, and nuclear forces (B-2 and B-52 bombers) for STRATCOM.

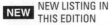 

NEW Directorate of Requirements
http://www.dr.langley.mil/

★ ACC Center for Lessons Learned
http://redwood.do.langley.af.mil

Air Education and Training Command (AETC)
Randolph AFB, TX 78150-4324

AETC Homepage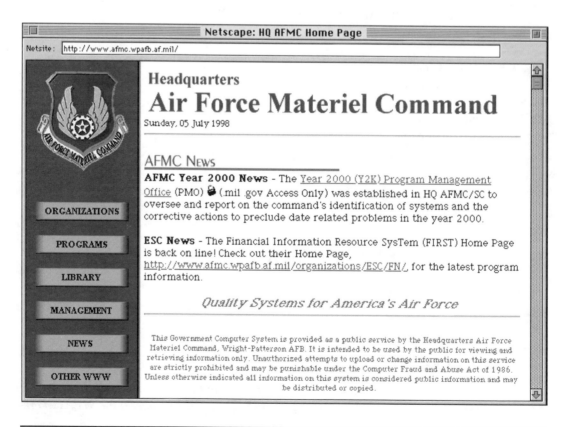
http://www.aetc.af.mil/

Responsible for Air Force flying and specialty training and Air Force higher education.

Air Force Materiel Command (AFMC)
Wright-Patterson, OH 45433-5006

★ AFMC Home 🔍 📖 $
http://www.afmc.wpafb.af.mil/

Particularly well-organized and well-presented website, though it is filled with numerous military-only restricted links.

Netscape: HQ AFMC Home Page

Netsite: http://www.afmc.wpafb.af.mil/

Headquarters
Air Force Materiel Command
Sunday, 05 July 1998

ORGANIZATIONS

PROGRAMS

LIBRARY

MANAGEMENT

NEWS

OTHER WWW

AFMC News

AFMC Year 2000 News - The Year 2000 (Y2K) Program Management Office (PMO) 📧 (.mil .gov Access Only) was established in HQ AFMC/SC to oversee and report on the command's identification of systems and the corrective actions to preclude date related problems in the year 2000.

ESC News - The Financial Information Resource SysTem (FIRST) Home Page is back on line! Check out their Home Page, http://www.afmc.wpafb.af.mil/organizations/ESC/FN/, for the latest program information.

Quality Systems for America's Air Force

This Government Computer System is provided as a public service by the Headquarters Air Force Materiel Command, Wright-Patterson AFB. It is intended to be used by the public for viewing and retrieving information only. Unauthorized attempts to upload or change information on this service are strictly prohibited and may be punishable under the Computer Fraud and Abuse Act of 1986. Unless otherwise indicated all information on this system is considered public information and may be distributed or copied.

NEW Directorate of Requirements
http://www.afmc.wpafb.af.mil/HQ-AFMC/DR/

AFMC Publishing Distribution Library and Command Publications
http://www.afmc.wpafb.af.mil/pdl/

> *One of the best electronic publications libraries, with Air Force and AFMC documents and links to other commands and bases.*

Science & Technology Planning Information
http://stbbs.wpafb.af.mil/STBBS

> *Includes access to Air Force Technology Area Plans (TAPS).*

Technology Transition Office
http://tto.wpafb.af.mil/TTO/

Air Force Reserve Command (AFRES)
Robins AFB, GA 31098-1635

Air Force Reserves Homepage
http://www.afres.af.mil/

> *Major command activated 17 February 1997 (formerly field operating agency).*

Air Force Space Command (AFSPC)
Peterson AFB, CO 80914-3010

AFSPC Home
http://www.spacecom.af.mil/hqafspc/

> *Air Force component of U.S. Space Command (SPACECOM) and Strategic Command (STRATCOM), operating Air Force land-based ballistic missiles.*

Air Force Special Operations Command (AFSOC)
Hurlburt Field, FL 32544-5273

AFSOC Homepage
http://www.hqafsoc.hurlburt.af.mil/

Air Mobility Command (AMC)
Scott AFB, IL 62225

AMC Public Affairs
http://www.safb.af.mil/hqamc/pa/

> *Air Force component of U.S. Transportation Command (TRANSCOM).*

Pacific Air Forces (PACAF)
Hickam AFB, HI 96853-5420
☎ 808-471-7110

HQ PACAF
http://www.hqpacaf.af.mil/

Air Force component of U.S. Pacific Command (PACOM).

PACAF Director of Operations/Command Center
http://www.cidss.af.mil/

PACAF Publications
http://www.hqpacaf.af.mil/im/publications

★ U.S. Air Forces in Europe (USAFE)
(Ramstein AB, Germany)
APO AE 09094-0501

USAFE Homepage
http://www.usafe.af.mil/

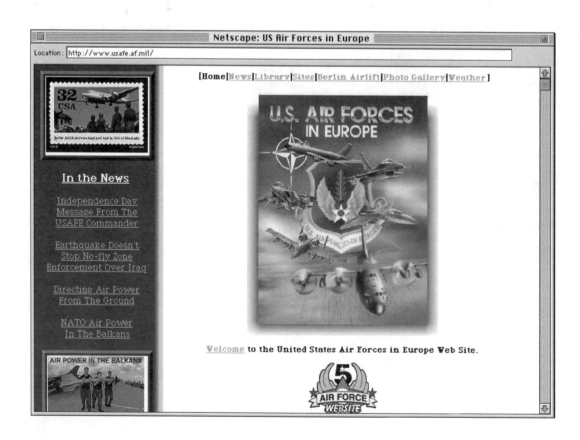

BASE SCHEDULED TO CLOSE $ COMMERCIAL, BUSINESS OPPORTUNITY   E-MAIL ADDRESS   INTERNAL SEARCH ENGINE

Directorate of Intelligence
http://www.usafe.af.mil/direct/in/in.htm

Directorate of Operations
http://www.usafe.af.mil/direct/do/

Directorate of Logistics
http://www.usafe.af.mil/direct/lg/

NEW Directorate of Plans and Programs
http://www.usafe.af.mil/direct/xp/xp.htm

USAFE Publications
http://www.usafe.af.mil/direct/foas/css/sb/scbp/pdl/publish.htm

Air Force Field Operating Agencies

A number of minor Air Force field operating agencies still have no apparent Internet presence. They include the Air Force Frequency Management Agency (Arlington, VA), Air Force Legal Services Agency (Bolling AFB, Washington, DC), Air Force Operations Group (Washington, DC), Air Force Pentagon Communications Agency, Air Force Personnel Operations Agency (Washington, DC), Air Force Program Executive Office (Washington, DC), Air Force Real Estate Agency (Bolling AFB, Washington, DC), and Air Force Review Boards Agency (Andrews AFB, MD).

NEW **Air Force Agency for Modeling and Simulation**
http://www.afams.af.mil

Air Force Audit Agency (AFAA)
Washington, DC 20330-1125
http://www.afaa.hq.af.mil/

Address and E-mail directory, the newsletter "Audit Facts," and links to other auditing sites.

NEW **Air Force Base Conversion Agency (AFBCA)**
1700 N. Moore Street, Arlington, VA 22209
http://www.afbca.hq.af.mil

Air Force Center for Environmental Excellence
Brooks AFB, TX 78235-5318
http://www.afcee.brooks.af.mil

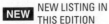 

Air Force Center for Quality and Management Innovation
Randolph AFB, TX 78150
http://www.afcqmi.randolph.af.mil

> *"The Innovation Center," created in December 1996, merging the Air Force Quality Institute (Maxwell AFB, AL) and the Air Force Management Engineering Agency.*

Air Force Civil Engineering Support Agency (AFCESA)
Tyndall AFB, FL 32403-5319
http://www.afcesa.af.mil/

Air Force Communications Agency (AFCA)
Scott AFB, IL 62225-5219
http://infosphere.safb.af.mil/

> *Name changed from the Air Force Command, Control, Communications and Computers Agency in June 1996. A once helpful website has been transformed into a restricted bastion.*

`NEW` Air Force Cost Analysis Agency (AFCAA)
Arlington, VA 22202
http://www.saffm.hq.af.mil/SAFFM/afcaa/afcaa.html

Air Force Flight Standards Agency
Andrews AFB, MD 20330-1480
http://www.andrews.af.mil/tenants/affsa/AFFSA.htm

Air Force Historical Research Agency (AFHRA)
Maxwell AFB, AL 36112-6424
http://www.au.af.mil/au/afhra/

`NEW` Air Force History Support Office
Bolling AFB, Washington, DC
http://www.airforcehistory.hq.af.mil

Air Force Inspection Agency (AFIA)
Kirtland AFB, Albuquerque, NM 87117-5000
http://www-afia.saia.af.mil

Air Force Logistics Management Agency (AFLMA)
501 Ward Street
Maxwell AFB, Gunter Annex, AL 36114-3236
http://www hq.af.mil/AFLG/AFLMA/aflma2/manage.html

Air Force Medical Support Agency (AFMSA)
Brooks AFB, TX 78235-5121
http://usafsg.satx.disa.mil:90/master.html

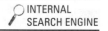

BASE SCHEDULED TO CLOSE $ COMMERCIAL, BUSINESS OPPORTUNITY   E-MAIL ADDRESS   INTERNAL SEARCH ENGINE

NEW Air Force National Security Emergency Preparedness Agency
Ft. McPherson, GA 30330
http://www-afnsep.forscom.army.mil

Air Force News Agency
Kelly AFB, TX 78241-5601
http://www.dtic.mil/airforcelink/pa/AirForceNewsAgency.html

Air Force Office of Scientific Research (AFOSR)
http://web.fie.com/fedix/afosr.html

Being incorporated into the new Air Force Research Laboratory structure.

NEW Air Force Office of Special Investigations
Bolling AFB, Washington, DC
http://www.dtic.mil/afosi

★ **Air Force Personnel Center (AFPC)**
Randolph AFB, TX 78150
http://www.afpc.af.mil/
ftp://ftp.afpc.af.mil

Air Force Safety Center
Kirtland AFB, NM 87117
http://www-afsc.saia.af.mil

Air Force Security Forces Center
Lackland AFB, TX
http://www.lak.aetc.af.mil/AFSF\index.html

Air Force Services Agency
Randolph AFB, TX 78150-4755
http://www.afsv.af.mil/

Air Force Studies and Analyses Agency
The Pentagon
Washington, DC 20330-1570
http://www.afsaa.hq.af.mil/

Air Force Technical Applications Center (AFTAC)
Patrick AFB, FL 32925-3002
http://www.aftac.gov/

Air Force Weather Agency (AFWA)
Scott AFB, IL 62225-5206
http://www.safb.af.mil/afwa

Formerly the Air Weather Service (AWS), formed and redesignated 15 October 1997.

 NEW LISTING IN THIS EDITION   ONLINE FACT SHEET    PUBLICATION REPOSITORY OR LIBRARY    RECOMMENDED SITE   TELEPHONE NUMBER

Air Intelligence Agency (AIA)
Kelly AFB, San Antonio, TX 78243-7009
http://www.aia.af.mil

Air National Guard Readiness Center
Andrews AFB, MD 20331-5157
http://www.ang.af.mil/

NEW Air Reserve Personnel Center
Denver, CO
http://www.arpc.org

Air Force Direct Reporting Units

11th Wing
Bolling AFB, Washington, DC 20332
http://www.bolling.af.mil/

> *Formerly Air Force District of Washington, provides support for Washington-based Air Force personnel and units.*

Air Force Communications and Information Center

> *Created in late 1996 to focus on systems management and design issues.*

Air Force Doctrine Center
Maxwell, AFB, AL
http://www.hqafdc.maxwell.af.mil

> *Upgraded to a direct reporting unit and activated at Maxwell on 17 May 1997 to focus Air Force doctrinal development. It moved from Langley AFB, VA, to incorporate elements of Air University.*

Air Force Operational Test and Evaluation Center
Kirtland AFB, NM 87117-5558
http://www.afotec.af.mil/

U.S. Air Force Academy
Colorado Springs, CO 80840-5001
http://www.usafa.af.mil/
ftp://ftp.usafa.af.mil/

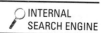

8

Department of the Army

Headquarters Department of the Army is composed of the Office of the Secretary of the Army; the Office of the Chief of Staff, Army; the Army Staff; and designated staff support agencies performing "national headquarters" functions, regardless of geographic location.

The Secretary of the Army is responsible for and has the authority to conduct all affairs of the Department of the Army, including its organization, administration, operation, efficiency, and such other activities. Certain civilian functions, such as comptroller, acquisition, inspector general, auditing, and information management, are under the authority of the Secretary. Additionally, the Secretary is responsible for civil functions, such as oversight of the Panama Canal Commission and execution of the Panama Canal Treaty, the civil works program of the Corps of Engineers, and Arlington and Soldiers' Home National Cemeteries.

Department of the Army
The Pentagon
Washington, DC 20310

Army Homepage
http://www.army.mil/

NEW Army Reserve Homepage
http://www.army.mil/usar

Secretary of the Army

HQDALINK—Headquarters Department of the Army Homepage
http://www.hqda.army.mil/

Links to Army Secretariat offices and the Army staff.

Deputy Under Secretary of the Army, Operations Research
http://www.odusa-or.army.mil

Deputy Under Secretary of the Army, International Affairs

Assistant Secretary of the Army, Civil Works
http://www.hqda.army.mil/asacw/

★ Assistant Secretary of the Army, Financial Management and Comptroller 📖
http://www.asafm.army.mil

> *Complete website dealing with the Army budget and financial issues (see Chapter 5).*

NEW Assistant Secretary of the Army, Installations, Logistics and Environment
http://www.hqda.army.mil/asaile

NEW Assistant Secretary of the Army, Manpower and Reserve Affairs
http://134.11.7.5

Assistant Secretary of the Army, Research, Development and Acquisition
(SARDA) 🔍 📖
http://www.sarda.army.mil/

Director of Information Systems for Command, Control, Communications and
Computers (ODISC4)
http://www.army.mil/disc4/default.htm

> **NEW** Army Chief Information Office (CIO)
> http://www.army.mil/disc4/cio

> **NEW** Army Command and Control Protect Division
> http://www.army.mil/disc4/isec/c2p/c2p.htm

> **NEW** Army DOIM Homepage 🔍
> http://www.army.mil/doim

NEW Office of the Chief of Legislative Liaison
http://www.army.mil/date_official.htm

The Army Science Board
http://www.sarda.army.mil/sard-asb/asb.htm

Army Staff

The Army Staff, presided over by the Chief of Staff, is the military staff of the Secretary of
the Army. The Chief of Staff is the principal military adviser to the Secretary of the Army
and is charged with the planning, development, execution, review, and analysis of the Army

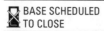 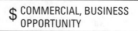

programs. The Chief supervises the members and organization of the Army and is directly responsible to the Secretary for the efficiency of the Army, its state of preparation for military operations, and plans.

Chief of Staff of the Army (CSA)
http://www.hqda.army.mil/ocsa/chief.htm

> *Includes biography, speeches, presentations, articles, interviews, and Congressional testimony.*

Deputy Chief of Staff, Operations and Plans

NEW Deputy Chief of Staff, Personnel
http://www.odcsper.army.mil

Army Retirement Services
http://www.odcsper.army.mil/retire/retire.htm

Deputy Chief of Staff, Logistics
http://www.hqda.army.mil/logweb/docs/

Deputy Chief of Staff, Intelligence
http://134.11.36.7/

Assistant Chief of Staff for Installation Management
http://www.hqda.army.mil/acsim

Principal Advisers to the Army Staff

Office of the Sergeant Major of the Army
http://www.hqda.army.mil/sma/smamenu/htm

Chief, Army Reserve
http://www.army.mil/usar/ocar.htm

★ Chief of Engineers and Commanding General, Army Corps of Engineers 🔍
http://www.usace.army.mil/

> *See Army Corps of Engineers below under Army Major Commands.*

Surgeon General and Commanding General, Army Medical Command (MEDCOM)
http://www.armymedicine.army.mil/otsgmaininfo.htm

NEW Army Medical Department 🔍
http://www.armymedicine.army.mil/armymed/index.htm

Judge Advocate General of the Army
http://www.jagc.army.mil/jagc2.htm

NEW JAG Corps Website
http://jagcnet.army.mil/jagcnet/jagcnetsitel.nsf/?open

Army Quartermaster General
http://www.lee.army.mil/quartermaster

Chief of Signal
http://www.gordon.army.mil/index.htm

Chief, National Guard Bureau ("GuardLink")
http://www.ngb.dtic.mil/

Made up of the Army and Air National Guards.

Assistant Chief of Staff, Army National Guard
http://leav-www.army.mil/arng

Army Major Commands

Army Corps of Engineers (USACE)
20 Massachusetts Avenue, NW
Washington, DC 20314-1000
☎ 202-761-0660

★ Army Corps Homepage/Information Network 🔍 📖
http://www.usace.army.mil/

The model for a well-organized, full-searchable, fact-filled website.

Regional Headquarters

Great Lakes Regional Headquarters (CELRD-GL) (former North Central Division)
http://www.usace.army.mil/ncd/

Ohio River Regional Headquarters (CELRD-OR) (former Ohio River Division)
http://www.usace.army.mil/lrd/

Missouri River Regional Headquarters (CENWD) (former Missouri River Division)
http://www.mrd.usace.army.mil/

North Pacific Regional Headquarters (CENWD-NP) (former North Pacific Division)
http://www.nwd.usace.army.mil/np/

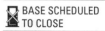 BASE SCHEDULED TO CLOSE    $ COMMERCIAL, BUSINESS OPPORTUNITY   E-MAIL ADDRESS    INTERNAL SEARCH ENGINE

Divisions

Great Lakes and Ohio River Division (CELRD)
http://www.usace.army.mil/lrd/lrd.htm

Mississippi Valley Division (CEMVD) (former Lower Mississippi Valley Division)
http://www.mvd.usace.army.mil

North Atlantic Division (CENAD)
http://www.usace.army.mil/nad/nad.htm

Northwestern Division (CENWD)
http://www.nwd.usace.army.mil/

Pacific Ocean Division (CEPOD)
http://www.pod.usace.army.mil

South Atlantic Division (CESAD)
http://www.sad.usace.army.mil/

South Pacific Division (CESPD)
http://www.spd.usace.army.mil/

Southwestern Division (CESWD)
http://www.swt.usace.army.mil/swd/

Army Criminal Investigation Command (CIDC)
6010 6th Street
Fort Belvoir, VA 22060
☎ 703-806-0400

CIDC Home
http://www.belvoir.army.mil/cidc/index.htm

Army Forces Command (FORSCOM)
Fort McPherson, GA 30330-6000
☎ 404-669-5750

★ FORSCOM Homepage 🔍 📖 $
http://www.forscom.army.mil

Army component of U.S. Atlantic Command (ACOM).

FORSCOM Publications
http://www.forscom.army.mil/pubs/default.htm

Full-text access to FORSCOM supplements to Army Regulations, pamphlets, circulars, and forms.

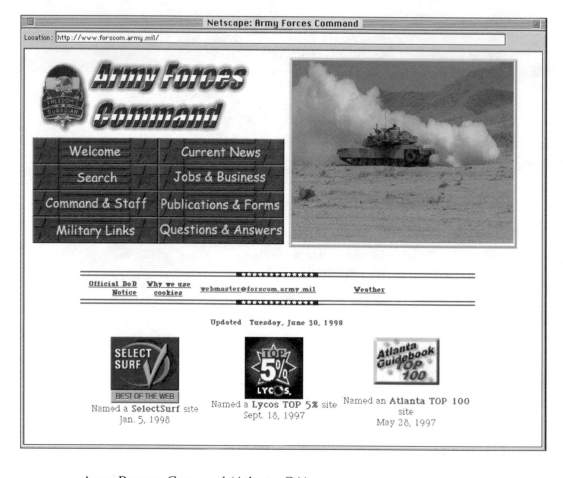

Army Reserve Command (Atlanta, GA)
http://www.usarc.army.mil
http://160.136.109.3/

Army Intelligence and Security Command (INSCOM)
Nolan Building
Fort Belvoir, VA 22060
☎ 703-706-1603

INSCOM Home
http://www.vulcan.belvoir.army.mil

Army Materiel Command (AMC)
5001 Eisenhower Avenue
Alexandria, VA 22333-0001
☎ 703-617-0125

AMC Home ⌕ ▱ $
http://www.amc.army.mil/

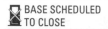 BASE SCHEDULED TO CLOSE

 COMMERCIAL, BUSINESS OPPORTUNITY

 E-MAIL ADDRESS

 INTERNAL SEARCH ENGINE

AMC Publications
http://amc.citi.net/amc/ci/pub_index.html

Army Medical Command (MEDCOM)
Fort Sam Houston, TX 78234-5000

Army Medical Command
http://www.armymedicine.army.mil/armymed/data/medcom.htm

Army Veterinary Services
http://vetpath1.afip.org/Vet_Services/VSg.html

Army Dental Command
http://www.dencom.army.mil/dencom.dir/index.html

Army Space and Missile Defense Command (SMDC)
1941 Jefferson Davis Highway, CM 4
Arlington, VA 22215-0280
☎ 703-607-1938

Space and Missile Defense Homepage $
http://www.smdc.army.mil/

*Army major command activated 1 October 1997 and replacing the Army Space
and Strategic Defense Command (SSDC), which was established in August 1992
combining Army Space Command and elements of the Army Strategic Defense
Command. Under Army downsizing plans, SSDC was to have reorganized under
Training and Doctrine Command.*

Army Special Operations Command
Fort Bragg, Fayetteville, NC 28307-5000

ARSOC Home $
http://www.usasoc.soc.mil
http://137.29.194.201

*Includes the Army Special Operations Support Command, John F. Kennedy
Special Warfare Center and School, Special Warfare Training Group (Airborne),
Special Forces Groups (Airborne), Army Civil Affairs/Psychological Operations
Command (Airborne), and subordinate special forces, psychological operations,
and civil affairs units.*

Army Training and Doctrine Command (TRADOC)
Fort Monroe, VA 23651-5000

★ TRADOC Home 🔍 📖 $
http://www.-tradoc.army.mil/

Deputy Chief of Staff for Combat Developments
http://www-tradoc.army.mil/dcscd/index.html

NEW Deputy Chief of Staff for Doctrine 🔎
http://www-tradoc.army.mil/dcsdoc

Includes the Army Doctrine Development Homepage.

Deputy Chief of Staff for Simulations and Analysis
http://www-tradoc.army.mil/dcssa/index.html

NEW Deputy Chief of Staff for Space and Information Operations
http://www-tradoc.army.mil/dcscd/spaceweb/index.html

Deputy Chief of Staff for Training
http://www-dcst.monroe.army.mil/

TRADOC Publications
http://www-tradoc.army.mil/publica.htm

Online index of TRADOC regulations, supplements to Army Regulations, pamphlets, TRADOC commanding general documents and quarterly command updates.

Eighth U.S. Army (EUSA)

(Yongsan Army Garrison, Seoul, South Korea)
APO AP 96205

EUSA Home
http://www.korea.army.mil/usfk/eusa/eusa.htm

> *Highest-level Korean-based Army command and Army component of U.S. Forces Korea (USFK), including the 2nd Infantry Division and a variety of subordinate and support commands.*

Military District of Washington (MDW)

Fort McNair, 4th & P Streets NW
Washington, DC 20319-5000
☎ 202-685-2807

MDW Home
http://www.mdw.army.mil

Military Traffic Management Command (MTMC)

5611 Columbia Pike
Falls Church, VA 22041-5050
☎ 800-756-MTMC

MTMC
http://mtmc.army.mil
http://baileys-mtmcwww.army.mil

> *Army component of U.S. Transportation Command (TRANSCOM).*

U.S. Army Europe (USAREUR) and Seventh Army

(Campbell Barracks, Heidelberg, Germany)
APO AE 09403

HQ USAREUR 📖
http://www.hqusareur.army.mil/

> *Major European-based Army command and Army component of U.S. European Command (EUCOM), including V Corps; Southern European Task Force (SETAF), Vicenza, Italy; and support commands in Belgium, Germany, and Italy.*

Deputy Chief of Staff for Operations
http://www.odcsops.hqusareur.army.mil/

> *Includes the ★ USAREUR Lessons Learned homepage and repository.*

NEW USAREUR Publications 📖
http://www.aeaim.hq.usareur.army.mil

NEW NEW LISTING IN THIS EDITION	✎ ONLINE FACT SHEET	📖 PUBLICATION REPOSITORY OR LIBRARY	★ RECOMMENDED SITE	☎ TELEPHONE NUMBER

U.S. Army Pacific (USARPAC)
Fort Shafter, Honolulu, Oahu, HI 96858
☎ 808-438-2206

USARPAC
http://www.usarpac.army.mil/

Major Pacific-based Army command and Army component of U.S. Pacific Command (PACOM), including U.S. Army Japan, U.S. Army Alaska, 25th Infantry Division (Light), and Johnston Atoll.

U.S. Army South (USARSO)
Fort Clayton (Panama), APO AA 34004

USARSO Homepage
http://www.army.mil/USARSO/default.htm

Army component command of U.S. Southern Command (SOUTCOM).

Army Field Operating Agencies

There are myriad minor Army field operating agencies that have no apparent Internet presence. They include the Civilian Personnel Evaluation Agency (Arlington, VA), Army Claims Service (Ft. Meade, MD), Command and Control Support Agency (Pentagon); Communications-Electronics Service Office (Alexandria, VA), Equal Employment Opportunity Agency (Washington, DC), Equal Employment Opportunity Compliance and Complaint Review Agency (Arlington, VA), Finance Command (Indianapolis, IN), Force Integration Support Agency (Ft. Belvoir, VA), Legal Services Agency (Falls Church, VA), Military Policy Support Agency (Falls Church, VA), Special Operations Agency (Washington, DC), U.S. Military Entrance Processing Command (Chicago, IL), and U.S. Military Observers Group (Washington, DC).

Army Aeronautical Services Agency
9325 Gunston Road, Suite N319
Fort Belvoir, VA 22060-5582
http://leav-www.army.mil/usaasa/usaasa.htm

Agency of the Deputy Chief of Staff for Operations; the Army airspace representative and liaison to the FAA dealing with special-use airspace, Open Skies Treaty, air shows, and paradrops.

Army Artificial Intelligence Center
http://www.pentagon-ai.army.mil

Army Staff field operating agency responsible for military artificial-intelligence-related programs (e.g., machine learning, speech recognition, fuzzy logic, natural language, virtual reality) as well as technology and Internet-related software and links.

Army Audit Agency
3101 Park Center Drive
Alexandria, VA 22302-1596
  http://www.hqda.army.mil/webs/AAAWEB/aaa.htm

  Summary and Index of Army Audit Agency Reports
    http://www-tradoc.army.mil/irac/index.html

Army Center of Military History (CMH)
1099 14th Street NW
Washington, DC 20005-3402
  http://www.army.mil/cmh-pg/

Army Community and Family Support Center
Alexandria, VA
  http://www.armymwr.com

  Morale, Welfare, and Recreation (MWR) gateway.

Army Concepts Analysis Agency
8120 Woodmont Avenue
Bethesda, MD 20814-2797

  Bibliography of Concepts Analysis Agency Studies
    http://carlisle-www.army.mil/usamhi/RefBibs/research/concepts.htm

Army Cost and Economic Analysis Center
Falls Church, VA
  http://134.11.192.15/ceac.htm

Army Environmental Center
Aberdeen Proving Ground, MD 21005
  http://aec-www.apgea.army.mil:8080/

Army Logistics Integration Agency
5001 Eisenhower Avenue
Alexandria, VA 22333
  http://lia.army.mil

Army Model Improvement and Study Management Agency (MISMA)
1725 Jefferson Davis Highway, CS 2, Suite 808
Arlington, VA 22202

Army Operational Test and Evaluation Command (OPTEC)
4501 Ford Avenue, Park Center IV
Alexandria, VA 22302-1458
  http://www.optec.army.mil/

★ **Army Publishing Agency**
2461 Eisenhower Avenue, Room 1050
Alexandria, VA 22331-0301
http://www-usappc.hoffman.army.mil

Formerly Army Publications and Printing Command, with a full repository of Army regulations and orders.

Army Recruiting Command
Fort Knox, KY 40121-2726
http://www.goarmy.mil/

Army Research Institute for Behavioral and Social Sciences
5001 Eisenhower Avenue
Alexandria, VA 22333-5600
http://www.ari.army.mil

Army Safety Center
Fort Rucker, AL 36362-5363
http://safety.army.mil/

Army Test and Experimentation Command
Fort Hood, TX 96544
http://texcom-www.army.mil/

Army War College ✎
Carlisle Barracks, PA 17013-5050
http://carlisle-www.army.mil

See Chapter 3.

★ **Total Army Personnel Command (PERSCOM)** ✎
Hoffman II Building
200 Stovall Street
Alexandria, VA 22332-0400
http://www-perscom.army.mil/

"PERSCOM Online" includes Army selection boards and promotions, as well as detailed branch (e.g., armor, infantry, military intelligence) personnel and assignment newsletters.

U.S. Military Academy
West Point, NY 10996
914-938-3301
http://www.usma.edu

Department of the Navy

The Department of the Navy is composed of the Office of the Secretary of the Navy, the Chief of Naval Operations, the administrative and operational organizations of the Navy, and the U.S. Marine Corps. The Secretary of the Navy is appointed by the President as the head of the department and is responsible to the Secretary of Defense for the operation of the Navy, including its organization, administration, functioning, and efficiency.

The Chief of Naval Operations (CNO), under the Secretary of the Navy, takes precedence above all other officers of the Navy and exercises command over certain central executive organizations, assigned shore activities, and the Operating Forces of the Navy. The CNO plans for and provides the manpower, material, weapons, facilities, and services to support the needs of the Navy, with the exception of Marine Forces, and exercises area coordination authority over all shore activities of the Department of the Navy.

Headquarters Department of the Navy
The Pentagon
Washington, DC 20350

   Navy Online
      http://www.navy.mil/

   Navy Organization
      http://www.chinfo.navy.mil/navpalib/organization/org-top.html
      Organizational diagrams of Navy staff, shore establishments, and operating forces, with embedded hyperlinks.

Secretary of the Navy

Secretary of the Navy
   http://www.chinfo.navy.mil/navpalib/people/secnav/secnavpg.html

   Under Secretary of the Navy

   Assistant Secretary of the Navy, Manpower and Reserve Affairs

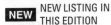 

Assistant Secretary of the Navy, Research, Development, and Acquisition

NEW Assistant Secretary of the Navy, Financial Management and Comptroller
http://navweb.secnav.navy.mil/

> *Includes the full budget justification materials of the Navy and Marine Corps (see Chapter 5).*

Assistant Secretary of the Navy, Installations and Environment
http://www.enviro.navy.mil/asn.htm

Navy Environmental and Safety Programs
http://www.enviro.navy.mil

NEW General Counsel
http://www.ogc.secnav.navy.mil

NEW Chief Information Officer of the Navy
http://www.doncio.navy.mil

Judge Advocate General (JAG)

Auditor General of the Navy and Commander, Naval Audit Service

Office of the Naval Inspector General 🔎
http://www.ig.navy.mil

Chief of Naval Operations

The Office of the Chief of Naval Operations is the headquarters of the Navy which advises and assists the Secretary, the Under Secretary, the Assistant Secretaries, and the Chief of Naval Operations in the discharge of their responsibilities.

Chief of Naval Operations (CNO)
http://www.ncts.navy.mil/navpalib/people/cno/
http://www.chinfo.navy.mil/navpalib/organization/org-cno.html

Vice Chief of Naval Operations

Deputy Chief of Naval Operations, Manpower and Personnel (N1)

Director of Naval Intelligence (N2)

Deputy Chief of Naval Operations, Plans, Policy and Operations (N3/N5)

Strategy and Concepts Branch (N513)
http://n4.opnav.navy.mil/N3_N5/N513/n513r~1.html

Deputy Chief of Naval Operations, Logistics (N4)
    http://n4.nosc.mil
    http://www.n4.hq.navy.mil/n4main.htm

> **NEW** Environmental Protection Safety and Occupational Health Division
> http://www.n4.hq.navy.mil/n45/n45main.htm

★ Deputy Chief of Naval Operations, Space, Information Warfare, and
Command and Control (N6)
    http://copernicus.hq.navy.mil/

> *Well-designed website with access to explanatory materials, briefings, speeches, documents, etc.*

Director of Naval Training (N7)

> Office of Training Technology (N75)
> http://www.ott.navy.mil

> **NEW** Catalog of Naval Training Courses (CANTRAC)
> http://www.cnet.navy.mil/netpdtc/cantrac/

Deputy Chief of Naval Operations, Resources, Warfare Requirements and Assessments (N8)
http://www.chinfo.navy.mil/navpalib/organization/org_n8.html

>   NEW Expeditionary Warfare Division (N85)
>   http://www.chinfo.navy.mil/navpalib/cno/n85/

>   NEW Surface Warfare Division (N86)
>   http://www.chinfo.navy.mil/navpalib/cno/n86/n86-main.html

>   Submarine Warfare Division (N87)
>   http://www.chinfo.navy.mil/navpalib/cno/n87/n87.html

>   Air Warfare Division (N88)
>   http://www.hq.navy.mil/Airwarfare/

NEW Director, Test and Evaluation and Technology Requirements (N091)
http://www.hq.navy.mil/N091/

Chief of Navy Chaplains (N097)
http://www.navy.mil/homepages/bupers/pers-04/pers-04.html

Oceanographer of the Navy
http://oceanographer.navy.mil/main.html

Major Fleet Commands/Operating Forces

The Operating Forces of the Navy include the several fleets, seagoing forces, Marine Forces and other assigned Marine Corps forces, the Military Sealift Command, and other forces and activities as may be assigned by the President or the Secretary of the Navy. The Chief of Naval Operations is responsible for the command and administration of the Operating Forces of the Navy.

Military Sealift Command (MSC)
Washington Navy Yard, Building 210
901 M Street SE
Washington, DC 20398-5540
☎ 1-800-MSC-2112

>   MSC Home $
>   http://www.msc.navy.mil

Mine Warfare Command
325 Fifth Street, SE
Corpus Christi, TX 78419-5032

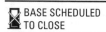 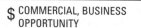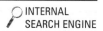

NEW Mine Warfare Command
http://www.cnsl.navy.mil/cmwc/cmwc.htm

> *Established in 1991 to command all mine countermeasures forces—air, surface, and explosive ordnance disposal.*

Naval Reserve Force (NRF)
4400 Dauphine Street
New Orleans, LA 70146-5046

Naval Reserve
http://www.navy.mil/homepages/navresfor/navres.html

> *Organization, public affairs, and information about the Naval Reserve, including job opportunities.*

Naval Surface Reserve Force
http://www.ncts.navy.mil/navresfor/navsurf/navsurf.html

Naval Air Reserve Force
http://www.ncts.navy.mil/navresfor/navair/navair.html

NEW Naval Reserve Information Systems Office
http://www.navriso.nola.navy.mil

Naval Special Warfare Command
2000 Trident Way
Naval Amphibious Base Coronado
San Diego, CA 92155-5000
☎ 619-437-3947

NEW NAVSOC Home
http://www.navsoc.navy.mil

Operational Test and Evaluation Force (OPTEVFOR)
7970 Diven Street
Norfolk, VA 23505-1498
☎ 757-444-5546

NEW OPTEVFOR Home
http://www.cotf.navy.mil

U.S. Atlantic Fleet
1562 Mitscher Avenue, Suite 250
Norfolk, VA 23511
☎ 757-322-5832

NEW NEW LISTING IN THIS EDITION   ONLINE FACT SHEET   PUBLICATION REPOSITORY OR LIBRARY ★ RECOMMENDED SITE   TELEPHONE NUMBER

LANTFLT Home
http://www.lantflt.navy.mil

> *Navy component command of U.S. Atlantic Command (ACOM) and Strategic Command (STRATCOM), including Fleet Marine Forces and the Second Fleet, as well as subordinate Type Commands (Naval Air, Submarine, and Naval Surface Force).*

U.S. Naval Forces Central Command (USNAVCENT)
(Manama, Bahrain)
FPO AE 09501-6008

> *Navy component command of U.S. Central Command (CENTCOM), includes the newly formed Fifth Fleet.*

U.S. Naval Forces Europe (USNAVEUR)
(London, UK)
FPO AE 09499-0152

NEW NAVEUR
http://199.208.201.37

> *Navy component command of U.S. European Command (EUCOM), including the Sixth Fleet.*

U.S. Pacific Fleet (PACFLT)
250 Makalapa Drive
Pearl Harbor, HI 96860-7000
☎ 808-471-9727

★ PACFLT
http://www.cpf.navy.mil/

> *Navy component command of U.S. Pacific Command (PACOM) and Strategic Command (STRATCOM). One of the more extensive and informative Navy Internet sites. Including Fleet Marine Forces and the Third and Seventh Fleets, as well as subordinate Type Commands (Naval Air, Submarine, and Naval Surface Force).*

Major Shore Establishments

The shore establishment provides support to the operating forces (known as "the fleet") in the form of facilities for the repair of machinery and electronics; communications centers; training areas and simulators; ship and aircraft repair; intelligence and meteorological support; storage areas for repair parts, fuel, and munitions; medical and dental facilities; and air bases.

 BASE SCHEDULED TO CLOSE $ COMMERCIAL, BUSINESS OPPORTUNITY   E-MAIL ADDRESS    INTERNAL SEARCH ENGINE

Bureau of Medicine and Surgery (BUMED)
23rd and E Streets NW
Washington, DC 20372-5120
☎ 202-653-1327

BUMED Home 🔍 📖
http://support1.med.navy.mil/bumed/

The Surgeon General of the Navy is also the Chief, Bureau of Medicine and Surgery.

Naval Medical Information Management Center
http://www-nmimc.med.navy.mil/

Navy Pharmacy Homepage
http://support1.med.navy.mil/navyphar/

Navy Psychiatry
http://164.167.49.31/psych/npsyhom.htm

Bureau of Naval Personnel (BUPERS)/Chief of Naval Personnel
Naval Support Activity Memphis
Millington, TN 38054-5045
☎ 901-874-5509

BUPERS Home
http://www.bupers.navy.mil/

The Chief of Naval Personnel is also the Deputy Chief of Naval Operations, Manpower and Personnel. The excellent website includes personnel news, selection board results, and Navy administration and personnel policy, as well as links to BUPERS magazines Link, Perspective, *and* Shift Colors. *BUPERS headquarters moved from Washington, DC in 1998.*

Engineering Duty Officers Homepage
http://www.bupers.navy.mil/edo

Naval Air Systems Command (NAVAIR)
NAS Patuxent River, MD 20670

★ Naval Aviation Team $
http://www.navair.navy.mil/

NAVAIR headquarters moved from Arlington, VA, in 1998. Extensive website with excellent information.

NEW Air Systems Program
http://asp.navair.navy.mil

NEW The Greenshirt 🔍
http://greenshirt.nalda.navy.mil

> *The naval aviation maintenance homepage.*

Naval Computer and Telecommunications Command
4401 Massachusetts Avenue NW
Washington, DC 20390
☎ 202-282-0357

> Naval Computer and Telecommunications Command Home
> http://www.nctc.navy.mil/

Naval Doctrine Command
1540 Gilbert Street
Norfolk, VA 23511-2785
☎ 757-445-0555

> NEW Naval Doctrine Command
> http://www.ndc.navy.mil

Naval Education and Training Command
250 Dallas Street
Pensacola, FL 32508
☎ 904-452-4858

> CNET Home 🔍
> http://www.cnet.navy.mil/
>
> > *The Director, Naval Training is also the Chief of Naval Education and Training (CNET).*

Naval Facilities Engineering Command (NAVFAC)
200 Stovall Street
Alexandria, VA 22332-2300
☎ 703-325-0589; ☎ 703-325-0310

> ★ NAVFAC
> http://www.navy.mil/homepages/navfac/
>
> > *One of the most extensive Navy Internet sites, with links to subordinate divisions and field activities, the Navy Construction Battalion Centers, and Navy Public Works Centers.*

> NEW Directorate of Public Works
> http://www.fac131.navfac.navy.mil

Naval Legal Service Command
200 Stovall Street
Alexandria, VA 22332-2400
☎ 703-325-9820

Naval Meteorology and Oceanography Command (NAVMETOCCOM)
Stennis Space Center
Bay St. Louis, MS 39529-5002
☎ 601-688-4726

> METOC Home
> http://www.cnmoc.navy.mil/
>
> *Links to Navy meteorology, oceanography, mapping, charting, and geodesy.*

Naval Safety Center
Naval Air Station Norfolk
9420 Third Avenue
Norfolk, VA 23511

> Navy Safety
> http://www.norfolk.navy.mil/safecen/

Naval Sea Systems Command (NAVSEA)
2531 Jefferson Davis Highway, Building NC3
Arlington, VA 22242
☎ 703-602-6920

> ★ NAVSEA $
> http://www.navsea.navy.mil/
>
> *Super-organized site with excellent organizational and project-related
> information.*
>
> NEW LogTools Homepage 🔎
> http://www.logtools.navsea.navy.mil

Naval Security Group Command
9800 Savage Road
Fort Meade, MD 20755
☎ 301-617-3698

> NEW NSGC
> http://www.nsg.navy.mil/Home.html

Naval Space Command (NAVSPACECOM)
5280 Fourth Street
Dahlgren, VA 22448-5300
☎ 540-653-6100

> Navy Space
> http://www.navspace.navy.mil
>
> > *Navy component command of U.S. Space Command (SPACECOM).*

Naval Supply Systems Command (NAVSUP)
1931 Jefferson Davis Highway, CM3
Arlington, VA 22241
☎ 703-695-4009

> NAVSUP Home
> http://www.navsup.navy.mil/newsup
>
> Naval Logistics Reference Library
> http://quads-www.std.caci.com/navdoc3/

Office of Naval Intelligence (ONI)
National Maritime Intelligence Center
4251 Suitland Road
Washington DC 20395
☎ 301-669-3005

> `NEW` Naval Intelligence Home
> http://oni.nmic.navy.mil
>
> > *Though located in Suitland, MD, the National Maritime Intelligence Center*
> > *maintains a Washington, DC, address.*

Space and Naval Warfare Systems Command (SPAWAR)
2451 Crystal Drive, CP 5
Arlington, VA 22245-5200
☎ 703-602-8954

> SPAWAR Home $ 📖
> http://www.spawar.navy.mil/spawar/welcome.page
>
> SPAWAR/NRaD Publications 📖
> http://www.nosc.mil/nrad/publications
>
> SPAWAR Information Systems Security Program Office
> http://infosec.nosc.mil/infosec.html

Navy Field and Shore Activities

Department of the Navy Information Network Program Office
http://www.inpo.navy.mil/

> *Under the authority of the Deputy Assistant Secretary of the Navy (C4I/EW/Space).*

Naval Audit Service/Auditor General of the Navy
5611 Columbia Pike
Falls Church, VA 22041-5080
☎ 703-681-9117

Naval Center for Cost Analysis
1111 Jefferson Davis Highway, Suite 400 West Tower
Arlington, VA 22202-4306
☎ 703-604-0312
http://www.ncca.navy.mil/

Naval Criminal Investigative Service (NCIS)
Washington Navy Yard
901 M Street SE
Washington, DC 20388
http://www.ncts.navy.mil/homepages/ncis/

> *Reporting to the Under Secretary of the Navy.*

Naval District Washington (NDW)
Washington Navy Yard
901 M Street SE
Washington, DC 20374
http://www.ndw.navy.mil/

Navy Recruiting Command
4015 Wilson Boulevard
Arlington, VA 22203
☎ 1-800-USA-NAVY
http://www.nrc.navy.mil
http://www.navyjobs.com

Office of Naval Research (ONR) ⌕ $
Ballston Tower 1, 800 North Quincy Street
Arlington, VA 22217-5660
☎ 703-696-5031
http://www.onr.navy.mil/
http://web.fie.com/fedix/onr.html

> *Reporting to the Assistant Secretary of the Navy, Research, Development, and Acquisition; the Chief of Naval Research is also the Commander of the Naval Meteorology and Oceanography Command.*

U.S. Marine Corps

Headquarters U.S. Marine Corps
Washington, DC 20380-0001
☎ 703-614-8010

Marine Corps Homepage
http://www.usmc.mil

Headquarters Marine Corps
http://www.hqmc.usmc.mil/hqmc/default.htm
http://www.hqmc.usmc.mil/hqmcmain/hqmc.htm

Marine Corps Headquarters is moving out of the Arlington Annex and is scheduled to take up residence in the Pentagon or at other bases and facilities by the end of the decade.

Commandant of the Marine Corps
http://www.usmc.mil/cmc.nsf/cmc

Assistant Commandant of the Marine Corps

Deputy Chief of Staff for Aviation

NEW Deputy Chief of Staff for Installations and Logistics
http://www.hqmc.usmc.mil/ilweb.nsf

Marine Corps Environmental Program
http://www.hqmc.usmc.mil/enviro1/default.htm

Deputy Chief of Staff for Manpower and Reserve Affairs

Deputy Chief of Staff for Plans, Policies and Operations

Deputy Chief of Staff for Programs and Resources

NEW Assistant Chief of Staff for Command, Control, Communications and Computers/Director of Intelligence
http://issb-www1.quantico.usmc.mil/c4i/index.html

Chief Information Officer
http://www.cio.usmc.mil

NEW Staff Judge Advocate
http://www.hqi.usmc.mil/jaweb/hqmc/ja.nsf

U.S. Marine Corps Health Services
http://www.hqmc.usmc.mil/opages/health1.htm

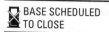 BASE SCHEDULED TO CLOSE

 $ COMMERCIAL, BUSINESS OPPORTUNITY

 E-MAIL ADDRESS

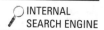 INTERNAL SEARCH ENGINE

Marine Corps Operating Forces

The Operating Forces of the Marine Corps include Marine Security Forces and Marine Detachments Afloat, those Marines aboard naval aircraft carriers and other major ships.

Marine Forces Atlantic
Norfolk, VA

> MARFORLANT
> http://www.nfd.usmc.mil

Marine Forces Pacific
Camp H. M. Smith, HI 96861

> MARFORPAC
> http://www.mfp.usmc.mil/
>
> **NEW** Marine Forces Pacific G2 Site
> http://www.mfp.usmc.mil/g2/html/marfor_top_nav.htm

Marine Forces Reserve
Naval Support Activity New Orleans
2300 General Meyer Avenue
New Orleans, LA 70142-5007

> MARFORRES
> http://www.marforres.usmc.mil/
>
> **NEW** Reserve Information Network
> http://www.met.marforres.usmc.mil

Marine Corps Supporting Establishments

Marine Corps Combat Development Command (MCCDC)
3250 Catlin Avenue, Suite 107
Quantico, VA 22134-5001

> MCCDC Home
> http://ismo-www1.mqg.usmc.mil/quantico/
>
> *Includes the Marine Corps University and the Marine Corps Warfighting Laboratory (see Chapter 3).*
>
> **NEW** Amphibious Warfare Technology Directorate
> http://www.usmc-awt.brtrc.com
>
> **NEW** Concepts Division
> http://138.156.107.3/concepts

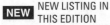 NEW LISTING IN THIS EDITION   ONLINE FACT SHEET   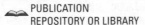 PUBLICATION REPOSITORY OR LIBRARY   RECOMMENDED SITE   TELEPHONE NUMBER

NEW Doctrine Division
http://138.156.107.3/docdiv

Training and Education Division
http://138.156.15.33/tediv/tande.html

★ CDC Domino 🔍
http://138.156.112.14/CDCHome.nsf/?OpenDatabase

Marine Corps Recruiting Command
Headquarters, U.S. Marine Corps
4104 Arlington Annex
Arlington, VA 22204
☎ 1-800-MARINES

Marine Corps Systems Command (MarCorSysCom)
2033 Barnett Avenue, Suite 315
Quantico, VA 22134-5010

Marine Corps Systems Command $
http://www.marcorsyscom.usmc.mil

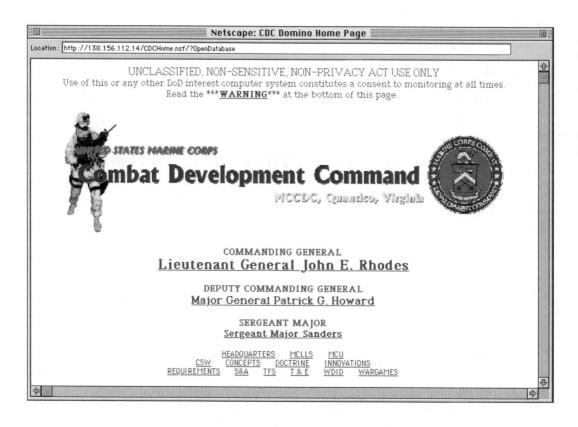

Netscape: CDC Domino Home Page

Location: http://138.156.112.14/CDCHome.nsf/?OpenDatabase

UNCLASSIFIED, NON-SENSITIVE, NON-PRIVACY ACT USE ONLY
Use of this or any other DoD interest computer system constitutes a consent to monitoring at all times.
Read the ***WARNING*** at the bottom of this page.

UNITED STATES MARINE CORPS
Combat Development Command
MCCDC, Quantico, Virginia

COMMANDING GENERAL
Lieutenant General John E. Rhodes

DEPUTY COMMANDING GENERAL
Major General Patrick G. Howard

SERGEANT MAJOR
Sergeant Major Sanders

HEADQUARTERS MCLLS MCU
CSW CONCEPTS DOCTRINE INNOVATIONS
REQUIREMENTS S&A TFS T & E WDID WARGAMES

⧗ BASE SCHEDULED TO CLOSE $ COMMERCIAL, BUSINESS OPPORTUNITY   ✉ E-MAIL ADDRESS   🔍 INTERNAL SEARCH ENGINE

Major Military Bases in the United States, by State

Alabama

Anniston Army Depot, 7 Frankfurt Avenue, Anniston, AL 36201-5000
☎ 205-235-7501

Anniston Army Depot (IOC)
http://www-anad.army.mil
http://www-ioc.army.mil/home/elements/anniston.html 🖎

NEW Anniston Chemical Activity (CBDCOM)
http://www.cbdcom.army.mil/storage/Anniston/index.html

⌛ **Fort McClellan,** Anniston, AL 36205-5000
☎ 205-848-4611

Home also to the Department of Defense Polygraph Institute and the Air Force Disaster Preparedness Technical Training School. The base is scheduled to close by October 1999; the schools will move to Ft. Leonard Wood, MO.

Army Chemical and Military Police Centers (TRADOC) 🔎
http://www.mcclellan.army.mil/

Army Chemical School
http://www.mcclellan.army.mil/usacmls/index.htm

Army Military Police School
http://www.mcclellan.army.mil/usamps/default.htm
http://160.148.50.20/

Fort Rucker, AL 36362-5000
☎ 334-255-1100

Base tenants include the Army Aviation Technical Test Center, the Army School of Aviation Medicine, the Air Maneuver Battle Lab, the Aviation Technical Library, and the Aviation Museum.

Army Aviation Center and Fort Rucker (TRADOC) 📖
http://www-rucker.army.mil/

Army Aeromedical Center (MEDCOM)
http://www.rucker.amedd.army.mil

Army Safety Center (Army field operating agency)
http://safety.army.mil/

Gunter Annex, Maxwell AFB, AL 36114-5000
☎ 334-416-1110

Air Force Logistics Management Agency (AF field operating agency)
http://www.il.hq.af.mil/AFLMA/index.html

Standard Systems Group (SSG) (AFMC) 🔍 📖 $
http://www.ssg.gunter.af.mil/

Defense Megacenter Montgomery (DISA)
http://www.dmcgun.disa.mil

Maxwell AFB, AL 36112-5000
☎ 334-953-1110

★ Air University (AU) (AETC) 📖
http://www.au.af.mil/

Air University colleges, institutes, and activities include the Air War College; Air Command and Staff College; School of Advanced Airpower Studies; Squadron Officer School; Officer Training School; College of Aerospace Doctrine, Research and Education (CADRE), Air Force Wargaming Institute; Ira C. Eaker College for Professional Development; Air Force Judge Advocate General School; Community College of the Air Force; and Air University Press (see Chapter 3)

Civil Air Patrol–USAF
http://www.cap.af.mil/

NEW Air Force Doctrine Center (AF direct reporting unit) 📖
http://www.hqafdc.maxwell.af.mil

Air Force Reserve Officer Training Corps (ROTC)
http://www.afoats.af.mil/ROTC/ROTC_in_Frames.htm

Air Force Historical Research Agency (AF field operating agency)
http://www.au.af.mil/au/afhra/

Missile Defense and Space Technology Center (SMDC), PO Box 1500, Huntsville, AL 35807-3801
(located at 106 Wynn Drive, Huntsville, AL 35805-1990)

SMDC Technology Center Home
http://www.smdc.army.mil/MDSTC.html

Space and Missile Defense Command Simulation Center $
http://sc-www.army.mil/

Redstone Arsenal, Huntsville, AL 35898-5000
☎ 205-876-2151

Redstone Arsenal and Army Aviation and Missile Command (AMCOM)
(AMC) $
http://www.redstone.army.mil/
http://wwwsun.redstone.army.mil/

AMCOM changed its name from Army Missile Command (MICOM) in 1997 with expanded responsibilities. The website includes a searchable database of regulations, supplements to Army Regulations, pamphlets, circulars, etc.

★ Redstone Arsenal Historical Information
http://wwwsun.redstone.army.mil/history/welcome.html

Missile Research, Development and Engineering Center
http://www.mrdec.redstone.army.mil/

★ Redstone Scientific Information Center (RSIC)
http://rsic3.redstone.army.mil/
http://library.redstone.army.mil/

NEW Redstone Technical Test Center
http://www.atc.army.mil/~rttc/

Army Logistics Support Activity
http://www.logsa.army.mil/

Army Ordnance, Missile and Munitions Center and School/59th Ordnance Brigade
(TRADOC)
http://www.logsa.army.mil/ommcs

Huntsville Engineering and Support Center (USACE) $
http://www.hnd.usace.army.mil

Ordnance and Explosives Mandatory Center of Expertise and Design Center
http://w2.hnd.usace.army.mil/oew/oewindex.html

Technologies and ongoing work related to risks from unexploded ordnance, explosives, and recovered chemical weapons at current and formerly used defense sites.

Engineering Data Management Office/Army JEDMICS Component Office
http://wwwedms.redstone.army.mil

Defense Megacenter Huntsville (DISA)
http://www.westhem.disa.mil/~WEH/dmch.html

Missile and Space Intelligence Center (DIA)
http://msic.dia.mil/

Alaska

Eareckson Air Station, Shemya, AK 99506-2270
☎ 907-552-1814

NEW Eareckson Homepage
http://www.topcover.af.mil/orgs/eareck/EARhome.htm

Eielson AFB, Fairbanks, AK 99702-1830
☎ 907-377-1110

Eielson AFB and 354th Fighter Wing (PACAF)
http://www.eielson.af.mil
http://midnight.eielson.af.mil/

Elmendorf AFB, Anchorage, AK 99506-2530
☎ 907-552-1110

Elmendorf AFB and 3rd Wing
http://www.topcover.af.mil

NEW Alaskan Command
http://www.topcover.af.mil/alcom/alcom.html

Eleventh Air Force (PACAF)
http://www.topcover.af.mil/orgs/11af/index.html

Commander serves as the head of Alaskan Command, Joint Task Force–Alaska (PACOM), and the Alaskan NORAD Region.

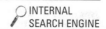

Fort Greely, Fairbanks, APO AK 96508
☎ 907-873-1121

> NEW Fort Greely
> http://143.213.12.254/3posts/fgapage.htm

> Northern Warfare Training Center
> http://143.213.12.254/3posts/NWTC.htm

> Army Cold Regions Test Activity (Yuma Proving Ground, TECOM)
> http://143.212.201.6/
> http://crta-www.army.mil/

Fort Richardson, Anchorage, AK 99505-5900
☎ 907-384-1110, ✉ postmaster@richardson-emh2.army.mil

> NEW Fort Richardson and Arctic Support Brigade
> http://143.213.12.254/3posts/frapage.htm

Fort Wainwright/Wainwright Army Airfield, Fairbanks, AK 99703-5000
☎ 907-353-1110

> Fort Wainwright
> http://143.213.12.254/3posts/fwapage.htm

> U.S. Army Alaska (PACOM)
> http://143.213.12.254/home.htm

> 1st Brigade, 6th Infantry Division (Arctic Warrior)
> http://143.214.20.26/1bde/index.htm

> *Aligned with the 10th Mountain Division (Light Infantry), Ft. Drum, NY.*

Arizona

Davis-Monthan AFB, Tucson, AZ 85707
☎ 520-228-3900

> Davis-Monthan AFB and 355th Wing
> http://www.dm.af.mil

> Twelfth Air Force (ACC)
> http://www.12af.dm.af.mil/

> *Also serves as the headquarters for the U.S. Southern Air Force (USSOUTHAF),*
> *the air component of SOUTHCOM.*

Aerospace Maintenance and Regeneration Center ("The Boneyard") (AFMC)
http://www.dm.af.mil/amarc/default.htm

Fort Huachuca, Sierra Vista, AZ 85613-6000
☎ 520-538-7111

Fort Huachuca
http://huachuca-www.army.mil/
http://138.27.209.61/teamhua/

Army Intelligence Center and Fort Huachuca (TRADOC)
http://huachuca-usaic.army.mil/
http://138.27.209.71/teamhua/icfh.htm

Home of a variety of Army intelligence units and intelligence and electronic warfare (IEW) development and test directorates, including the 111th Military Intelligence Brigade.

Military Intelligence Warrant Officer Homepage
http://huachuca-usaic.army.mil/miwarrant/wohpl.htm/

Army Signal Command (FORSCOM)
http://138.27.190.13/

Activated 16 September 1996 and formerly the Army Information Systems Command (ISC).

NEW 11th Signal Brigade
http://www.asc.army.mil/11th

NEW Army Network and System Operation Center
http://www.ansoc.army.mil

Army Information Systems Engineering Command $
http://www.hqisec.army.mil/

Electronic Proving Ground (WSMR, TECOM)
http://www.epgC4i.com
http://www.epg.army.mil/epg

Military Affiliate Radio System (MARS)
http://www.asc.army.mil/mars/

Joint Interoperability Test Command (DISA)
http://jitc-emh.army.mil/

Luke AFB, Litchfield, AZ 85309-5000
☎ 602-856-7411

    56th Fighter Wing (AETC)
    http://www.luke.af.mil

Marine Corps Air Station Yuma, AZ 85369-9113
☎ 520-341-2011

    MCAS Yuma
    http://192.156.46.130
    http://www.eltoro.usmc.mil/YUMA/IDXYUMA.htm

      Home of Marine Aircraft Group 13 (MAG-13), part of the 3rd MAW.

    NEW Marine Aviation Weapons and Tactics Squadron One
    http://www.tediv.quantico.usmc.mil/mawts1/index.htm

Yuma Proving Ground, AZ 85365
☎ 520-328-3287

    Yuma Proving Ground (TECOM)
    http://www.yuma.army.mil

Arkansas

Little Rock AFB, AR 72099-5026
☎ 501-988-3131

    314th Airlift Wing (ACC) 📖
    http://www.littlerock.af.mil/

Pine Bluff Arsenal, Pine Bluff, AR 71602-9500
☎ 501-540-3000
    http://www.pba.army.mil
    http://www-ioc.army.mil/home/elements/pinebl.html ✎

    NEW Pine Bluff Chemical Activity (CBDCOM)
    http://www.cbdcom.apgea.army.mil/storage/PineBluff/index.html

---

 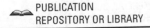

California

Beale AFB, CA 95903-5000
☎ 916-634-3000; ✉ 9rwpa@acchost.acc.af.mil

>Beale AFB
>http://www.beale.af.mil/

>9th Reconnaissance Wing (ACC)
>http://www.beale.af.mil/9rw

Edwards AFB, CA 93524-1115
☎ 805-277-1110

>Edwards AFB and Air Force Flight Test Center (AFFTC) (AFMC) 🔎 $
>http://www.edwards.af.mil/
>http://www.elan.af.mil/
>http://afftc.edwards.af.mil/

>>Time Space Position Information
>>http://www.tspi.elan.af.mil/

>>>*Explanation of the various tracking methods used to determine the exact position of a test vehicle in time and space.*

>Air Force Research Laboratory Propulsion Directorate
>http://www.ple.af.mil

>>*Formerly Phillips Laboratory Directorate, part of the newly formed Air Force superlab.*

Fort Irwin, CA 92310-5000
☎ 760-256-1071; ✉ afzj-po@irwin-emh1.army.mil

>National Training Center and Fort Irwin (FORSCOM) 🔎
>http://www.irwin.army.mil/

>11th Armored Cavalry Regiment (FORSCOM) 🔎
>http://www.irwin.army.mil/11acr/sitemap.htm

Los Angeles AFB, El Segundo, CA 90245-4687
☎ 310-363-1110

>Los Angeles AFB
>http://www.laafb.af.mil/

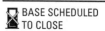 BASE SCHEDULED TO CLOSE   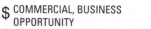 $ COMMERCIAL, BUSINESS OPPORTUNITY   E-MAIL ADDRESS    INTERNAL SEARCH ENGINE

Space and Missile Systems Center (SMC) (AFMC) $
http://www.laafb.af.mil/SMC/

SMC Systems Acquisition
http://ax.laafb.af.mil/

SMC/XR Developmental Planning Directorate
http://www.afbmd.laafb.af.mil/

Marine Corps Air-Ground Combat Center Twentynine Palms, CA 92278-8100
☎ 760-830-6000; ✉ pnzhz2@mqgsmtp3.usmc.mil

Base tenants include the 7th Marines and the Marine Corps Communications-Electronics School.

Marine Corps Air-Ground Combat Center
http://www.mcagcc.usmc.mil

Marine Corps Air Facility Tustin, CA 92710-5001
☎ 714-726-2100
http://www.eltoro.usmc.mil/TUSTIN/IDXTUS.htm

Home to the last elements of Marine Aircraft Group 11 (MAG-11), in the process of moving to MCAS Miramar. The base is scheduled to close in 1999.

Marine Corps Air Station El Toro, Santa Ana, CA 92709-5010
☎ 714-726-2100

MCAS El Toro
http://www.eltoro.usmc.mil/

Marine Corps Air Bases Western Area (I MEF) and the 3rd Marine Aircraft Wing (3rd MAW) moved to MCAS Miramar. The base is scheduled to close in 1999.

Marine Corps Air Station Miramar, 45249 Miramar Way, San Diego, CA 92145-5000
☎ 619-537-1011

Formerly Naval Air Station (NAS), transitioned to Marine control on 1 October 1991. The Marine Corps elements moved from MCAS El Toro and Tustin, both scheduled to close.

NEW MCAS Miramar
http://www.eltoro.usmc.mil/MIRAMAR/IDXMIR.htm

NEW Marine Corps Airbases Western Area and 3rd Marine Aircraft Wing (3rd MAW) (I MEF)
http://www.3maw.usmc.mil

Marine Corps Base Camp Joseph H. Pendleton, Oceanside, CA 92055-5001
☎ 760-725-4111

Camp Pendleton $
http://www.cpp.usmc.mil/default.htm

Home to the School of Infantry and the Assault Amphibian School.

I Marine Expeditionary Force (I MEF) (FMFPAC)
http://www.cpp.usmc.mil/imef/index.htm

1st Force Service Support Group (1st FSSG)
1st Marine Division (1st MarDiv)
Marine Aircraft Group 39 (MAG-39) (3rd MAW)
http://www.cpp.usmc.mil/home.htm

*Because of bad Web design, these major unit homepages can be accessed
directly only through the Camp Pendleton major units page.*

Marine Corps Tactical Systems Support Activity
http://www.mctssa.usmc.mil

Field Hospital Operations and Training Command
http://truenorth.med.navy.mil/~fhotc/

Formerly Field Medical Service School.

Marine Corps Recruit Depot San Diego, CA 92140-5093
☎ 619-524-8762

MCRD San Diego
http://www.sdo.usmc.mil

Marine Corps Mountain Warfare Training Center, Bridgeport, CA 93517
☎ 619-932-7761

Mountain Warfare Training Center
http://mwtc.cpp.usmc.mil
http://138.156.4.23/

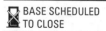 **McClellan AFB,** CA 95652
☎ 916-643-4113

The base is scheduled to close by 2001.

Sacramento Air Logistics Center (SM-ALC) (AFMC) $
http://www.mcclellan.af.mil/

⌛ BASE SCHEDULED
   TO CLOSE

$ COMMERCIAL, BUSINESS
   OPPORTUNITY

✉ E-MAIL
   ADDRESS

○ INTERNAL
   SEARCH ENGINE

Space & C3I Systems Directorate
http://www.mcclellan.af.mil/LH/

NEW Defense Microelectronics Activity (DMEA)
http://www.dmea.osd.mil

Defense Megacenter Sacramento (DISA)
http://www.westhem.disa.mil/~WET41/dmcsac.html

Moffett Federal Air Field, Moffett Field, CA 94035
☎ 415-604-3645

Formerly Naval Air Station (NAS) Moffett Field.

Aeroflight Dynamics Directorate, Aviation Research, Development and Engineering
Center (AMCOM)
http://AFDD.arc.nasa.gov/

Naval Air Station Alameda, 250 Mall Square, CA 94501-5000
☎ 510-263-3012

The base is officially closed.

Fleet Hospital Support Office (NAVSUP)
http://www.fhso.navy.mil/

Naval Air Station Lemoore, 700 Avenger Avenue, Lemoore, CA 93246-5000
☎ 209-998-0100

*Home to Strike Fighter Wing Pacific and Carrier Air Wings 2, 9, 11, and 14 (when not
at sea).*

NEW NAS Lemoore
http://www.lemoore.navy.mil

NAS Lemoore (Unofficial)
http://cnetech.cnetech.com/davide/

Naval Air Station North Island, Coronado, CA 92135
☎ 619-545-8123

NAS North Island
http://www.nasni.navy.mil/

Naval Air Force U.S. Pacific Fleet (NAVAIRPAC) (PACFLT)
http://www.airpac.navy.mil

> *Includes Helicopter Antisubmarine Wing U.S. Pacific Fleet, Helicopter Tactical Wing U.S. Pacific Fleet, and Seacontrol Wing U.S. Pacific Fleet. Carrier Air Wing headquarters and elements are based at North Island and Lemoore when not at sea.*

> USS Kitty Hawk (CV 63)
> http://trout.spawar.navy.mil/~cv63pao/

`NEW` Naval Aviation Depot North Island
http://www.nadepni.navy.mil

Defense Megacenter San Diego (DISA)
http://www.westhem.disa.mil/~WES/dmcsd.html

Naval Air Weapons Station China Lake, China Lake, CA 93555-6001
☎ 619-939-9011

Naval Air Warfare Center Weapons Division (NAWC WD) China Lake
(NAVAIR) 🔍 $ 📖
http://www.nawcwpns.navy.mil/

Naval Air Weapons Stations Point Mugu, CA 93042-5001
☎ 805-989-1110

Naval Air Warfare Center Weapons Division (NAWC WD) Point Mugu (NAVAIR)
http://salmon.mugu.navy.mil/
http://143.113.21.51/About_NAWC_Mugu.html

`NEW` Naval Weapons Test Squadron Point Mugu
http://eabb.pt.mugu.navy.mil/weptest/

Antarctic Development Squadron 6 (VXE-6)
http://www.navy.mil/homepages/vxe6

Naval Amphibious Base Coronado, San Diego, CA 92155-5000
☎ 619-545-8123; ✉ amphib@scn.com

Naval Surface Force U.S. Pacific Fleet (NAVSURFPAC) (PACFLT)
http://www.surfpac.navy.mil

`NEW` Amphibious Group 3
http://www.cpg3.navy.mil

`NEW` Expeditionary Warfare Training Group Pacific
http://www.ewtgpac.navy.mil

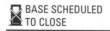 BASE SCHEDULED TO CLOSE    COMMERCIAL, BUSINESS OPPORTUNITY   E-MAIL ADDRESS   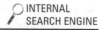 INTERNAL SEARCH ENGINE

NEW Commander Naval Special Warfare Command
http://www.navsoc.navy.mil

> *Includes the Naval Special Warfare Center, Naval Special Warfare Group 1 and subordinate Special Boat Squadron 1, and Seal Teams 1, 3, and 5.*

NEW Official Navy Seals Website
http://webix.nosc.mil/seals

Naval Base San Diego
937 N. Harbor Drive, San Diego, CA 92132
☎ 619-553-1011

NEW Commander Naval Base San Diego
http://www.cnbsd.navy.mil

> *Includes the combined activities of NAS North Island, Naval Amphibious Base Coronado, Naval Station San Diego, Naval Submarine Base, the Naval Training Center, and other bases and facilities.*

Fleet and Industrial Supply Center San Diego, 937 North Harbor Drive,
San Diego, CA 92132-5044
http://www.sd.fisc.navy.mil/

NEW Fleet Combat Training Center (Point Loma)
http://fctcpac.navy.mil

NEW Fleet Imaging Command Pacific
http://www.ficp.navy.mil

NEW Fleet Technical Support Center Pacific
http://www.ftscpac.navy.mil

NEW Naval Computer and Telecommunications Station San Diego (NCTC)
http://www.nctssd.navy.mil

Naval Facilities Engineering Command Southwest Division
http://www.edfswest.navfac.navy.mil

Public Works Center San Diego
http://nanu.nosc.mil/

Naval Construction Battalion Center Port Hueneme, CA 93043-4301
☎ 805-982-4711

Naval Construction Battalion Center
http://www.cbcph.navy.mil/

Includes the 1st Naval Construction Regiment and the 31st Naval Construction Regiment (Training), Naval Mobile Construction Battalions 3, 4, 5, and 40, and Underwater Construction Team (UCT) 2.

Naval Surface Warfare Center Port Hueneme Division (NAVSEA) 🔎 $
http://www.nswses.navy.mil/

Naval Facilities Engineering Service Center
http://www.nfesc.navy.mil

Naval Medical Center San Diego, 34800 Bob Wilson Drive, San Diego, CA 92134-5000
☎ 619-532-6400; ✉ navmed@scn.com

NEW Naval Medical Center San Diego
http://www-nmcsd.med.navy.mil

Naval Health Research Center (NMRDC) 📖
http://www.nhrc.navy.mil/

Naval Postgraduate School, Monterey, CA 93943-5000
☎ 408-656-2441

★Naval Postgraduate School (NPS) 📖
http://www.nps.navy.mil/
gopher://peacock.nps.navy.mil/

See Chapter 3.

Naval Security Group Detachment Monterey (NSGC)
http://www.nsgdmry.navy.mil

Fleet Numerical Meteorology and Oceanography Center
http://152.80.56.203/index.html
http://www.fnoc.navy.mil/

Naval Research Laboratory Marine Meteorology Division 🔎
http://www.nrlmry.navy.mil/

Naval Station San Diego, 3445 Surface Navy Boulevard, San Diego, CA 92136-5059
☎ 619-556-1246; ✉ 32street@scn.com

Naval Submarine Base, 150 Sylvester Road, San Diego, CA 92106-3521
☎ 619-553-7100

NEW Commander Submarine Base San Diego
http://www.subasesd.navy.mil

Includes the Naval Training Facility.

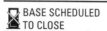 BASE SCHEDULED TO CLOSE    $ COMMERCIAL, BUSINESS OPPORTUNITY   E-MAIL ADDRESS    INTERNAL SEARCH ENGINE

Commander Third Fleet (PACFLT)
   http://www.comthirdflt.navy.mil/

   Located aboard the flagship USS Coronado (AGF-11).

Fleet Anti-Submarine Warfare Training Center, 32444 Echo Lane, San Diego, CA 92147-5199

Navy Personnel Research and Development Center (Point Loma)
   http://www.nprdc.navy.mil/

   To move to Tennessee with the Bureau of Naval Personnel.

Naval Training Center San Diego, 32224 Roosevelt Road, San Diego CA 92133
☎ 619-524-4851

   Fleet Training Center
   http://www.cnet.navy.mil/cnet/ftcsd/index.htm

   Training Command U.S. Pacific Fleet (PACFLT)
   http://www.cnet.navy.mil/trapac/ctp.html

Naval Warfare Assessment Station, 2300 Fifth Street, Norco, CA 91718-5000
☎ 909-273-5000

   Naval Warfare Assessment Division (NAVSEA)
   http://www.corona.navy.mil/

   Fleet Marine Force Metrology
   http://marines.corona.navy.mil/

Naval Weapons Station Concord, CA 94520-5100
☎ 510-246-2000

   Naval Sea Logistics Center Pacific Detachment (NAVSEA)
   http://www.seacosd.navy.mil/
   http://www.nslcpacific.navy.mil

Naval Weapons Support Facility Seal Beach, CA 90740
☎ 213-594-7011

   Formerly Naval Weapons Station.

   Naval Ordnance Center Pacific Division (NAVSEA)
   http://www.sbeach.navy.mil/sbeach.htm

Onizuka Air Station, Sunnyvale, CA 94089-1235
☎ 408-752-3000

> Onizuka AFS
> http://www.oafb.af.mil

> 750th Space Group (14th Air Force, AFSPC)
> http://www.oafb.af.mil/75osg/index.html

Presidio of Monterey, CA 93944-5006
☎ 408-242-5119

> Presidio of Monterey
> http://pom-www.army.mil

> Defense Language Institute/Foreign Language Center
> http://dli-www.army.mil

>> LingNet (The Linguist's Bulletin Board System)
>> http://lingnet.army.mil/

>>> *Devoted to military linguists. The website includes foreign language materials and programs.*

Public Works Center San Francisco Bay, Oakland, CA 94623-1000
> http://www.pwcsfb.navy.mil/

⌛ **Sacramento Army Depot Activity,** Sacramento, CA 95813

> *The depot has closed, and only minor activities remain.*

> Television-Audio Support Activity (AFIS)
> http://tasa2.army.mil/

Sierra Army Depot Activity, Herlong, CA 96113-5000
☎ 916-827-4111

> Sierra Army Depot Activity
> http://www.sierra.army.mil
> http://www-ioc.army.mil/home/elements/sierra.html ✎

Space and Naval Warfare Systems Center (SSC San Diego)
53690 Tomahawk Drive, San Diego, CA 92147-5042

> SSC San Diego (SPAWAR) $ 📖
> http://www.nosc.mil/nrad/welcome.page

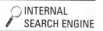

⌛ BASE SCHEDULED TO CLOSE $ COMMERCIAL, BUSINESS OPPORTUNITY   ✉ E-MAIL ADDRESS   🔍 INTERNAL SEARCH ENGINE

Formerly the Naval Command Control and Ocean Surveillance Center (NCCOSC) and the NCCOSC RDT&E Division, which was formed in March 1996 when the NCCOSC In-Service Engineering West Coast Division (NISE West) and NRaD merged.

Travis AFB, CA 94535-2127
☎ 707-424-1110

Travis AFB
http://www.travis.af.mil/

Home to the Fifteenth Air Force (AMC) and the 60th Air Mobility Wing.

Vandenberg AFB, Lompoc, CA 93437-6267
☎ 805-734-8232

Vandenberg AFB and the 30th Space Wing 📖
http://www.vafb.af.mil

NEW Fourteenth Air Force (AFSPC)
http://www.vafb.af.mil/orgs/14af/index.htm

Colorado

Air Force Academy, Colorado Springs, CO 80840-5151
☎ 719-333-1110

U.S. Air Force Academy (AF direct reporting unit) 📖
http://www.usafa.af.mil/
ftp://ftp.usafa.af.mil/

Includes the Institute for National Security Studies and the Frank J. Seiler Research Laboratory.

Cheyenne Mountain Air Station, Colorado Springs, CO 80914
☎ 719-554-2239

NEW http://www.spacecom.af.mil/usspace/cmocfb.htm
http://www.spacecom.af.mil/usspace/fbcmas.htm✎

The Cheyenne Mountain Operations Center (SPACECOM/NORAD) is a combined underground command center of SPACECOM and NORAD containing the Space Control Center, Missile Warning Center, Air Defense Operations Center, and Space Operations Intelligence Center.

Defense Megacenter Denver (DISA), 6760 East Irvington Place, Denver, CO 80279-8000
☎ 303-676-7004
http://199.49.191.26/~WEE/Home.html

Falcon AFB, CO 80912-3024
☎ 719-567-1110

Falcon AFB 🔎
http://www.fafb.af.mil

Home of the Space Warfare Center (AFSPC), the Joint National Test Facility, and the 50th Space Wing (Fourteenth Air Force, AFSPC).

Space BattleLab (Space Warfare Center)
http://www.fafb.af.mil/swc/battlelab

Fort Carson, Colorado Springs, CO 80913-5000
☎ 719-526-5811

Fort Carson
http://www.carson.army.mil/
http://155.214.81.209

Home of the 3rd Armored Cavalry Regiment, a FORSCOM unit that relocated from Ft. Bliss, TX; the 10th Special Forces Group (Airborne), an Army Special Operations Command unit relocated from Ft. Devens, MA; and the 3rd Brigade, 4th Infantry Division (Mechanized). The headquarters of the division moved to Ft. Hood, TX, in 1995.

Peterson AFB, Colorado Springs, CO 80914-1294
☎ 719-556-7321; ✉ helpdsk@spacecom.af.mil

Peterson AFB
http://www.spacecom.af.mil/usspace

U.S. Space Command (SPACECOM)
http://www.spacecom.af.mil/usspace/index.htm

The Commander-in-Chief SPACECOM is also the commander of Air Force Space Command and the North American Aerospace Defense Command.

Air Force Space Command (AFSPC) 🔎
http://www.spacecom.af.mil/hqafspc/index.htm

21st Space Wing (Fourteenth Air Force, AFSPC)
http://www.spacecom.af.mil/21sw/index.htm

Defense Information Systems Agency SPACECOM Field Office (DISA)
http://www.disa.mil/line/spacecm.html

⌛ BASE SCHEDULED TO CLOSE $\qquad$ $ COMMERCIAL, BUSINESS OPPORTUNITY $\qquad$ ✉ E-MAIL ADDRESS $\qquad$ 🔎 INTERNAL SEARCH ENGINE

Army Space Command (SMDC) $
http://www.armyspace.com

NEW North American Aerospace Defense Command (NORAD)
http://www.spacecom.af.mil/norad/index.htm

Joint U.S.-Canadian command responsible for the air defense of North America.

Pueblo Chemical Depot, CO 81001-5000
☎ 719-549-4111

Formerly Pueblo Army Depot Activity, shifted to the control of Army Chemical and Biological Defense Command in October 1995.

NEW Pueblo Chemical Depot (CBDCOM)
http://www.cbdcom.apgea.army.mil/FactSheets/fs_ped.html ✎

Pueblo Army Depot Activity
http://www-ioc.army.mil/home/elements/pueblo.htm ✎

Rocky Mountain Arsenal, CO 80022
☎ 303-289-0140

Program Manager for Rocky Mountain Arsenal
http://pmrma-www.army.mil

Connecticut

Naval Submarine Base New London, Groton, CT 06349-5000
☎ 860-449-4636

NEW Commander Naval Submarine Base New London
http://www.subase.nlon.com

Home also to the Naval Submarine Support Facility, Naval Undersea Medical Institute (Naval School of Health Sciences), and Naval Submarine Medical Research Laboratory (NMRDC).

NEW Submarine Group 2
http://www.csg2.navy.mil

NEW Naval Submarine School
http://www.cnet.navy.mil/newlondn/ns1.htm

Submarine Development Squadron 12
http://www.devron12.com/

Delaware

Dover AFB, DE 19902-7219
☎ 302-677-3000

Dover AFB and 436th Airlift Wing (AMC)
http://www.dover.af.mil/

District of Columbia

Command and Agency Headquarters in the District of Columbia
Air Force History Support Office (AF field operating agency): see Bolling AFB
Air Force Legal Services Agency (AF field operating agency): see Bolling AFB
Air Force Office of Special Investigations (AF field operating agency): see Bolling AFB
Air Force Office of Scientific Research: see Bolling AFB
Army Center of Military History (Army field operating agency): see Chapter 3
Army Corps of Engineers: see Chapter 8
Bureau of Medicine and Surgery (BUMED) (Navy): see Chapter 9
Defense Intelligence Agency: see Bolling AFB
Military District of Washington: see Fort McNair
Military Sealift Command: see Naval Station Washington
National Defense University: see Fort McNair and Chapter 3
Naval Computer and Telecommunications Command: see Chapter 9
Naval Criminal Investigative Service: see Naval Station Washington
Naval District Washington: see Naval Station Washington
Naval Research Laboratory: see below

Bolling AFB, Washington, DC 20332-5100
☎ 703-545-6700

Bolling AFB is also host to the Air Force Legal Services Agency (AF field operating agency).

11th Wing (AF direct reporting unit)
http://www.bolling.af.mil/

NEW Air Force History Support Office (AF field operating agency)
http://www.airforcehistory.hq.af.mil

NEW Air Force Office of Special Investigations (AF field operating agency)
http://www.dtic.mil/afosi

Air Force Office of Scientific Research (AFOSR) (AFMC) 🔍 $
http://web.fie.com/fedix/afosr.html
http://www.afosr.af.mil/

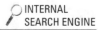

Defense Intelligence Analysis Center (DIA)
http://www.dia.mil/

> *Home of the Defense Intelligence Agency and the Joint Military Intelligence College.*

Fort McNair, 4th & P Streets NW, Washington, DC 20319-5050
☎ 202-685-3089

Military District of Washington (MDW)
http://www.mdw.army.mil

National Defense University (NDU) 📖
http://www.ndu.edu/

> *NDU colleges and institutes include the Counter Proliferation Center, Industrial College of the Armed Forces, Information Resources Management College, Institute for National Strategic Studies, Inter-American Defense College, and National War College (see Chapter 3).*

Naval Research Laboratory (NRL), 4555 Overlook Avenue SW,
Washington, DC 20375-5000; ✉ nrl1230@ccf.nrl.navy.mil

★ NRL 📖 $
http://www.nrl.navy.mil/

> *A well-organized, fact-filled site, including extensive organizational and scientific links, publications, and contract opportunities. Organizations include the Systems Directorate, Material Science and Components Technology Directorate, Ocean and Atmospheric Science and Technology Directorate, and Naval Center for Space Technology.*

NRL Organizational Directory
http://www.nrl.navy.mil/nrl/nrl.org.html

NRL Center for High Assurance Computer Systems
http://www.itd.nrl.navy.mil/ITD/5540

Naval Center for Space Technology
http://ncst-www.nrl.navy.mil

Naval Station Washington, 2701 South Capitol Street SW, Washington, DC 20374
☎ 202-433-2231; ✉ ndwpao@opnav-emh.navy.mil

*Created in 1996 and encompassing the Washington Navy Yard (WNY)
(901 M Street SE, Washington, DC 20374) and the formerly named Naval Station
Anacostia.*

Naval District Washington (NDW)
http://www.ndw.navy.mil/

> *Includes the Public Works Center Washington and the U.S. Navy Band/Navy Ceremonial Guard in Anacostia.*

★ Naval Historical Center
http://www.history.navy.mil

Military Sealift Command (MSC) 🔍 $
http://www.msc.navy.mil

Naval Criminal Investigative Service (NCIS)
http://www.ncis.navy.mil

White House Communications Agency (DISA)
http://www.disa.mil/line/whca.html

> *The main elements and headquarters are located at the Washington Navy Yard, with operating elements at the Old Executive Office Building, Washington, DC 20500.*

U.S. Naval Observatory, 3450 Massachusetts Avenue NW, Washington, DC 20392-5420 ☎ 202-653-1541

Oceanographer of the Navy and Superintendent, U.S. Naval Observatory 📖
http://www.usno.navy.mil/

Astronomical Applications
http://aa.usno.navy.mil/AA

Time Service
http://tycho.usno.navy.mil/
ftp://tycho.usno.navy.mil/

National Earth Orientation Service
http://maia.usno.navy.mil/eo/
ftp://maia.usno.navy.mil/

Walter Reed Army Medical Center, 6825 16th Street NW, Washington, DC 20307-5001 ☎ 202-782-3501

> *Home also to the Army Physical Disability Agency, a field operating agency.*

Walter Reed Army Medical Center 🔍 📖
http://www.wramc.amedd.army.mil

Walter Reed Army Institute of Research 🔎
http://wrair-www.army.mil/

Armed Forces Institute of Pathology/Armed Forces Medical Examiner
http://www.afip.org/

Florida

Army Simulation, Training and Instrumentation Command (STRICOM),
12350 Research Parkway, Orlando, FL 32826-3276
☎ 407-380-8334

STRICOM (AMC) 🔎 $
http://www.stricom.army.mil/home.html

Army Materiel Command organization activated in 1992. The homepage contains information on Army simulation policies, links to other modeling and simulation sites, and organizational data.

Naval Air Warfare Center Training Systems Division (NAWCTSD) (NAVAIR) 🔎
http://www.ntsc.navy.mil/

Formerly Naval Training Systems Center.

NEW Air Force Agency for Modeling and Simulation (AF field operating agency) 🔎
http://www.afams.af.mil

Eglin AFB, Fort Walton Beach, FL 32542-5000
☎ 850-882-1110

Eglin AFB 🔎 $
http://www.eglin.af.mil/

NEW 33rd Fighter Wing (ACC)
http://33fw.eglin.af.mil

Air Force Development Test Center (AFMC) $
http://www.eglin.af.mil/afdtc/afdtc.html

46th Test Wing
http://tw1.eglin.af.mil/

Aeronautical Systems Center Eglin
http://www.asc.eglin.af.mil/

NEW Munitions Directorate, Air Force Research Laboratory 📖 $
http://www.munitions.eglin.af.mil

> *Formerly the Wright Laboratory Armament Directorate.*

53rd Wing (Air Warfare Center, ACC)
http://www.wg53.eglin.af.mil/

NEW Unmanned Aerial Vehicle Battlelab
http://www.wg53.eglin.af.mil/battlelab/default.htm

NEW Air Force Armament Museum
http://www.wg53.eglin.af.mil/armmus/default.htm

Hurlburt Field, Fort Walton Beach, FL 32544-5000
☎ 850-884-1110

Hurlburt Field
http://www.hurlburt.af.mil

Air Force Special Operations Command (AFSOC)
http://www.afsoc.af.mil/

16th Special Operations Wing
http://www.hurlburt.af.mil/16sow.html

720th Special Tactics Group
http://www.hurlburt.af.mil/stn

Air Force Special Operations School
http://www.hurlburt.af.mil/usafsos/

NEW Air Force Combat Weather Center
http://www.hurlburt.af.mil/afcwc

MacDill AFB, Tampa, FL 33621-5502
☎ 813-828-1110; ✉ nscmacdill@ddn-conus.ddn.mil

MacDill AFB and 6th Air Base Wing (ACC)
http://www.macdill.af.mil

U.S. Central Command (CENTCOM) (see Chapter 6)
http://www.centcom.mil

NEW U.S. Special Operations Command (SOCOM) (see Chapter 6)
http://www.dtic.mil/socom

Joint Communications Support Element (ACOM)
http://www.jcse.macdill.af.mil/

JCS Agency transferred to ACOM control as of 1 October 1998.

Naval Air Station Cecil Field, Jacksonville, FL 32215-5000
☎ 904-778-5627; ✉ cecilpao@pera18.spear.navy.mil

The base is scheduled to close by October 2000.

NAS Cecil Field
http://www.cecilfield.com/

Home to the Strike Fighter Wing U.S. Atlantic Fleet and the Strike Fighter Weapons School Atlantic. Cecil Field is also Carrier Air Wing headquarters for Mayport-based aircraft carriers.

Naval Air Station Jacksonville, FL 32212-5000
☎ 904-772-2345; ✉ jaxpao@pera18.spear.navy.mil

Air station tenants include Helicopter Antisubmarine Wing U.S. Atlantic Fleet and Patrol Wing 11. The Sea Control Wing U.S. Atlantic Fleet moved from NAS Cecil Field as of 1 October 1997.

Naval Base Jacksonville
http://www.nasjax.org/

NEW Fleet and Industrial Supply Center
http://www.fiscjax.com

NEW Naval Aviation Depot Jacksonville
http://www.nadjx.navy.mil

Public Works Center Jacksonville
http://www.navy.mil/pwcjax/

Naval Computer and Telecommunications Station Jacksonville (NCTC)
http://www.nctsjax.navy.mil/

Naval Air Facility Key West, Boca Chica, FL 33040-5000
☎ 305-293-2268

Home of Joint Interagency Task Force East, Joint Task Force Four/Caribbean Regional Operations Center (ACOM).

NCTAMS Lant Detachment Key West
http://www.chips.navy.mil/code19.html ✎

Naval Air Station Pensacola, 190 Radford Boulevard, Pensacola, FL 32508-5217
☎ 850-452-0111

> *Base tenants include the Fleet and Industrial Supply Center, Public Works Center Pensacola, Naval Aviation Depot, and Training Air Wing 6 (CNATRA).*

NAS Pensacola
http://www.cnet.navy.mil/naspcola/naspcola.htm

Naval Education and Training Command (NETC)
http://www.cnet.navy.mil/

> *The commander of NETC is also the chief of Naval Education and Training (CNET). NETC organizations on base include the Naval Aviation Schools Command and Naval Financial Management Career Center.*

Naval Education and Training Professional Development and Technology Center
http://www.cnet.navy.mil/netpdtc/

> *Formerly the Naval Education and Training Program Management Support Activity (NETPMSA).*

Naval Education and Training Security Assistance Field Activity
http://penu0011.netsafa.navy.mil/

Naval Reserve Officer Training Corps (ROTC)
http://www.cnet.navy.mil/nrotc/nrotc.htm

Naval Aerospace Medical Research Laboratory (NMRDC)
http://www.namrl.navy.mil/

Naval Computer and Telecommunications Station Pensacola (NCTC)
http://www.ncts.navy.mil/ncts/index.html

> *The physical home of Navy Online.*

Defense Photography School (AFIS)
http://www.dphsch.osd.mil/

Naval Air Station Whiting Field, Milton, FL 32570-6155
☎ 850-623-7011

Training Air Wing 5 (CNATRA)
http://www.navy.mil/vt6/

> *Home of naval aviation pilot training.*

Naval Coastal Systems Station Panama City, FL 32407-7001
☎ 850-234-4011

 BASE SCHEDULED TO CLOSE
 COMMERCIAL, BUSINESS OPPORTUNITY
E-MAIL ADDRESS
 INTERNAL SEARCH ENGINE

Home also to the Naval Diving and Salvage Training Center and the Navy Experimental Diving Unit.

Naval Surface Warfare Center Dahlgren Division Coastal Systems Station (NAVSEA) 🔎
http://www.ncsc.navy.mil/

Naval Station Mayport, FL 32228-0112
☎ 904-270-5011

Mayport is a major surface ship home port. Base tenants include the Helicopter Antisubmarine Light Wing U.S. Atlantic Fleet.

NEW Fleet Training Center Mayport/Fleet Training Group
http://www.cnet.navy.mil/tralant/ftcmay/ftcmptm.htm

Naval Technical Training Center Corry Station, Pensacola, FL 32511-5138
☎ 850-452-2000; ✉ nttc-pen.pao@netpmsa.cnet.navy.mil

NTTC Corry Station
http://www.navy.mil/homepages/nttc/main1.html

NEW Naval Security Group Activity Pensacola (NSGC)
http://www.nsg.navy.mil/top.html

Patrick AFB, FL 32925
☎ 407-494-1110

Patrick AFB and 45th Space Wing (Fourteenth Air Force, AFSPC)
http://www.pafb.af.mil/

Air Force Technical Application Center (AFTAC) (AF field operating agency)
http://www.aftac.gov

Joint Test Force JSTARS
http://www.pafb.af.mil/tenants/jstars.htm

Defense Equal Opportunity Management Institute (OSD)
http://www.pafb.af.mil/deomi/deomi.htm

Tyndall AFB, Panama City, FL 32403-5425
☎ 850-283-1110

Tyndall AFB and 325th Fighter Wing (AETC) 🔎
http://www.tyndall.af.mil/

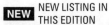 

First Air Force (ANG) (ACC)
http://www.1staf.tyndall.af.mil

Air Force Civil Engineering Support Agency (AF field operating agency)
http://www.afcesa.af.mil/

U.S. Southern Command (SOUTHCOM), 3511 NW 91st Avenue, Miami, FL 33172
☎ 1-888-547-4025

> NEW U.S. Southern Command (SOUTHCOM)
> http://www.ussouthcom.mil/southcom/
>
> *The headquarters for the unified command relocated to Florida from Quarry
> Heights, Panama, in 1998.*

Georgia

Army Environmental Policy Institute
430 Tenth Street, NW, Atlanta, GA 30318-5768
☎ 404-892-5768

> AEPI Homepage 🔍
> http://aepi.army.mil
>
> *Located at Georgia Tech University.*

Fort Benning, GA 31905-5000
☎ 706-545-2011

> *Fort Benning is home also to the 3rd Brigade, 3rd Infantry Division (Mech), and 75th
> Ranger Regiment.*
>
> Army Infantry Center and School (TRADOC) 🔍 📖
> http://www.benning.army.mil/
>
> *The Army Infantry Center includes offices relating to infantry policy, training,
> and doctrine development, the Officer Candidate School, and the Ranger
> Training Brigade.*
>
> School of the Americas
> http://192.153.150.25/usarsa/index.html

Fort Gillem, Forest Park, GA 30050-5000

> NEW Fort Gillem Homepage
> http://www.mcpherson.army.mil/Fort_Gillem.htm

`NEW` First U.S. Army (FORSCOM)
http://www-first.army.mil/

Fort Gordon, GA 30905-5000
☎ 706-791-0110; ✉ atzhpao@gordon-emh1.army.mil

Home also to the 513th Military Intelligence Brigade and the 702nd Military Intelligence Group.

Army Signal Center (TRADOC)
http://www.gordon.army.mil/home/

> *The Army Signal Center is responsible for combat developments and doctrine relating to Army communications.*

NAG-OnLine: Signal Corps Network Advisory Group
http://nag.gordon.army.mil/

Naval Security Group Activity Fort Gordon (NSGC)
http://www.gordon.army.mil/nsgafg/

Eisenhower Army Medical Center
http://www.ddeamc.amedd.army.mil/

Signal Corps Museum
http://www.gordon.army.mil/museum/

Fort McPherson, Atlanta, GA 30330-5000
☎ 404-464-3113

Fort McPherson 🔍
http://www.mcphersn.army.mil/
http://160.136.15.22/

Army Forces Command (FORSCOM)
http://www.forscom.army.mil
http://160.136.17.213

> *FORSCOM is the Army component command of ACOM. The headquarters also serves as headquarters for Army Forces, U.S. Central Command (ARCENT) (CENTCOM) and as Third U.S. Army headquarters. The Deputy Commanding General of Army Forces Command is also the Commander, Third U.S. Army.*

`NEW` Army Forces Central Command (ARCENT)
http://www.arcent.army.mil

Fort Stewart, Hinesville, GA 31314-5000 (and Hunter Army Airfield)
☎ 912-767-1411

> *Formerly home to the 24th Infantry Division. The 3rd Infantry Division relocated from Germany.*

> 3rd Infantry Division (Mechanized)
> http://www.stewart.army.mil/

Marine Corps Logistics Base, 814 Radford Boulevard, Albany, GA 31704-1128
☎ 912-439-5000

> MCLB Albany
> http://www.ala.usmc.mil/

Moody AFB, Valdosta, GA 31699-5000
☎ 912-257-4211

> Moody AFB and 347th Wing (ACC) 🔎
> http://www.moody.af.mil/

Naval Submarine Base Kings Bay, GA 31547-2606
☎ 912-673-2001; ✉ pao@subasekb.navy.mil

> NSB Kings Bay
> http://www.subasekb.navy.mil

> > *The ballistic missile submarine base includes Submarine Group 10 and the Strategic Weapons Facility Atlantic, Trident Refit Facility, and Trident Training Facility.*

Robins AFB, GA 31098
☎ 912-926-1113

> *Base tenants include the 19th Air Refueling Wing (AMC).*

> Robins AFB and Warner Robins Air Logistics Center (WR-ALC) (AFMC)
> http://www.robins.af.mil/
> http://137.244.199.129/

> Air Force Reserve Command (AFREC)
> http://www.afres.af.mil/

> > *Air Force major command activated 17 February 1997, formerly called Air Force Reserve (AFRES).*

> 93rd Air Control Wing/JSTARS Homepage (ACC) 🔎
> http://www.jstars.af.mil

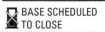 BASE SCHEDULED TO CLOSE    COMMERCIAL, BUSINESS OPPORTUNITY   E-MAIL ADDRESS    INTERNAL SEARCH ENGINE

Defense Megacenter Warner Robins (DISA)
http://www.wr.disa.mil

Robins Museum of Aviation
http://www.museum.robins.af.mil/

Hawaii

Camp H. M. Smith, Halawa Heights, HI 96861-5001
☎ 808-477-8365

U.S. Pacific Command (PACOM) (see Chapter 5)
http://www.pacom.mil/

Marine Forces Pacific (MarForPac) (PACOM)
http://www.mfp.usmc.mil/

The commander of MarForPac is also the commander of Fleet Marine Forces, Pacific (FMFPAC), a component of U.S. Pacific Fleet, and of Marine Corps Bases Pacific.

Marine Forces, U.S. Central Command (USMARCENT)
http://ccfs1.centcom.mil/marcent.htm

Fort Shafter, Honolulu, Oahu, HI 96858-5100
☎ 808-471-7110

Home also to the Pacific Ocean Division, Army Corps of Engineers.

U.S. Army Pacific (USARPAC) (PACOM)
http://www.usarpac.army.mil/

Hickam AFB, Honolulu, HI 96853-5328
☎ 808-471-7110

Hickam AFB and 15th Air Base Wing
http://www.hickam.af.mil/

Pacific Air Forces (PACAF) (PACOM)
http://www.hqpacaf.af.mil/

Maui Optical Station, 535 Lipoa Parkway, Kihei, HI 96753
☎ 808-874-1541

Air Force Maui Optical Station (AMOS) (AFRL, AFMC)
http://ulua.mhpcc.af.mil

Marine Corps Base Hawaii/Marine Corps Air Facility Kaneohe Bay,
Kaneohe Bay, HI 96863-3002
☎ 808-471-7110

> *Formerly Marine Corps Air Station.*

Deputy Commanding General, III MEF/Marine Corps Bases Hawaii
http://www.mcbh.usmc.mil/

>> NEW 1st Marine Aircraft Wing (1st MAW)
>> http://www.mcbh.usmc.mil/ase/ase.htm

>> NEW 3rd Marines
>> http://www.mcbh.usmc.mil/3mar/3rframe.htm

Naval Air Station Barbers Point, HI 96862-5050
☎ 808-684-6266

> *The base is scheduled to close by end of July 1999. Aircraft and helicopter squadrons will move to MCBH Kaneohe Bay and NAS Whidbey Island, WA.*

> NEW NAS Barbers Point
> http://www.bpt.nas.navy.mil

Naval Base Pearl Harbor, HI 96860-5020
☎ 808-471-7110; ✉ pao@cpf.navy.mil

Commander Naval Base Pearl Harbor
http://www.hawaii.navy.mil/

> *Home to numerous subordinate organizations and tenants, such as Naval Submarine Base Pearl Harbor, Submarine Training Center Pacific, Naval Shore Intermediate Maintenance Facility Pearl Harbor, Fleet and Industrial Supply Center, and Joint Intelligence Center Pacific (PACOM).*

> NEW Naval Station Pearl Harbor
> http://www.pearlharbor.navy.mil

> NEW Public Works Center Hawaii
> http://www.pwcpearl.navy.mil

Commander-in-Chief U.S. Pacific Fleet (PACFLT) (PACOM)
http://www.cpf.navy.mil/

> *Other subordinate elements in Hawaii include the ASW Force U.S. Pacific Fleet (CTF-12).*

> Submarine Force U.S. Pacific Fleet (SUBPAC)
> http://csp.navy.mil/

NEW Naval Surface Force Middle Pacific
http://www.midpac.navy.mil

NEW Pearl Harbor Naval Shipyard (NAVSEA)
http://www.phnsy.navy.mil

Naval Security Group Activity Pearl Harbor (NSGC)
http://www.nsgaph.navy.mil/

SPAWAR Systems Activity Pacific (SPAWAR)
http://lono.nosc.mil/

> *Formerly the NRaD Activity, Pacific (NCCOSC).*

Naval Computer and Telecommunications Area Master Station Eastern Pacific,
Wahiawa, HI 96786-3050
☎ 808-653-5385

NCTAMS EASTPAC (NCTC)
http://nctamsep.navy.mil/

Naval Security Group Activity Kunia, Kunia, Oahu, HI 96854

Located at the Kunia Tunnel, an intelligence-processing center of the NSA and Pacific Command.

NEW NSGA Kunia (NSGC)
http://www.nsgakunia.com

Schofield Barracks, Wahiawa, Oahu, HI 96857-6000
☎ 808-471-7110; ✉ acofsg1@schofield-emh1.army.mil

Home to the 703rd Military Intelligence Brigade.

NEW U.S. Army Hawaii (USARPAC)
http://150.137.10.101
http://www-25idl.army.mil

NEW 25th Infantry Division (Light)
http://www.usarpac.army.mil/docs/25id(L).htm

> *Formerly a full division; the 3rd Brigade has been inactivated and the 1st Brigade is at Ft. Lewis, WA.*

Tripler Army Medical Center, Honolulu, Oahu, HI 96859-5000
☎ 808-433-2778

Tripler Army Medical Center
http://www.tamc.amedd.army.mil

Idaho

Mountain Home AFB, ID 83648-5000
☎ 208-828-1110

> Mountain Home AFB and 366th Wing (ACC)
> http://www.mountainhome.af.mil/

> Air Expeditionary Force (AEF) Battlelab
> http://www.mountainhome.af.mil/AEFB/default.htm

Illinois

Army Construction Engineering Research Laboratory (USACE), PO Box 9005, Champaign, IL 61826-9005
☎ 800-USA-CERL

> CERL 🔎 $
> http://www.cecer.army.mil/

Naval Training Center Great Lakes, Great Lakes, IL 60088-5000
☎ 847-688-3500; ✉ ntc-grl.pao@stmp.cnet.navy.mil

> Naval Training Center Great Lakes (CNET)
> http://www.ntcpao.com

> Naval Dental Research Institute (NMRDC)
> http://support1.med.navy.mil/NDRI/

Rock Island Arsenal, IL 61299-5000
☎ 309-782-4149; ✉ SIORI-APA@ria-emh2.army.mil

> Rock Island Arsenal
> http://www.ria.army.mil/
> http://www-ioc.army.mil/rm/IOCfact/ria.htm ✎

> Army Industrial Operations Command (IOC) (AMC) 🔎
> http://www-ioc.army.mil/home/index.htm

>> *Established in January 1994 by combining Depot Systems Command and Army Armament, Munitions and Chemical Command.*

>> Army War Reserve Support Command
>> http://www.ioc.army.mil/war_reserve/

 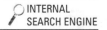

Armament and Chemical Acquisition and Logistics Agency (TACOM)
http://www-acala1.ria.army.mil/

Defense Megacenter Rock Island (DISA)
http://www.ri.disa.mil/

Savanna Army Depot Activity, IL 61074-9639
☎ 815-273-8000

The base is scheduled to close by October 2000; the activities will move to McAlester Army Ammunition Plant, OK.

Savanna Army Depot Activity
http://www-ioc.army.mil/rm/IOCfact/svda.htm

Defense Ammunition Center and School (IOC)
http://www.dac.army.mil

Scott AFB, IL 62225-5000
☎ 618-256-1110; ✉ wgpa@wing.safb.af.mil

Scott AFB and 375th Airlift Wing (AMC)
http://www.safb.af.mil/

U.S. Transportation Command (TRANSCOM) (see Chapter 6)
http://ustcweb.safb.af.mil/

Air Mobility Command (AMC) (TRANSCOM) $
http://www.safb.af.mil/hqamc/pa/

Air Force Communications Agency (AF field operating agency)
http://infosphere.safb.af.mil/homepage

Air Force Weather Agency (AF field operating agency)
http://www.safb.af.mil/afwa

Air Force Combat Climatology Center
http://thunder.scott.af.mil/

Indiana

Naval Surface Warfare Center Crane Division, 300 Highway 361, Crane, IN 47522
☎ 812-854-2511

★ Naval Surface Warfare Center Crane Division (NAVSEA) $
http://www.crane.navy.mil/

 NEW LISTING IN THIS EDITION    ONLINE FACT SHEET   PUBLICATION REPOSITORY OR LIBRARY   ★ RECOMMENDED SITE   TELEPHONE NUMBER

Crane Army Ammunition Activity (IOC)
http://www.crane.army.mil
http://www-ioc.army.mil/home/elements/crane.html ✎

Newport Chemical Depot/Army Ammunition Plant, Newport, IN 47966

Newport Chemical Activity (CBDCOM)
http://www.cbdcom.apgea.army.mil/Storage/Newport/index.htm
http://www.cbdcom.apgea.army.mil/FactSheets/fs_ncd.html ✎
http://www-ioc.army.mil/home/elements/newport.htm ✎

Base and activities transferred to Army Chemical and Biological Defense Command in 1995.

Kansas

Fort Leavenworth, KS 66027-5000
☎ 913-684-4021

Home also to the U.S. Disciplinary Barracks, the famous "Fort Leavenworth."

★ Combined Arms Center and Fort Leavenworth (TRADOC) 📖 🔍
http://leav-www.army.mil/
ftp://leav-ftp.army.mil/

Colleges, institutes, and activities include Command and General Staff School, Combined Arms and Services Staff School, School of Advanced Military Studies (SAMS), School for Command Preparation, School of Corresponding Studies, Center for Army Leadership, Military Review *magazine, and the Foreign Military Studies Office (see Chapter 3).*

Army Command and General Staff College
http://www-cgsc.army.mil

★ Center for Army Lessons Learned (CALL) 🔍
http://www.call.army.mil/call.html

Force Design Directorate (Combined Arms Center)
http://www-leav.army.mil/fdd

TRADOC Analysis Center (TRADOC)
http://purple.army.mil

National Simulation Center
http://www-nsc.army.mil/

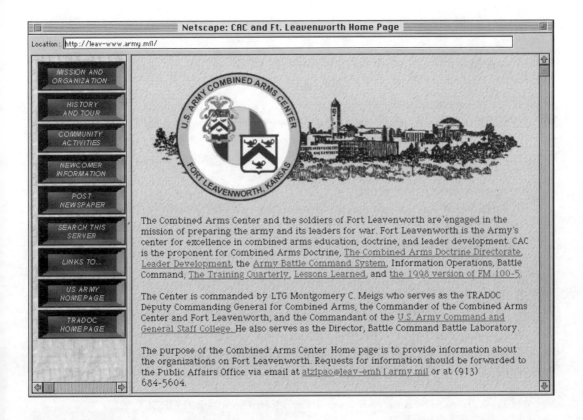

The Combined Arms Center and the soldiers of Fort Leavenworth are engaged in the mission of preparing the army and its leaders for war. Fort Leavenworth is the Army's center for excellence in combined arms education, doctrine, and leader development. CAC is the proponent for Combined Arms Doctrine, The Combined Arms Doctrine Directorate, Leader Development, the Army Battle Command System, Information Operations, Battle Command, The Training Quarterly, Lessons Learned, and the 1998 version of FM 100-5.

The Center is commanded by LTG Montgomery C. Meigs who serves as the TRADOC Deputy Commanding General for Combined Arms, the Commander of the Combined Arms Center and Fort Leavenworth, and the Commandant of the U.S. Army Command and General Staff College. He also serves as the Director, Battle Command Battle Laboratory.

The purpose of the Combined Arms Center Home page is to provide information about the organizations on Fort Leavenworth. Requests for information should be forwarded to the Public Affairs Office via email at atzlpao@leav-emh1.army.mil or at (913) 684-5604.

Air Force Joint Programs Office (ACC)
http://leav-www.army.mil/usaf/usafacc.htm

Frontier Army Museum
http://www-leav.army.mil/museum

Fort Riley, Junction City, KS 66442-5016
☎ 785-239-2672

Home to 3rd Brigade, 1st Armored Division, and 1st Brigade, 1st Infantry Division (Mechanized). The headquarters for the division is in Germany.

Fort Riley
http://www.riley.army.mil
http://144.246.28.35/

McConnell AFB, Wichita, KS 67221-5000
☎ 316-652-6100

22nd Air Refueling Wing (AMC)
http://www.mcconnell.af.mil

Kentucky

Blue Grass Army Depot, Richmond, KY 40475-6001
☎ 606-625-6246

Base tenants include the Special Operations Forces Support Activity, which conducts aircraft, watercraft, and communications-electronics repair, modifications, reconfigurations, and logistics for SOCOM and service special operations forces.

BGAD
http://www-bgad.army.mil
http://www-ioc.army.mil/home/elements/bluegras.html ✎

Blue Grass Chemical Activity (CBDCOM)
http://www.cbdcom.apgea.army.mil/storage/BlueGrass/index.html ✎

Fort Campbell, KY 42223-5000
☎ 502-798-2151; ✉ afzb-po@campbell-emh1.army.mil

Base tenants include the 5th Special Forces Group (Airborne) and 160th Special Operations Aviation Regiment (Airborne), both Army Special Operations Command units.

101st Airborne Division (Air Assault) and Fort Campbell (FORSCOM) $
http://www.campbell.army.mil/

NEW Pratt Museum
http://www.campbell.army.mil/pratt/index.html

Fort Knox, KY 40121-5000
☎ 502-624-1181

Army Armor Center and Fort Knox (TRADOC) 🔎
http://147.238.100.101/

Responsible for the development of armor doctrine and the publication of Armor *Magazine.*

NEW Inside the Turret
http://www.turret.com

Army Recruiting Command (Army field operating agency)
http://www.goarmy.mil/

⧗ **Naval Ordnance Station,** 5403 Southside Drive, Louisville, KY 40214
☎ 502-364-5456

The base is scheduled to close.

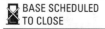 BASE SCHEDULED TO CLOSE    $ COMMERCIAL, BUSINESS OPPORTUNITY   E-MAIL ADDRESS    INTERNAL SEARCH ENGINE

Naval Surface Warfare Center Crane Division Louisville Det (NAVSEA)
http://www.crane.navy.mil/organization/code30.htm

Louisiana

Barksdale AFB, Bossier City, LA 71110-5000
☎ 318-456-2252; ✉ 2bw@bw2.barksdale.mil

Barksdale AFB and 2nd Bomb Wing (ACC)
http://www.barksdale.af.mil/

Eighth Air Force (ACC)
http://hq8af.barksdale.af.mil/

Fort Polk, Leesville, LA 71459-5000
☎ 318-531-2911

Home to the 2nd Armored Cavalry Regiment (Light), the Warrior Brigade, and the Louisiana Maneuvers Task Force.

Joint Readiness Training Center and Fort Polk (FORSCOM)
http://146.53.33.3

Naval Support Activity New Orleans, New Orleans, LA 70146
☎ 504-678-5001; ✉ cnfrpao%cnrf10s@navresfor.navy.mil

Commander Naval Reserve Force
http://www.navy.mil/navresfor/

Marine Forces Reserve
http://www.marforres.usmc.mil/

Includes an extensive listing of reserve websites by location and major command.

Maine

Naval Air Station Brunswick, 551 Fitch Avenue, Brunswick, ME 04011-5000
☎ 207-921-1110

NEW Patrol Wing 5
http://www.flightdeck.airlant.navy.mil/public/cpw5.htm

Base tenants include the Air Force Survival, Evasion, Resistance and Escape (SERE) School.

Naval Computer and Telecommunications Station Cutler,
East Machias, ME 04630-1000

> NCTS Cutler (NCTC)
> http://www.norfolk.navy.mil/cutler/nctscut.htm

Naval Security Group Activity Winter Harbor, ME 04693-7001
☎ 207-963-5534; ✉ ns-gaxo@downeast.net

> NSGA Winter Harbor (NSGC)
> http://www.navy.mil/homepages/nsgawh/

Maryland

Aberdeen Proving Ground, MD 21005
☎ 410-278-5201; ✉ amstepa@apg-9.apg.army.mil

> Aberdeen Proving Ground
> http://www.apg.army.mil/
>
> Aberdeen Test Center 🔍 $
> http://www.atc.army.mil
>
> Army Test and Evaluation Command (TECOM) (AMC) $ 📖
> http://www.atc.army.mil/~tecom/
>
> > Virtual Proving Ground
> > http://vpg.apg.army.mil
>
> **NEW** Army Ordnance Center and School/Army Ordnance Corps (TRADOC)
> http://130.114.88.10
>
> Army Center for Health Promotion and Preventive Medicine (CHPPM) (MEDCOM)
> http://chppm-www.apgea.army.mil/
>
> Army Environmental Center (Army field operating agency)
> http://aec-www.apgea.army.mil:8080/
>
> Army Materiel Systems Analysis Activity (AMC)
> http://amsaa-www.arl.mil/
>
> > *Includes the Joint Technical Coordinating Group/Munitions Effectiveness Office.*

Edgewood Area

Edgewood Enterprise
http://www.cbdcom.apgea.army.mil/RDA/

Edgewood Research, Development and Engineering Center (ERDEC)
http://www.cbdcom.apgea.army.mil/RDA/erdec/

> *Comprehensive center responsible for chemical weapons, chemical and biological defense, smoke/obscurants, and arms control and treaty compliance.*

Army Chemical and Biological Defense Command (CBDCOM) (AMC) 🔎
http://www.cbdcom.apgea.army.mil/

Army Medical Research Institute of Chemical Defense
http://chemdef.apgea.army.mil/

NEW Edgewood Chemical Activity (CBDCOM)
http://www.cbdcom.apgea.army.mil/storage/Edgewood/index.html

Andrews AFB, Camp Springs, MD 20331-5000
☎ 301-981-1110

> *Home also to the Air Force Review Boards Agency (AF field operating agency).*

Andrews AFB
http://www.andrews.af.mil
http://www.aon.af.mil

89th Airlift Wing (AMC)
http://www.andrews.af.mil/89AW/89thaw.htm

Air Force Flight Standards Agency (AF field operating agency)
http://www.andrews.af.mil/tenants/affsa/AFFSA.htm

Air National Guard/ANG Readiness Center (AF field operating agency) 🔎 📖
http://www.ang.af.mil/

Army Research Laboratory (ARL), 2800 Powder Mill Road, Adelphi, MD 20783
☎ 301-394-2515

Adelphi Laboratory Center
http://w3.arl.mil/home/index.html
http://www.arl.mil/EA/alcvistpg.html ✎

Army Research Laboratory (ARL) (AMC)
http://www.arl.mil/
http://info.arl.mil/

NEW Advanced Technology and Concepts Network (ARTAC-Online)
http://tiu.arl.mil/artac

Fort Detrick, Frederick, MD 21701
☎ 301-619-8000

Base tenants include the Armed Forces Medical Intelligence Center (DIA). With the closure of Ft. Ritchie, Detrick will provide support for the Alternate Joint Communications Center (JCS), Joint Data Systems Support Center (JCS), and Joint Coordination Center (STRATCOM), all located nearby at Site R, an underground command facility.

Fort Detrick
http://www.armymedicine.army.mil/detrick

Army Medical Research and Materiel Command (MEDCOM)
http://mrmc-www.army.mil/

Formerly the Army Medical Research and Development Command, an Army field operating agency.

Army Medical Materiel Agency
http://140.139.12.250/usamma/index.htm

Army Medical Materiel Development Activity
http://www.armymedicine.army.mil/usammda/

Army Medical Research Acquisition Agency
http://www-usamraa.army.mil/

NEW Army Medical Research Institute of Infectious Diseases
http://140.149.42.105

NEW Air Force Medical Logistics Office
http://www.medicine.af.mil/afmlo

DOD Telemedicine Test Bed 🔍
http://www.matmo.org/

Naval Medical Logistics Command 🔍
http://www-nmlc.med.navy.mil/

Army Information Systems Engineering Command—Ft. Ritchie Engineering Office (ISEC-CONUS)
http://isec-conus.army.mil/

Moved from Ft. Ritchie, which is closing.

Fort George G. Meade, Odenton, MD 20755-5025
☎ 301-677-6261

Base tenants include the 694th Intelligence Group (AIA) and the Defense Courier Service.

| ⧗ BASE SCHEDULED TO CLOSE | $ COMMERCIAL, BUSINESS OPPORTUNITY | ✉ E-MAIL ADDRESS | 🔍 INTERNAL SEARCH ENGINE |

Fort Meade
http://www.mdw.army.mil/meade/meade.htm

National Security Agency/Central Security Services (NSA/CSS)
http://www.nsa.gov:8080/

704th Military Intelligence Brigade (INSCOM)
http://www.meade-704mi.army.mil/

NEW Naval Security Group Command
http://www.nsg.navy.mil/Home.html

Defense Information School (AFIS)
http://www.dinfos.osd.mil/home.html

Fort Ritchie, Cascade, MD 21719-5010
☎ 301-878-1300

> *Fort Ritchie is in the process of closing (by October 1998), with support for command facilities shifting to Fort Detrick.*

Fort Ritchie
http://www.mdw.army.mil/ritchie/intro.htm

Naval Maritime Intelligence Center, 4251 Suitland Road, Washington, DC 20395
☎ 301-669-3005

Office of Naval Intelligence
http://oni.nmic.navy.mil

★ Marine Corps Intelligence Activity
http://ismo-www1.mqg.usmc.mil/mcia/index.htm
http://138.156.107.3/mcia/index.htm

> *Links to open source country and regional information, maps, news sources, and travel information.*

National Naval Medical Center, 8901 Wisconsin Avenue, Bethesda, MD 20889-5600
☎ 301-295-4611

NEW National Naval Medical Center
http://www.nnmc.med.navy.mil

Naval Medical Research and Development Command (NMRDC) ◢◣
http://www.dmso.mil/NMRDC/

Naval Medical Research Institute
http://131.158.70.70
http://www.nmri.nnmc.navy.mil/

Naval School of Health Sciences
http://www-nshs.med.navy.mil/

National Naval Dental Center
http://131.158.67.146/

Uniformed Services University of the Health Sciences (USUHS) 🔍 📖
http://www.usuhs.mil/

> *Includes the Medical School, Graduate School, and Graduate School of Nursing.*

> Armed Forces Radiobiology Research Institute
> http://www.afrri.usuhs.mil/

Naval Air Station Patuxent River, MD 20670-5409
☎ 301-342-3000

> ★ Naval Air Warfare Center Aircraft Division (NAWC AD) (NAVAIR) 🔍 $
> http://www.nawcad.navy.mil/nawcad/

> **NEW** Air Test and Evaluation Squadron One (VX-1)
> http://www.navy.mil/homepages/vx-1/

> Naval Air Systems Command (NAVAIR)
> http://www.navair.navy.mil

>> *Moved from Arlington, VA.*

Naval Computer and Telecommunications Station Washington, Cheltenham, MD 20623
☎ 301-238-2335

> Information Technology Services Center (InTec) Washington (NCTC)
> http://www.nctsw.navy.mil

Naval Explosive Ordnance Disposal Technology Center, 2008 Stump Neck Road,
Indian Head, MD 20640
☎ 301-743-4304/6505; ✉ pao@smtphost.nosih.sea06.navy.mil

> Naval Surface Warfare Center Indian Head Division (NAVSEA) $
> http://www.ih.navy.mil/

> Army Technical Detachment (AMC)
> http://www.pica.army.mil/orgs/fsac/eod/techdet.htm

> **NEW** Naval Ordnance Center (NAVSEA)
> http://www.navordcen.navsea.navy.mil

Naval Ship Research and Development Center, Carderock, MD 20034

Naval Surface Warfare Center Carderock Division (NAVSEA) $
http://www.dt.navy.mil/
http://ollie.dt.navy.mil/pao.html

Created from the merger of the David W. Taylor Research Center and the Naval Ship Systems Engineering Station.

Hydromechanics Directorate (formerly David W. Taylor Model Basin)
http://www50.dt.navy.mil/

U.S. Naval Academy, Annapolis, MD 21402-5000
☎ 410-293-1000; ☎ 410-293-3972; ✉ pao@nadn.navy.mil

US Naval Academy 🔍 📖
http://www.nadn.navy.mil/

Massachusetts

Hanscom AFB, Lexington, MA 01731-5000
☎ 617-377-4441

Electronic Systems Center (ESC) (AFMC) $
http://www.hanscom.af.mil/

Projects include the Combat Air Forces System Program Office (formerly Theater Battle Management), Expeditionary Force Experiment (EFX), JSTARS, and information operations.

Alphabetical Listing of ESC Projects
http://www.hanscom.af.mil/Orgs/O_Orgs/XR/TechX/Programs/Programs.listing.html

Hanscom Research Site, AFRL
http://www.plh.af.mil/

Formerly the Phillips Laboratory Geophysics Directorate.

Natick Army Research Center, Kansas Street, Natick, MA 01760-5000
☎ 508-651-4300

Home also to the Army Research Institute of Environmental Medicine and the Navy Clothing and Textile Research Facility.

Army Soldier Systems Command (AMC) $
http://www-sscom.army.mil

Michigan

Defense Logistics Services Center, 74 Washington Avenue N, Battle Creek, MI 49017
☎ 616-961-4000; ✉ dlsc-cso@dlsc.dla.mil

Defense Logistics Information Service (DLA)
http://www.dlsc.dla.mil/

Formerly the Defense Logistics Services Center.

Defense Reutilization and Marketing Service (DLA)
http://www.drms.dla.mil/

Air Force Cataloging and Standardization Center (AFMC)
http://www.casc.af.mil

Detroit Arsenal, Warren, MI 48397-5000
☎ 313-574-5000

Tank-Automotive and Armaments Command (TACOM) (AMC)
http://www.tacom.army.mil/

Tank-Automotive Research, Development and Engineering Center (TARDEC)
http://www.tacom.army.mil/tardec/

Mississippi

Army Waterways Experimental Station (WES), 3909 Halls Ferry Road,
Vicksburg, MS 39180
☎ 601-634-3111

Waterways Experimental Station (USACE) 📖 $
http://www.wes.army.mil/

Responsible for coastal, environmental, geotechnical, and structures research and development.

Columbus AFB, MS 39810-7901
☎ 601-434-7322

14th Flying Training Wing (AETC)
http://www.col.aetc.af.mil/

Keesler AFB, Biloxi, MS 39534-2603
☎ 228-377-1110

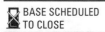 

Keesler AFB and 81st Training Wing 🔍
http://www.kee.aetc.af.mil/

Second Air Force (AETC)
http://hq2af.kee.aetc.af.mil/

NEW 53rd Weather Reconnaissance Squadron ("Hurricane Hunters")
http://www.hurricanehunters.com

Naval Air Station Meridian, 1155 Rosenbaum Avenue, Meridian, MS 39309-5003
☎ 601-679-2211

Base tenants include the Naval Technical Training Center and the Regional Counter-drug Training Academy.

Training Air Wing 1 (CNATRA)
http://www.cnet.navy.mil/meridian

Naval Construction Battalion Center, 5200 CBC 2nd Street, Gulfport, MS 39501-5001
☎ 601-871-2555

Home of the Construction Battalion Center and the Construction Training Center.

Stennis Space Center (NASA), Bay St. Louis, MS 39529
☎ 601-688-4726

Naval Meteorology and Oceanography Command (NAVMETOCCOM)
http://www.cnmoc.navy.mil/

Naval Oceanographic Office
http://www.navo.navy.mil/

Naval Research Laboratory Stennis Space Center (NRL)
http://www.nrlssc.navy.mil/

Missouri

Army Aviation and Missile Command, 4300 Goodfellow Boulevard,
St. Louis, MO 63120-1798
☎ 314-263-9075; ✉ satasca@st-louis-emh4.army.mil

Army Aviation and Missile Command (AMCOM) (AMC)
http://www.stl.army.mil/

Aviation Research, Development and Engineering Center
http://avrdec1.redstone.army.mil/avrdec.html

Defense Megacenter St. Louis (DISA)
http://www.stl.disa.mil/

Fort Leonard Wood, St. Robert, MO 65473-5000
☎ 573-596-0131

Army Engineer Center and School (TRADOC) 🔍 📖
http://www.wood.army.mil/

Whiteman AFB, Knob Noster, MO 65305-5000
☎ 816-687-1100

509th Bomb Wing (ACC)
http://www.whiteman.af.mil/

Home of the B-2 "Spirit" stealth bomber.

Montana

Malmstrom AFB, Great Falls, MT 59402-5000
☎ 406-731-1110

341st Space (Missile) Wing (Twentieth Air Force, AFSPC)
http://www.malmstrom.af.mil/

Nebraska

Offutt AFB, Omaha, NE 68113-4029
☎ 402-294-1110

Offutt AFB
http://www.offutt.af.mil/

U.S. Strategic Command (STRATCOM) $ (see Chapter 6)
http://www.stratcom.af.mil

55th Wing (Twelfth Air Force, ACC)
http://www.offutt.af.mil/55thwg.htm

| ⬛ BASE SCHEDULED TO CLOSE | $ COMMERCIAL, BUSINESS OPPORTUNITY | ✉ E-MAIL ADDRESS | 🔍 INTERNAL SEARCH ENGINE |

Air Force Weather Agency
http://afwin.offutt.af.mil:443/

> *Formerly Air Force Global Weather Central.*

Strategic Air Command Museum
http://omahafreenet.org/sacmuzm

Nevada

Hawthorne Army Depot, Hawthorne, NV 89415
☎ 702-945-7001

Hawthorne Army Depot
http://www-ioc.army.mil/home/elements/hawthorn.html

Naval Air Station Fallon, NV 89496-5000
☎ 702-426-5161

> *Home of the Naval Strike and Air Warfare Center and the Carrier Airborne Early Warning Weapons School.*

Nellis AFB, NV 89191-5000
☎ 702-652-1110

Air Warfare Center (ACC)
http://www.nellis.af.mil/

> *Includes the subordinate 57th Wing and 99th Air Base Wing.*

Air-Ground Operations School
http://nova.agos.hurlburt.af.mil

> *Moved from Hurlburt Field, FL, in November 1997.*

New Hampshire

Army Cold Regions Research and Engineering Laboratory, 72 Lyme Road, Hanover, NH 03755
☎ 603-646-4100; ✉ info@crrel.usace.army.mil

CRREL (USACE)
http://www.crrel.usace.army.mil

NEW NEW LISTING IN THIS EDITION ✎ ONLINE FACT SHEET 📖 PUBLICATION REPOSITORY OR LIBRARY ★ RECOMMENDED SITE ☎ TELEPHONE NUMBER

Portsmouth Naval Shipyard (NAVSEA), Portsmouth, NH 03804-5000
☎ 207-438-1000

> Submarine Maintenance Engineering, Planning and Procurement Activity (NAVSEA)
> http://www.submepp.navy.mil/

New Jersey

Fort Dix, NJ 08640-5000
☎ 609-562-1011

> Fort Dix
> http://www.dix-emh5.army.mil
>
> Air Mobility Warfare Center (Air Mobility Command)
> http://www.maguire.af.mil/amc/index.html

Fort Monmouth, NJ 07703
☎ 908-532-9000; ✉ amsel-io@monmouth-emh3.army.mil

> ★ Fort Monmouth ("Team C4IEWS")
> http://www.monmouth.army.mil/
> http://www.monmouth.army.mil/ftp.html
> gopher://gopher.monmouth.army.mil/
>
> Army Communications-Electronics Command (CECOM) (AMC) $
> http://www.monmouth.army.mil/cecom/cecom.html
>
>> CECOM Research, Development and Engineering Center
>> http://www.monmouth.army.mil/CECOM/rdec/rdec.html

McGuire AFB, NJ 08641-5000
☎ 609-724-1110

> McGuire AFB and 305th Air Mobility Wing
> http://www.mcguire.af.mil
>
> **NEW** Twenty-first Air Force (AMC)
> http://www.mcguire.af.mil/21af/index.html

Naval Air Engineering Station, Highway 547, Lakehurst, NJ 08733-5000
☎ 908-323-2011

> Naval Air Warfare Center Aircraft Division Lakehurst 🔎 $
> http://www.lakehurst.navy.mil/

⌛ BASE SCHEDULED TO CLOSE $ COMMERCIAL, BUSINESS OPPORTUNITY   ✉ E-MAIL ADDRESS   🔎 INTERNAL SEARCH ENGINE

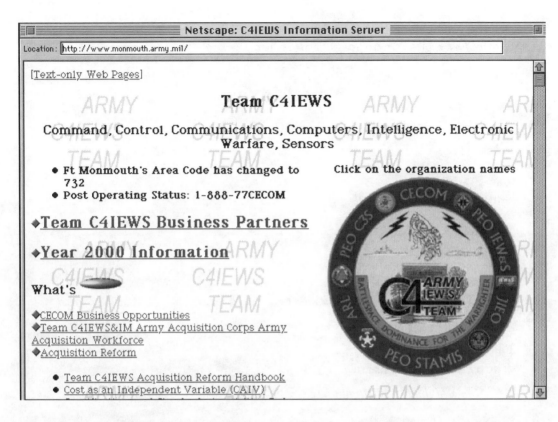

Netscape: C4IEWS Information Server

Location: http://www.monmouth.army.mil/

[Text-only Web Pages]

Team C4IEWS

Command, Control, Communications, Computers, Intelligence, Electronic Warfare, Sensors

- Ft Monmouth's Area Code has changed to 732
- Post Operating Status: 1-888-77CECOM

Click on the organization names

◆**Team C4IEWS Business Partners**

◆**Year 2000 Information**

What's

◆CECOM Business Opportunities
◆Team C4IEWS&IM Army Acquisition Corps Army Acquisition Workforce
◆Acquisition Reform

- Team C4IEWS Acquisition Reform Handbook
- Cost as an Independent Variable (CAIV)

Naval Weapons Station Earle (NAVSEA), 201 Highway 34 South, Colts Neck, NJ 07722-5001
☎ 908-866-2661

> NWS Earle
> http://www.noclant.navy.mil/earle/index.html
> http://www.spawar.navy.mil/nredo/wpnsta/wpnsta.html

Picatinny Arsenal, Dover, NJ 07806-5000
☎ 201-724-4021

> Picatinny Arsenal 🔎
> http://www.pica.army.mil

> Army Armaments Research, Development and Engineering Center (ARDEC) (TACOM) $
> http://www.pica.army.mil/ardec/top.html

>> Close Combat Armaments Center
>> http://www.pica.army.mil/orgs/ccac/top.html

>> Fire Support Armaments Center
>> http://www.pica.army.mil/orgs/fsac/top.html

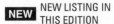 

Defense Ammunition Logistics Activity
http://www.pica.army.mil/orgs/dala/top.html

New Mexico

Cannon AFB, NM 88103-5216
☎ 505-784-3311

Cannon AFB
http://www.cannon.af.mil/

27th Fighter Wing (ACC)
http://ns2.cannon.af.mil/
http://www.cannon.af.mil/wing

Holloman AFB, Alamogordo, NM 88330-5000
☎ 505-475-6511

49th Fighter Wing (ACC)
http://www.holloman.af.mil/

Home of the F-117 Nighthawk stealth fighter.

Kirtland AFB, Albuquerque, NM 87117-5000
☎ 505-846-0011; ✉ pa@commgate.kirtland.af.mil

*Home also to the Defense Evaluation Support Activity, which previously had a website
at* http://www.kirtland.af.mil/organizations/DESA.htm.

377th Air Base Wing 📖 $
http://www.kirtland.af.mil

Phillips Research Site, AFRL (AFMC) 🔍 📖 $
http://www.plk.af.mil/

*Formerly Phillips Laboratory, now part of the Air Force Research Laboratory
superlab.*

Test and Evaluation Directorate, Space and Missile Systems Center (AFMC)
http://www.te.plk.af.mil

58th Special Operations Wing (Nineteenth Air Force, AETC)
http://www.irk.aetc.af.mil/

NEW Air Force Office of Aerospace Studies (HQ, AFMC)
http://prs.plk.af.mil/oas/

Air Force Center of Expertise for Analysis of Alternatives (AoA).

Air Force Operational Test and Evaluation Center (AF direct reporting unit)
http://www.afotec.af.mil/

Joint Advanced Distributed Simulation (JADS) JTF
http://jads.abq.com

Air Force Inspection Agency (AF field operating agency)
http://www-afia.saia.af.mil

Air Force Safety Center (AF field operating agency)
http://www-afsc.saia.af.mil

Defense Special Weapons Agency Field Command (DSWA)
http://www.dswa.mil/dswainfo/fcdswa.htm

White Sands Missile Range, NM 88002-5000
☎ 505-678-2121

Home to the Atmospheric Profiler Research Facility and the Battle Weather Division (ARL).

WSMR (TECOM) $
http://www.wsmr.army.mil/

High Energy Laser Systems Test Facility (SMDC)
http://wsmr-helstf-www.army.mil/

NEW Naval Aircraft Weapons Center WSMR Detachment
http://155.148.11.163

NEW Precision-Guided Weapons Countermeasures Test and Evaluation Directorate (OSD) 🔎
http://otd.osd.mil/

New York

Fort Drum, NY 13602-5000
☎ 315-772-6011; ✉ afzs-pao@drum-emh1.army.mil

10th Mountain Division (Light Infantry) (FORSCOM)
http://www.drum.army.mil

One of the division's brigades is the 1st Brigade, 6th Infantry Division, based in Alaska.

 NEW LISTING IN THIS EDITION    ONLINE FACT SHEET   PUBLICATION REPOSITORY OR LIBRARY   ★ RECOMMENDED SITE   ☎ TELEPHONE NUMBER

Fort Hamilton, Brooklyn, NY 11252-5700
☎ 718-630-4101

> **NEW** Fort Hamilton and HQ New York Army Command
> http://www.mdw.army.mil/hamilton/Hamilton.htm

Rome Laboratory, 26 Electronic Parkway, Rome, NY 13441-4514

> *Griffiss AFB closed on 30 September 1995, though Rome Laboratory remains.*

> Rome Research Site/Information Directorate, AFRL (AFMC) $ ➛
> http://www.rl.af.mil/

>> *Formerly the Rome Laboratory. Called the Air Force's "Super Lab for C4I Technology."*

⧗ **Seneca Army Depot Activity,** Romulus, NY 14541-5001
☎ 607-869-1110

> Seneca Army Depot Activity
> http://www-ioc.army.mil/home/elements/seneca.htm ✎

U.S. Military Academy, West Point, NY 10996-1788
(and Stewart Army Subpost, 12553-9000)
☎ 914-938-4011

> U.S. Military Academy (Army field operating agency)
> http://www.usma.edu

Watervliet Arsenal, NY 12189-4050
☎ 518-266-5111

> Watervliet Arsenal
> http://www.wva.army.mil
> http://www-ioc.army.mil/home/elements/watrvlit.html ✎

> Army Armaments Research, Development and Engineering Center, Benet Laboratories
> http://sgiserv.wva.army.mil/index.html

North Carolina

Army Research Office, PO Box 12211, Research Triangle Park, NC 27709-2211
☎ 919-549-0641

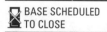 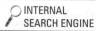

Army Research Office (ARO) (AMC) $
http://www.aro.army.mil

Army High Performance Computing Research Center
http://www.arc.umn.edu/

> *University-led consortium including the University of Minnesota as prime contractor and Howard, Jackson State, and Purdue universities; funded by the ARO's Division of Mathematical and Computer Sciences.*

Fort Bragg, Fayetteville, NC 28307-5000
☎ 910-396-0011; ✉ pao-corps@bbs.bragg.army.mil

> XVIII Airborne Corps and Fort Bragg (FORSCOM) 🔍
> http://www.bragg.army.mil/
>
> > **NEW** 82nd Airborne Division
> > http://www.bragg.army.mil/www-82DV/index.htm
> >
> > **NEW** 1st Corps Support Command
> > http://www.bragg.army.mil/coscom/wwwcos.htm
> >
> > XVIII Airborne Corps Artillery
> > http://www.bragg.army.mil/www-fa18/carty.htm
> >
> > 44th Medical Brigade
> > http://www.bragg.army.mil/www-44md/index.htm
> >
> > Fort Bragg Online File Libraries 📖
> > http://www.bragg.army.mil/18ABN/bbs.htm
> > telnet://bbs.bragg.army.mil
> >
> > > *Repository of directives and documents.*
>
> Army Special Operations Command
> http://army.usasoc.soc.mil
>
> Womack Army Medical Center
> http://www.bragg.army.mil/www-wamc/wamc.htm

Marine Corps Air Station Cherry Point, NC 28533-0003
☎ 919-466-2811; ✉ nadeppao@tecnet1.jcte.jcs.mil

> *Home of Marine Corps Air Bases East, headquarters of the 2nd Marine Aircraft Wing (2nd MAW), Marine Aircraft Group 14 (MAG-14), and Marine Aircraft Control Group 28 (MACG-28).*

MCAS Cherry Point
http://www.cherrypt.usmc.mil

Marine Corps Air Station New River, Jacksonville, NC 28545-1002
☎ 910-451-1113

Home of Marine Aircraft Group 26 (MAG-26) and Marine Aircraft Group 29 (MAG-29) (2nd MAW).

MCAS New River
http://www.mcasnewriver.com

Marine Corps Base Camp Lejeune, NC 28542-0004
☎ 910-451-1113

Also headquarters for the II Marine Expeditionary Force (II MEF), and the 2nd Marine Division (2nd MarDiv), with the subordinate 2nd, 6th, 8th, and 10th Marines.

Camp Lejeune
http://www.onslow.com/lejeune/

2nd Force Service Support Group (2nd FSSG)
http://158.241.16.252/

NEW Marine Corps Engineer Center
http://www.usmc-engr.com

NEW Chemical Biological Incident Response Force
http://www.cbirf.usmc.mil

Naval Hospital Lejeune
http://lej-www.med.navy.mil/

Pope AFB, NC 28308-5000
☎ 910-394-1110

Pope AFB
http://www.pope.af.mil/

43rd Airlift Wing
http://www.pope.af.mil/orgs/43aw

23rd Fighter Group (ACC)
http://www.pope.af.mil/orgs/23fg

Seymour Johnson AFB, NC 27531-2468
☎ 919-736-5400; ✉ pa@wg4.seymourjohnson.mil

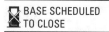 BASE SCHEDULED TO CLOSE   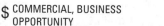 $ COMMERCIAL, BUSINESS OPPORTUNITY   E-MAIL ADDRESS   INTERNAL SEARCH ENGINE

Seymour Johnson AFB
   http://www.seymourjohnson.af.mil/

4th Fighter Wing (ACC)
   http://www.seymourjohnson.af.mil/4fw/4fw.html

North Dakota

Grand Forks AFB, Emerado, ND 58205-6231
☎ 701-747-3000

   Grand Forks is scheduled to close its missile operations by the end of 1998. The Minuteman III ICBMs are moved to Malmstrom AFB, MT.

   Grand Forks AFB

   321st Missile (Space) Group (Twentieth Air Force, AFSPC)
      http://www.grandforks.af.mil/321mg.htm

   319th Air Refueling Wing (AMC)
      http://www.grandforks.af.mil/base/ARW.htm

Minot AFB, ND 58705-5049
☎ 701-723-1110; ✉ 5bwpa@acchost.acc.af.mil

   Minot AFB
      http://www.minot.af.mil/

   5th Bomb Wing
      http://www.minot.af.mil/5BW/5bw.htm

   91st Space (Missile) Wing (Twentieth Air Force, AFSPC)
      http://www.minot.af.mil/91sw

Ohio

Defense Supply Center Columbus, PO Box 3990, Columbus, OH 43216-5000
☎ 614-238-2328

   DSC Columbus (DLA) $
      http://www.dscc.dla.mil/

      Formerly the Defense Construction Supply Center.

Defense Megacenter Columbus (DISA)
http://www.cols.disa.mil/

Wright-Patterson AFB, Dayton, OH 45433
☎ 937-257-1110

Home also to the National Air Intelligence Center (AIA), formerly the Foreign Technology Division (FTD) of Air Force intelligence.

Wright-Patterson AFB and 88th ABW
http://www.wpafb.af.mil/

★ Air Force Materiel Command (AFMC) 🔍 📖 $
http://www.afmc.wpafb.af.mil/

One of the best and most comprehensive websites maintained by the military, with organizational, planning, and procurement information, as well as extensive publications. Includes the Aeronautical Systems Center (ASC).

Development Planning Directorate
http://www.wpafb.af.mil/xr/index.htm

NEW Air Force Research Laboratory (AFRL) (AFMC) 🔍 📖
http://www.afrl.af.mil

Activated 1 November 1997 consolidating 22 directorates in four Air Force laboratories (Armstrong, Phillips, Rome, and Wright), as well as the Air Force Office of Scientific Research (AFOSR).

Materials and Manufacturing Directorate/Wright Research Site (AFRL) 🔍 📖
http://www.ml.afrl.af.mil/
http://www.wrs.afrl.af.mil

Formerly Wright Laboratory.

Human Effectiveness Directorate 🔍
http://www.al.wpafb.af.mil/

Formerly Armstrong Laboratory Wright-Patterson Crew Systems Directorate.

Materiel Systems Group (ESC, AFMC)
http://www.afmc.wpafb.af.mil/organizations/MSG/

Air Force Security Assistance Center (AFMC)
http://rock.afsac.wpafb.af.mil/

Joint Logistics Systems Center (AFMC)
http://www.jlsc.wpafb.af.mil/

Air Force Institute of Technology (AFIT) (AU)
http://www.afit.af.mil/

Defense Megacenter Dayton (DISA)
http://www.dmcdayton.day.disa.mil

Tri-Service Toxicology Consortium—Toxicology Division
http://www.navy.al.wpafb.af.mil/

74th Medical Group
http://wpmc1.wpafb.af.mil

★ US Air Force Museum
http://www.wpafb.af.mil/museum/

Oklahoma

Altus AFB, OK 73523-5000
☎ 405-482-8100

97th Air Mobility Wing (AETC)
http://www.lts.aetc.af.mil/

Fort Sill, Lawton, OK 73503-5000
☎ 405-442-8111

Army Field Artillery Center (TRADOC) 📖
http://sill-www.army.mil/

Includes field artillery doctrine development and publications.

Field Artillery Training Command
http://sill-www.army.mil/tngcmd/tc.htm

NEW Depth and Simultaneous Attack Battlelab
http://155.219.30.130/index.html

III Corps Artillery (FORSCOM)
http://155.219.52.3/index.htm
http://sill-www.army.mil/3corps/3cindex.htm

Fire Support Test Directorate (TEXCOM)
http://texcom-www.army.mil/fstd/fstd.htm

McAlester Army Ammunition Plant, McAlester, OK 74501

NEW McAlester AAP (IOC)
http://mcalestr-www.army.mil

Tinker AFB, OK 73145
☎ 405-732-7321

Tinker AFB and 72nd Air Base Wing (AFMC)
http://www1.tinker.af.mil/

Oklahoma City Air Logistics Center $
http://www1.tinker.af.mil/alcorg.htm

38th Engineering and Installation Wing (ESC, AFMC)
http://www.eiw38.af.mil/

552nd Air Control Wing (Twelfth Air Force, ACC)
http://www.awacs.af.mil

NEW Strategic Communications Wing One 🔍
http://www.tacamo.navy.mil

Defense Megacenter Oklahoma City (DISA)
http://www.okc.disa.mil

Vance AFB, OK 73705-5016
☎ 405-213-2121

71st Flying Training Wing (AETC)
http://www.vnc.aetc.af.mil/

Oregon

Umatilla Army Depot Activity, Hermiston, OR 97838-9544
☎ 503-564-8632

NEW Umatilla Chemical Depot (CBDCOM)
http://www.cbdcom.apgea.army.mil/FactSheets/fs_ucd.html ✎

Pennsylvania

Carlisle Barracks, PA 17013-5050
☎ 717-245-3131; ✉ AWCCI@carlisle-emh2.army.mil

Army War College (Army field operating agency) 🔍 📖
http://carlisle-www.army.mil

Institutes and centers include the Strategic Studies Institute, Center for Strategic Leadership, and Army Military History Institute (see Chapter 3).

Defense Distribution Region East, New Cumberland, PA 17070-5001
☎ 717-770-7401

Defense Distribution Center
http://www.ddre.dla.mil

Defense Distribution Depot Susquehana (DLA)
http://www.ddre.dla.mil/ddsphome.htm

Defense Personnel Support Center, 2800 South 20th Street, Philadelphia, PA 19101-8419
☎ 215-952-2000

DPSC (DLA) $
http://www.dpsc.dla.mil

Letterkenny Army Depot, Chambersburg, PA 17201-4150
☎ 717-267-8111/8300

Letterkenny Army Depot
http://www.letterkenny.army.mil

Industrial Logistics Systems Center (IOC)
http://www.ilsc.army.mil

Defense Megacenter Chambersburg (DISA)
http://www.westhem.disa.mil/~WEB12/Home.html

Naval Aviation Supply Office/Naval Inventory Control Point Compound
700 Robbins Avenue, Philadelphia, PA 19111-5098
☎ 215-697-2000

Naval Inventory Control Point (NAVSUP) $\mathcal{P}$ $
http://www.navicp.navy.mil/

> *Created in 1995 through the merger of the Aviation Supply Office and the Ships Parts Control Center Mechanicsburg. Includes the Naval Publications and Forms Center.*

Naval Aviation Engineering Service Unit
http://140.229.1.16:9102/

Defense Automated Printing Service Philadelphia
http://www.dodssp.daps.mil/
http://www.dtic.mil:80/dps-phila/

Defense Industrial Supply Center (DLA) $\mathcal{P}$ $
http://www.disc.dla.mil

Naval Facilities Engineering Command Northern Division
10 Industrial Highway, Lester, PA 19113
☎ 610-595-1000
http://www.efdnorth.navfac.navy.mil/

Naval Ships Parts Control Center, PO Box 2020, Mechanicsburg, PA 17055-0788
☎ 717-790-2000

Ships Support Directorate (NAVICP)
http://www.code05.icpmech.navy.mil/

Naval Sea Logistics Center/Naval Logistics Homepage (NAVSEA) $\mathcal{P}$
http://www.nslc.fmso.navy.mil/

Fleet Materiel Support Office (NAVSEA)
http://www.fmso.navy.mil/

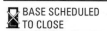 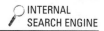

Defense Megacenter Mechanicsburg (DISA)
http://www.westhem.disa.mil/~WEP/DMCMechfrontpage.html

Tobyhanna Army Depot, PA 18466-5000
☎ 717-894-6660

Tobyhanna Army Depot (CECOM)
http://www.tobyhanna.army.mil/

Rhode Island

Naval Education and Training Center, Newport, RI 02841
☎ 401-841-3456; NWC ✉ nwcpao@ids.net

NETC Newport
http://www.cnet.navy.mil/newport/netc.htm

Naval War College
http://www.usnwc.edu/nwc/

NWC colleges, institutes, and academic schools include the Center for Naval Warfare Studies, College of Continuing Education, College of Naval Command and Staff, College of Naval Warfare, Naval Command College, Naval Staff College, Navy Senior Enlisted Academy, Naval Justice School, and Surface Warfare Officers School Command (see Chapter 3).

Naval Undersea Warfare Center (NUWC) (NAVSEA) (1126 Howell Street, Newport, RI 02841)
http://www.nuwc.navy.mil/

Naval Undersea Warfare Center Newport Division $
http://www.npt.nuwc.navy.mil/npt/

South Carolina

Charleston AFB, SC 29404-5000
☎ 1-800-438-2694; ☎ 803-566-5608

437th Airlift Wing (AMC)
http://www.charleston.af.mil

Fort Jackson, SC 29207-5060
☎ 803-751-7511

Army Training Center (TRADOC)
http://jackson-www.army.mil

> *Includes the Army Soldier Support Institute, Adjutant General School, Finance School, and Recruiting and Retention School.*

NEW Army Chaplain Center and School
http://usachcs-www.army.mil

NEW Army Recruiting and Retention School
http://jackson-www.army.mil/rr/rr.htm

Marine Corps Air Station Beaufort, SC 29904-5000
☎ 803-522-7100

> *Base tenants include Marine Aircraft Group 31 (MAG-31) (2nd MAW).*

Marine Corps Recruit Depot Parris Island, SC 29905-5001
☎ 803-525-2111

NEW MCRD Parris Island
http://www.parrisisland.com

Naval Base Charleston, 1690 Turnbull Avenue, Charleston, SC 29408-1955
☎ 803-743-4111; ✉ cnbchasnpao@pera18.spear.navy.mil

> *Base organizations include the Naval Station and the Fleet and Industrial Supply Center.*

Naval Facilities Engineering Command Southern Division
http://web.infoave.net/~southdiv/

Naval Weapons Station Charleston, Goose Creek, SC 29445-8601
☎ 803-764-7901

NWS Charleston (NAVSEA)
http://www.noclant.navy.mil/charles/index.html

SPAWAR Systems Center Charleston (SPAWAR) $
http://www-chas.spawar.navy.mil/

> *Formerly the NCCOSC In-Service Engineering East Coast Division (NISE East).*

Shaw AFB, SC 29152-5041
☎ 803-668-8110

20th Fighter Wing
http://www.shaw.af.mil

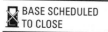 BASE SCHEDULED TO CLOSE    COMMERCIAL, BUSINESS OPPORTUNITY   E-MAIL ADDRESS   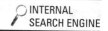 INTERNAL SEARCH ENGINE

Ninth Air Force (ACC)
  http://www.centaf.af.mil

> *Also serves as the headquarters for the U.S. Central Air Forces (CENTAF) (CENTCOM).*

South Dakota

Ellsworth AFB, Rapid City, SD 57706-5000
☎ 605-385-1000

Ellsworth AFB
  http://www.ellsworth.af.mil

> *Home to the 28th Bomb Wing (ACC) and the 99th Wing.*

Tennessee

Arnold AFB, Tullahoma, TN 37389
☎ 615-454-5586

Arnold Engineering Development Center (AFMC)
  http://info.arnold.af.mil/

NPARC Alliance
  http://info.arnold.af.mil/nparc/

> *Partnership between NASA Lewis Research Center and Arnold Engineering Center dedicated to computational fluid dynamics capability, centered on the NPARC computer program.*

Holston Army Ammunition Plant, Kingsport, TN 37662

NEW Holston AAP (IOC)
  http://holston-aap.com/hsaap/index.htm

Naval Support Activity Memphis, Millington, TN 38054-5045
☎ 901-874-5509

To be the new home of Bureau of Personnel (BUPERS) offices and the Navy Recruiting Command relocated from Washington, DC, as well as the Naval Personnel Research and Development Center, relocated from San Diego, CA.

Texas

Brooks AFB, San Antonio, TX 78235-5304
☎ 210-536-1110; ☎ hsc-pa@hqhsd.brooks.af.mil

Brooks AFB 🔎
http://www.brooks.af.mil/
http://xenon.brooks.af.mil/main.html

★ Human Systems Center (HSC) (AFMC) $ 📖 🔎
http://www.brooks.af.mil/HSC/hschome.html

　　NEW Development Planning Directorate
http://xrs10.brooks.af.mil/

　　NEW Human Systems Program Office
http://www.brooks.af.mil/HSC/YA/ya.htm

　　NEW Environmental, Safety and Occupational Health Service Center (ESOH)
http://www.brooks.af.mil/ESOH/esohhome.htm

　　NEW Office of Prevention and Health Services Assessment
http://www.ophsa.brooks.af.mil

Armstrong Laboratory
http://www.brooks.af.mil/HSC/AL/al-home.html
http://xenon.brooks.af.mil/HSC/AL/al-home.html

Air Force Surgeon General
http://usafsg.satx.disa.mil/

Air Force School of Aerospace Medicine
http://wwwsam.brooks.af.mil/

Air Force Medical Support Agency (AF field operating agency)
http://usafsg.satx.disa.mil:90/master.html

Air Force Center for Environmental Excellence (AF field operating agency)
http://www.afcee.brooks.af.mil

70th Air Base Group
http://www.brooks.af.mil/HSC/ABG/abg-home.html

Army Medical Research Detachment
http://www.brooks.af.mil/SGRD/usamrd.htm

⬛ BASE SCHEDULED TO CLOSE	$ COMMERCIAL, BUSINESS OPPORTUNITY	✉ E-MAIL ADDRESS	🔎 INTERNAL SEARCH ENGINE

Naval Medical Research Institute
http://www.brooks.af.mil/NMRI/nmri.htm

Corpus Christi Army Depot, TX 78419-5260
☎ 512-939-3626

CCAD
http://ccad-www.army.mil/
http://www-ioc.army.mil/home/elements/corpus.html

Dyess AFB, Abilene, TX 79607-1960
☎ 915-696-3113; ✉ 7wgpa@staff.wg7.dylan.af.mil

7th Bomb Wing (ACC)
http://www.dyess.af.mil/

Fort Bliss, El Paso, TX 79916-0058 (includes Biggs Army Airfield)
☎ 915-568-2121; ✉ pao@ftbliss-emh1.army.mil

★ Army Air Defense Artillery Center and School (TRADOC)
http://bliss-www.army.mil
http://bliss-www.army.mil/homepage/html/fbhome.htm

Responsible for air defense and theater ballistic missile defense doctrine, regulations, and publications. Units on base include the 6th, 11th, 31st, 35th, and 108th Air Defense Artillery Brigades.

Army Sergeants Major Academy (TRADOC)
http://bliss-usasma.army.mil

Fort Hood, TX 76544-5056
☎ 254-287-1110

III Corps and Fort Hood (FORSCOM)
http://www.hood-pao.army.mil/

1st Cavalry Division
http://www.hood-pao.army.mil/1stcavdiv

4th Infantry Division (Mechanized)
http://www.hood-pao.army.mil/Fort_Hood/4thID/4thid

13th Corps Support Command
http://www.hood-pao.army.mil/Fort_Hood/13COSCOM/13cc.htm

504th Military Intelligence Brigade (INSCOM)
http://www.hood-pao.army.mil/Fort_Hood/504thMI/504index.htm

Army Test and Experimentation Command (TEXCOM)
(Army field operating agency)
http://texcom-www.army.mil/

Fort Sam Houston, TX 78234-5000
☎ 210-221-1211; ✉ afzg@samhousbasops.army.mil

Fort Sam Houston 🔎
http://www.samhou-usag.army.mil

Army Medical Command (MEDCOM)
http://www.armymedicine.army.mil/armymed/default.htm

Army Medical Department Center and School 🔎
http://www.cs.amedd.army.mil/

NEW Fifth U.S. Army (FORSCOM)
http://www.5thArmy.army.mil

Goodfellow AFB, San Angelo, TX 76908-5000
☎ 915-654-3231

17th Training Wing (Second Air Force, AETC)
http://www.gdf.aetc.af.mil/

Kelly AFB, San Antonio, TX 78241
☎ 210-925-1110

Base organizations include the 67th Intelligence Wing, Information Warfare Battlelab, and Joint Command and Control Warfare Center (JC2WC) (ACOM)

Kelly AFB and the San Antonio Air Logistics Center (SA-ALC) (AFMC) $
http://www.kelly-afb.org

76th Air Base Wing
http://www.kelly-afb.org/links/orgs/kelly_afb/

NEW Air Force News Agency (AF field operating agency)
http://www.dtic.mil/airforcelink/pa/AirForceNewsAgency.html

Air Intelligence Agency (AIA) (AF field operating agency) 📖
http://www.aia.af.mil

Air Intelligence Agency Technology Demonstration Center
http://aia04.aia.af.mil

⬛ BASE SCHEDULED TO CLOSE	$ COMMERCIAL, BUSINESS OPPORTUNITY	✉ E-MAIL ADDRESS	🔎 INTERNAL SEARCH ENGINE

Air Force Information Warfare Center (San Antonio, Texas 78243-5000)
http://www.aia.af.mil/aialink/homepages/afiwc/index.htm

> *Created through the merger of the Air Force Electronic Warfare Center and the Air Force Cryptologic Support Center. Includes the 67th Intelligence Wing and the affiliated Joint Command and Control Warfare Center (JC2WC).*

Air Force INFOSEC Technical Assistance Center
http://itac05.kelly.af.mil

Defense Megacenter San Antonio (DISA)
www.satx.disa.mil
http://199.208.150.49

Lackland AFB, San Antonio, TX 78236-5110 (includes Medina Annex)
☎ 210-671-1110

37th Training Wing (Second Air Force, AETC)
http://www.lak.aetc.af.mil

> *Home of the Inter-American Air Forces Academy (SOUTHCOM).*

NEW Air Force Security Forces Center (AF field operating agency)
http://www.lak.aetc.af.mil/AFSF\index.html

> *Formerly Air Force Security Policy Agency and moved from Kirtland AFB, NM. Opened November 1997, includes the Force Protection Battlelab and 820th Security Forces Group.*

NEW Wilford Hall Medical Center/59th Medical Wing (AETC).
http://www.whmc.af.mil

Medina Annex

> *Medina Annex is host to the Medina Regional Security Operations Center, an NSA signals intelligence facility.*

NEW Naval Security Group Activity Medina (NSGC)
http://mrsoc.nsga.aia.af.mil

NEW 718th Military Intelligence Battalion (INSCOM)
http://749thmibn-www.army.mil

Laughlin AFB, TX 78843-5000
☎ 210-298-3511

Laughlin AFB and 47th Flying Training Wing (Nineteenth Air Force, AETC)
http://www.lau.aetc.af.mil/

Naval Air Station Corpus Christi, TX 78419-5021
☎ 512-939-2811

Chief of Naval Air Training (CNATRA)/Naval Air Training Command
http://www.cnet.navy.mil/cnatra/

NEW Training Air Wing 4
http://www.training4.org

NEW Mine Warfare Command (MINEWARCOM)
http://www.cnsl,spear.navy.mil/cnwc/cnwc.htm

Naval Air Station Kingsville, 554 McCain Street, Kingsville, TX 78363-5000
☎ 512-516-6136

NEW NAS Kingsville
http://209.127.66.12/nas/index.html

Training Air Wing 2 (CNATRA)
http://209.127.66.12/ctw2/index.html/

Naval Station Ingleside, 1455 Ticonderoga Road, Ingleside, TX 78362-5001
☎ 512-776-4200

*Home of the Mine Warfare Training Center (MINEWARCOM) and Mine
Countermeasures Group 3.*

Randolph AFB, TX 78150-4562
☎ 210-652-1110; ☎ 210-652-3946

Randolph AFB and 12th Flying Training Wing 🔎
http://www.rnd.aetc.af.mil

Air Education and Training Command (AETC) 📖
http://www.aetc.af.mil/

Nineteenth Air Force
http://www.rnd.aetc.af.mil/19af/index.htm

Air Force Recruiting Service
http://www.rs.af.mil

★ Air Force Personnel Center (AF field operating agency) 🔎
http://www.afpc.af.mil/
ftp://ftp.afpc.af.mil

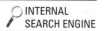

Air Force Center for Quality and Management Innovation (AF field operating agency)
http://www.afcqmi.randolph.af.mil

Air Force Services Agency (AF field operating agency)
http://www.afsv.af.mil/

Red River Army Depot, TX 75507-5000
☎ 903-334-2141

Red River Army Depot
http://www.redriver.army.mil
http://www-ioc.army.mil/home/elements/redriver.html

Army Materiel Command School of Engineering and Logistics
http://www.sel.army.mil/selhome2.htm

Sheppard AFB, TX 76311-2943
☎ 940-676-2511

Sheppard AFB and 82nd Training Wing (Second Air Force, AETC)
http://www.spd.aetc.af.mil

NEW 80th Flying Training Wing (Nineteenth Air Force, AETC).
http://www.spd.aetc.af.mil/80ftw

Utah

Dugway Proving Ground, Dugway, UT 84022
☎ 801-831-3757

Dugway Proving Ground
http://www.atc.army.mil/~dugway/

Hill AFB, Ogden, UT 84056
☎ 801-777-7221

Ogden Air Logistics Center (OO-ALC) and 75th Air Base Wing (AFMC) $
http://www.hill.af.mil/

388th Fighter Wing (ACC)
http://www.388fw.hill.af.mil/

Utah Test and Training Range
http://www.hill.af.mil/UTTR/index.htm

Defense Megacenter Ogden (DISA)
http://www.ogden.disa.mil

Tooele Army Depot, UT 84074-5000
☎ 801-833-3216

Tooele Army Depot $
http://www.tooele.army.mil
http://www-ioc.army.mil/home/elements/tooele.html ✎

NEW Deseret Chemical Depot (CBDCOM)
http://www.cbdcom.apgea.army.mil/storage/Deseret/index.html

Defense Non-tactical Generator and Rail Equipment Center (IOC)
http://www.tooele.army.mil/dgrc.htm
http://www-ioc.army.mil/home/elements/railshop.htm ✎

Virginia

Major Commands and Agencies in the Virginia Suburbs

Alexandria

American Forces Information Service (AFIS)

Army Audit Agency (Army field operating agency)

Army Civilian Personnel Center (Army field operating agency)

Army Logistics Integration Agency (Army field operating agency)

Army Materiel Command (AMC)

Army Operational Test and Evaluation Command (Army field operating agency)

Army Publishing Agency (Army field operating agency)

Army Research Institute (Army field operating agency)

Army Security Assistance Command (AMC)
http://www.amc.army.mil/amc/sac/index.html

Defense Acquisition University (see Chapter 3)

Defense Security Service (DSS) (see Chapter 6)

Defense Special Weapons Agency (DSWA) (see Chapter 6)

Naval Facilities Engineering Command (NAVFAC)

Naval Legal Service Command

Total Army Personnel Command (PERSCOM) (Army field operating agency)

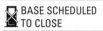 

Arlington

Air Force Base Conversion Agency (AF field operating agency)

Air Force Cost Analysis Agency (AF field operating agency)

Air Force Frequency Management Agency (AF field operating agency)

Army Space and Missile Defense Command (SMDC) (see Chapter 8)

Bureau of Naval Personnel (BUPERS)

Defense Advanced Research Projects Agency (DARPA) (see Chapter 6)

Defense Finance and Accounting Service (DFAS) (see Chapter 6)

Defense Information Systems Agency (DISA) (see Chapter 6)

Defense Security Assistance Agency (DSAA) (see Chapter 6)

Department of Defense Civilian Personnel Management Service

Department of Defense Education Activity (DODEA)

Naval Sea Systems Command (NAVSEA)

Naval Supply Systems Command (NAVSUP)

Naval Surface Warfare Center (NAVSEA) (see also Dahlgren, VA)

Navy Recruiting Command

Office of Naval Research (ONR)

Space and Naval Warfare Systems Command (SPAWAR)

Fairfax

National Imagery and Mapping Agency (see Chapter 6)

Falls Church

Defense Medical Program Activity (DMPA)

Military Traffic Management Command (MTMC)

Naval Audit Service

Defense Information Systems Agency Western Hemisphere (DISA)
http://www.disa.mil/line/westhm.html
http://www.westhem.disa.mil/~wes/home.html
(5600 Columbia Pike, Falls Church, VA 22041)

AEGIS Combat Systems Center, Wallops Flight Facility, Wallops Island, VA 23337-5000
☎ 804-824-2272
http://www.navy.mil/homepages/aegis/

 NEW LISTING IN THIS EDITION ONLINE FACT SHEET 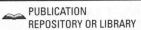 PUBLICATION REPOSITORY OR LIBRARY RECOMMENDED SITE TELEPHONE NUMBER

Army Judge Advocate General's School, 600 Massie Road, Charlottesville, VA 22903
☎ 804-972-6372; ☎ 1-800-552-3978

> NEW JAG School
> http://www.jagcnet.army.mil/jagcnet/ann_bull.nsf
>
> *Field operating agency of the Judge Advocate General of the Army.*

Defense Supply Center Richmond, 8000 Jefferson Davis Highway,
Richmond, VA 23297-5000
☎ 804-275-3209

> Defense Supply Center Richmond (DLA) ⌕ $
> http://www.dscr.dla.mil
>
> *Formerly the Defense General Supply Center.*

> DOD Security Institute (DSS)
> http://www.dtic.mil/dodsi/

Fleet and Industrial Supply Center Cheatham Annex, Williamsburg, VA 23185
☎ 804-887-7222

> *Tenants include the Naval Expeditionary Logistics Support Force and the Naval Cargo Handling and Port Group.*

> NEW FISC
> http://www.nor.fisc.navy.mil/home/page58.html

> Naval Inshore Undersea Warfare Group 2
> http://www.spawar.navy.mil/nr/cnsrf/iuwg2/

Fleet Combat Training Center Atlantic Dam Neck, Regulus Avenue,
Virginia Beach, VA 23461-2098
☎ 757-433-6234

> *Tenants include the Tactical Training Group Atlantic, Naval Ocean Processing Facility, Navy and Marine Corps Intelligence Training Center, and Naval Special Warfare Development Group.*

> NEW Fleet Combat Training Center Atlantic Dam Neck
> http://www.cnet.navy.mil/tralant/fctcl

> Naval Surface Warfare Center Port Hueneme Division Dam Neck (NAVSEA)
> http://www.damneck.navy.mil/

Fort Belvoir, VA 22060 (includes Davison Army Air Field)
☎ 703-545-6700

 BASE SCHEDULED TO CLOSE $ COMMERCIAL, BUSINESS OPPORTUNITY   E-MAIL ADDRESS   INTERNAL SEARCH ENGINE

Other base tenants include the Joint Services Survival, Evasion, Resistance and Escape (SERE) Agency (a DOD agency operated by the Air Force);the Belvoir Research, Development and Engineering Center (AMCOM); and the Defense Mapping School (NIMA).

Fort Belvoir
http://www.belvoir.army.mil

Defense Logistics Agency (DLA) $
http://www.dla.mil/

> **NEW** Defense Logistics Support Command $
> http://www.supply.dla.mil/
>
> Defense Contract Management Command
> http://www.dcmc.hq.mil/
>
> Defense Energy Support Center
> http://www.desc.dla.mil
>
> *Formerly the Defense Fuel Supply Center.*
>
> Defense National Stockpile Center
> http://www.dnsc.dla.mil
>
> ★ Defense Technical Information Center (DTIC) (see Chapter 2)
> http://www.dtic.mil/

Defense Contract Audit Agency (DCAA)
http://www.dtic.mil/dcaa

Defense Systems Management College (Defense Acquisition University)
http://www.dsmc.dsm.mil/

Army Criminal Investigation Command (CIDC)
http://www.belvoir.army.mil/cidc/index.htm

Army Intelligence and Security Command (INSCOM)
http://www.vulcan.belvoir.army.mil

Army Aeronautical Services Agency (Army field operating agency)
http://leav-www.army.mil/usaasa/usaasa.htm

Army Management Staff College
http://www.amsc.belvoir.army.mil

Army CECOM Software Engineering Center (ISC)
http://160.147.66.30/issc.htm

> *Formerly the Army Information Systems Software Center.*

Army Operational Support Airlift Command (OSACOM)
http://160.147.9.92/osacom.htm

Test and Evaluation Directorate—Belvoir Division (CECOM)
http://www.mnsinc.com/cnm/belvoir.html

NEW Defense Automated Printing Service
http://www.daps.mil/

Army Corps of Engineers Organizations

Humphreys Engineer Center Support Activity
http://www.hecsa.usace.army.mil/

Army Center for Public Works
http://www.usacpw.belvoir.army.mil

Army Topographic Engineering Center
http://www.tec.army.mil/

> Strategic Management and Innovations Division (CERM-S)
> http://www.usace.army.mil/essc/
>
> *Formerly the Engineer Strategic Studies Center.*

Fort Eustis, Newport News, VA 23604-5000
☎ 757-878-1212/1110

> Army Transportation Center and Fort Eustis (TRADOC)
> http://www.eustis.army.mil
>
> > Chief of Transportation Homepage
> > http://www.eustis.army.mil/ocot/index.html
>
> > Aviation Logistics School
> > http://www.usaals.com
> > http://www.eustis.army.mil/schools.htm
>
> Army Training Support Center (ATSC) (TRADOC)
> http://www.atsc-army.org/atschome.html-ssi

★ Army Doctrine and Training Digital Library
http://www.atsc-army.org/atdls.html

> *Repository of Army field manuals, training publications, and other doctrinal materials.*

Army Training Information Management Program
http://www.atimp.army.mil

Army Transportation Engineering Agency (MTMC)
http://www.tea-army.org

Aviation Applied Technology Directorate (AMCOM) $
http://155.217.5.78

Fort Lee, Petersburg VA 23801-5009
☎ 804-765-3000; ✉ atzmpao@lee-emh2.army.mil

Fort Lee
http://www.lee.army.mil

Combined Arms Support Command (TRADOC)
http://www.cascom.army.mil

Army Quartermaster Center and School (TRADOC)
http://www.lee.army.mil/quartermaster/

Army Logistics Management College (TRADOC)
http://www.almc.army.mil

NEW Defense Commissary Agency (DeCA) $
http://www.deca.mil

Fort Monroe, Hampton, VA 23651
☎ 757-727-2111

Fort Monroe
http://www-tradoc.monroe.army.mil/monroe

Army Training and Doctrine Command (TRADOC) $
http://www-tradoc.army.mil

> *Responsible for all aspects of Army combat development, doctrine, training, simulation, and analysis.*

Army Cadet Command
http://www-tradoc.army.mil/rotc/

`NEW` Joint Warfighting Center (ACOM)
http://www.jwfc.js.mil

JCS agency transferred to ACOM on 1 October 1998.

Fort Myer, Arlington, VA 22211-5050
☎ 703-545-6700

Fort Myer
http://www.mdw.army.mil/fmcc.htm

3rd U.S. Infantry (The Old Guard) (MDW)
http://www.mdw.army.mil/oldguard/index.htm

U.S. Army Band "Pershing's Own"
http://www.army.mil/armyband/

Joint Training, Analysis and Simulation Center (JTASC) 116 Lake View Parkway, Suite 150 Suffolk, VA 23435-2697
☎ 757-686-7522

`NEW` Joint C4ISR Battle Center (JBC) (ACOM)
http://www.jbc.js.mil

Langley AFB, VA 23665-2292
☎ 757-764-5615

Langley AFB
http://www.langley.af.mil/

Air Combat Command (ACC) 🔍
http://www.acc.af.mil/

`NEW` Air and Space Command and Control Agency
http://www.acc.af.mil/public/asc2a

1st Fighter Wing
http://www.langley.af.mil/1fw/

Air-Land-Sea Applications Center (ALSA)
http://www.dtic.mil/alsa/

Marine Corps Base Quantico, VA 22134
☎ 703-784-2121

MCB Quantico
http://ismo-www1.mqg.usmc.mil/
http://138.156.107.3/

★ Marine Corps Combat Development Command (MCCDC)
http://138.156.112.114
http://ismo-www1.mqg.usmc.mil/quantico/

Includes the Doctrine Division and the Concepts Branch.

Commandant's Warfighting Laboratory
http://www.mcwl.org/mcwl/Home/home.html
http://208.198.29.7

Marine Corps University 🔍 📖
http://138.156.203.52/
http://www.mcu.quantico.usmc.mil

MCU schools include the Marine Corps War College, Command and Staff College, School of Advanced Warfighting, and Amphibious Warfare School (see Chapter 3).

★ Marine Corps Systems Command (MarCorSysCom) $
http://www.marcorsyscom.usmc.mil

Marine Corps Computer and Telecommunications Activity
http://issb-www1.quantico.usmc.mil/mccta/index.html
http://mccta.cio.usmc.mil

NEW Marine Security Guard Battalion
http://www.quantico.usmc.mil/msg/msg.htm

Supplies Marine guards to U.S. embassies and consulates abroad.

National Ground Intelligence Center (NGIC), 220 Seventh Street, NE,
Charlottesville, VA 22901-5396

Formerly the Army Foreign Science and Technology Center.

Naval Air Station Norfolk, 9420 Third Avenue, Norfolk, VA 23511

Naval Air Force U.S. Atlantic Fleet
http://flightdeck.airlant.navy.mil/

NEW Carrier Group 4/Carrier Striking Force
http://flightdeck.airlant.navy.mil/public/ccg4/home.htm

USS Dwight D. Eisenhower (CVN 69)
http://www.navy.mil/homepages/cvn69/

USS John C. Stennis (CVN 74)
http://www.navy.mil/homepages/jcs/

Naval Safety Center 📖
http://www.norfolk.navy.mil/safecen/home.htm

Naval Air Station Oceana, Virginia Beach, VA 23460-5120
☎ 757-433-2366

*Base tenants include Fighter Wing U.S. Atlantic Fleet, Strike Weapons and Tactics
School Atlantic, and Carrier Air Wings 1, 3, 7, and 8.*

NEW NAS Oceana
http://oceana-navy.com

NEW Carrier Air Wing 3
http://www.ncts.navy.mil/homepages/cvn69/cvw3bio.htm

Naval Amphibious Base Little Creek, 2600 Tarawa Court, Norfolk, VA 23521-3229
☎ 757-464-7385

*Base tenants include the Naval Surface Warfare Development Group; Naval Special
Warfare Group 2 (Seal Teams 2, 4, and 8; Seal Delivery Vehicle Team 2; and Special
Boat Squadron 2); the 2nd Naval Construction Brigade; and the Fleet Information
Warfare Center, a Navy and Marine Corps center activated in October 1995.*

Naval Base Norfolk, VA 23511-2797
☎ 757-444-0000; ✉ cnbnpao@pera18.spear.navy.mil

The Flagship, *the Naval Base Norfolk authorized commercial newspaper, is online at* http://www.flagshipnews.com.

NEW Commander Naval Base Norfolk
http://www.cmar.navy.mil

Made up of the combined facilities of the NAS Norfolk, Naval Station, NAS Oceana, Naval Amphibious Base Little Creek, and other outlying bases.

NEW Naval Base Norfolk maps
http://www.nor.fisc.navy.mil/home/page65.html
http://www.lantflt.navy.mil/maps/maps.html

U.S. Atlantic Command (ACOM) 🔍
http://www.acom.mil/

See Chapter 6.

U.S. Atlantic Fleet (LANTFLT) (ACOM)
http://www.lantflt.navy.mil
http://www.clf.navy.mil

Naval Surface Force U.S. Atlantic Fleet (SURFLANT)
http://www.cnsl.spear.navy.mil/

Surflant Maintenance Page
http://www.spear.navy.mil/

NEW Submarine Force U.S. Atlantic Fleet (SUBLANT)
http://www.norfolk.navy.mil/sublant

Training Command U.S. Atlantic Fleet
http://www.cnet.navy.mil/tralant/tralant.htm

Marine Corps Forces Atlantic (MARFORLANT)
http://www.nfd.usmc.mil

Also Fleet Marine Force Atlantic (FMF Atlantic) and Commander Marine Corps Bases Atlantic.

Armed Forces Staff College (7800 Hampton Boulevard, Norfolk, VA 23511-1702)
http://www.afsc.edu/

NEW Naval Station Norfolk
http://naval-station.norfolk.va.us

 NEW LISTING IN THIS EDITION   ONLINE FACT SHEET   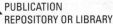 PUBLICATION REPOSITORY OR LIBRARY   ★ RECOMMENDED SITE   ☎ TELEPHONE NUMBER

Submarine Training Facility Norfolk (Naval Station Norfolk)
http://www.cnet.navy.mil/cnet/stf-nor/homepgc.htm

Fitting Out and Supply Support Assistance Center
http://www.norfolk.navy.mil/fossac/

Fleet and Industrial Supply Center Norfolk (Naval Station Norfolk) $
http://www.nor.fisc.navy.mil

★ Naval Computer and Telecommunications Area Master Station Atlantic
(NCTAMS LANT) (NCTC) 🔎
http://www.chips.navy.mil/

Naval Facilities Engineering Command Atlantic Division (NAVFAC)
http://www.efdlant.navfac.navy.mil/

Navy Public Works Center Norfolk (Naval Station Norfolk)
http://www.norfolk.navy.mil/pwc/

NISE East Detachment Norfolk (SPAWAR)
http://silk.nosc.mil/

Shore Intermediate Maintenance Activity
http://www.nor.mrms.navy.mil/

Naval Medical Center Portsmouth, VA 23708-5100
☎ 757-953-5000
http://www.nmcp.med.navy.mil/

Naval Security Group Activity Northwest, 1320 Northwest Boulevard,
Chesapeake, VA 23322-4094
☎ 757-421-8000

> *Base tenants include Naval Security Group Activity Northwest (NSGC), Fleet Surveil-lance Support Command, and the Marine Corps Security Force Training Company.*

SPAWAR Systems Center Chesapeake (SPAWAR)
http://www.massolant.navy.mil/

> *Formerly the Navy Management Systems Support Office (NCCOSC).*

Naval Surface Warfare Center, 17320 Dahlgren Road, Dahlgren, VA 22448-5100
☎ 540-653-8531

> *The Naval Space Command (NAVSPACECOM), the Navy component command of SPACECOM, is also headquartered at Dahlgren.*

★ Naval Surface Warfare Center Dahlgren Division (NSWCDD) (NAVSEA) 🔎 $
http://www.nswc.navy.mil/

NEW Aegis Training and Readiness Center
http://www.atrc.navy.mil

Naval Weapons Station Yorktown, VA 23691-0160
☎ 804-887-4545

> NWS Yorktown (NAVSEA)
> http://www.noclant.navy.mil/yorktown/index.html
>
> Naval Ordnance Center Atlantic Division (NAVSEA)
> http://www.noclant.navy.mil/
>
> NISE East Yorktown Technical Center (SPAWAR) 🔍 $
> http://ded-2-nt.nosc.mil/default.htm

Norfolk Naval Shipyard, Portsmouth, VA 23709-5000
☎ 757-396-3000

> NEW Norfolk Naval Shipyard (NAVSEA)
> http://www.nnsy1.navy.mil
> http://204.34.153.14

The Pentagon

Department of Defense, Washington, DC 20301
Joint Chiefs of Staff, Washington, DC 20301
Department of the Army, Washington, DC 20310
Department of the Air Force, Washington, DC 20330
Department of the Navy, Washington, DC 20350
Marine Corps, Washington, DC 20380
http://www.defenselink.mil/pubs/pentagon/index.html ✎

Commands Headquartered in the Pentagon

Ballistic Missile Defense Organization (BMDO)

Defense Legal Services Agency

Department of Defense (see Chapter 6)

Department of the Air Force (see Chapter 7)

Department of the Army (see Chapter 8)

Department of the Navy (see Chapter 9)

Single Agency Manager for Pentagon Information Technology Services
http://www.sam.pentagon.mil/

Army HQDA Information Management Support Center
http://www.hqda.army.mil/imcenweb/

Washington

Fairchild AFB, Airway Heights, WA 99011-5000
☎ 509-247-1212

    Fairchild AFB and 92nd Air Refueling Wing (AMC)
    http://www.fairchild.af.mil/

Fleet and Industrial Supply Center Puget Sound, 467 W Street,
Bremerton, WA 98314-5100

    FISC (NAVSUP)   ⌕ $
    http://www.puget.fisc.navy.mil/

Fort Lewis, WA 98433-5000
☎ 253-967-1110; ✉ af2zh-po@lewis-emh2.army.mil

    Home of the 1st Brigade, 25th Infantry Division (the 1st Brigade, 7th Infantry Division, often called the 9th Infantry Regiment [Manchu], realigned in FY 1995 at Ft. Lewis as 1st Brigade of the 25th Infantry Division); the 3rd Brigade, 2nd Infantry Division; and the 1st Special Forces Group (Airborne).

    Fort Lewis and I Corps (FORSCOM)
    http://www.lewis.army.mil

McChord AFB, WA 98438
☎ 253-984-1910

    `NEW` McChord AFB and 62nd Airlift Wing (AMC)
    http://www.mcchord.af.mil

Naval Air Station Whidbey Island, Oak Harbor, WA 98278-5100
☎ 360-257-2211

    NAS Whidbey Island
    http://www.naswi.navy.mil/

    `NEW` Electronic Combat Wing
    http://www.naswi.navy.mil/cvwp/vaqwing.htm

    `NEW` Patrol Wing 10
    http://www.naswi.navy.mil/cpw-10.html

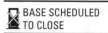 BASE SCHEDULED TO CLOSE    $ COMMERCIAL, BUSINESS OPPORTUNITY   E-MAIL ADDRESS    INTERNAL SEARCH ENGINE

Naval Hospital Bremerton, WA 98312-1898
☎ 360-479-6600
  http://nh_bremerton.med.navy.mil/

Naval Station Everett, WA 98207-5001
☎ 206-304-3000

> *Home to Naval Surface Group Pacific Northwest, the USS Abraham Lincoln (CVN 72), surface ships, and support facilities.*

  Naval Station Everett
    http://www.everett.navy.mil/

Naval Submarine Base Bangor, Silverdale, WA 98315-5000
☎ 360-396-48403

  ★ Naval Base Seattle
    http://www.cnbs.navy.mil

> *Responsible for Navy forces and bases in Washington state, Alaska, and Oregon.*

NSB Bangor
http://www.nsb.navy.mil/

> *The Ballistic Missile Submarine Base includes the Strategic Weapons Facility Pacific, Trident Refit Facility, and Trident Training Facility, and Submarine Development Group 1.*

NEW Submarine Group 9
http://www.csg9.trfb.navy.mil

Naval Undersea Warfare Engineering Station Keyport, 610 Dowell Street, Keyport, WA 98345
☎ 206-396-2699

Naval Undersea Warfare Center Keyport Division (NAVSEA)
http://www.nuwc.navy.mil/hq/keyport.html

Puget Sound Naval Shipyard, 1400 Farragut Avenue, Bremerton, WA 98314-5000
☎360-476-3711

USS *Carl Vinson* (CVN 70)
http://www.cvn70.navy.mil

> *Moved from Naval Air Station Alameda, CA, in early 1997.*

Wyoming

F. E. Warren AFB, Cheyenne, WY 82005-2271
☎ 307-775-1110

F. E. Warren AFB
http://www.warren.af.mil

Twentieth Air Force (AFSPC)
http://www.warren.af.mil/20af/index.html

NEW 90th Space (Missile) Wing
http://www.warren.af.mil/90sw

Major Military Bases
and Commands Overseas

Antarctica

McMurdo Station, FPO AA 96598

Antarctic Development Squadron 6 (VXE-6)
http://www.navy.mil/homepages/VXE6/vxe6main.html

Bahamas

Andros Island, FPO AA 34058

Atlantic Underwater Test and Evaluation Center (AUTEC) (NUWC)
http://www.npt.nuwc.navy.mil/autec/

Bahrain

Naval Support Facility Manama, FPO AE 09834-2800

U.S. Naval Forces Central Command (USNAVCENT) (CENTCOM) and
Commander Fifth Fleet
http://www.centcom.mil/new_pages/navcent.htm

Diego Garcia

Navy Support Facility, FPO AP 96464

NSF Diego Garcia
http://www.nctsdg.navy.mil/nsf.htm

Naval Computer and Telecommunications Station Diego Garcia (NCTC)
http://www.nctsdg.navy.mil/

NEW Naval Pacific Meteorology and Oceanography Detachment
http://www.npmocw.navy.mil/npmocw/dgar/index.html

Germany

Bad Kreuznach/Dexheim, APO AE 09111

1st Armored Division (V Corps)
http://www.1ad.army.mil

Elements of the division are stationed in Baumholder, Budingen, Friedburg/ Geissen, Hanau, Kirchgoens, and Wackernheim.

Bamberg, APO AE 09139

Bamberg Military Community
http://www.bamberg.army.mil

Consisting of major elements of the 1st Infantry Division, with headquarters in Wuerzburg.

Darmstadt, APO AE 09175

22nd Signal Brigade (V Corps)
http://www.22sigbde.army.mil/

Einsiedlerhof AS

Warrior Preparation Center (USAFE)
http://www.wpc.af.mil/

Garmisch, APO AE 09053

George C. Marshall European Center for Security Studies (EUCOM)
http://www.marshall.adsn.int/marshall.html

Grafenwoehr, APO AE 09114

Seventh Army Training Command (USAREUR)
http://www.grafenwoehr.army.mil

 BASE SCHEDULED TO CLOSE

$ COMMERCIAL, BUSINESS OPPORTUNITY

 E-MAIL ADDRESS

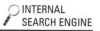 INTERNAL SEARCH ENGINE

Heidelberg, APO AE 09014

U.S. Army Europe and Seventh Army (USAREUR) (EUCOM)
http://www.hqusareur.army.mil

The online USAREUR Telephone Directory is at http://www.5sigcmd.army.mil/.

V Corps (USAREUR)
http://www.hq.c5.army.mil

Kaiserslautern, APO AE 09067

21st Theater Army Area Command (TAACOM) (USAREUR)
http://www.21taacom.army.mil
http://147.35.210.53/

Kitzingen, APO AE 09031

NEW 1st Infantry Division Support Command (DISCOM)
http://www.discom.1id.army.mil

Mannheim, APO AE 09267

NEW Mannheim Military Community
http://www.mannheim.army.mil

★ 5th Signal Command and USAREUR Information Management
http://www.5sigcmd.army.mil/

NEW 2nd Signal Brigade
http://www.2sigbdg.army.mil

7th Signal Brigade
http://www.7sigbde.army.mil/

Ramstein AB, APO AE 09094

Ramstein AB and 86th Airlift Wing
http://www.usafe.af.mil/bases/ramstein/ramstein.htm

U.S. Air Forces in Europe (USAFE) (EUCOM) 🔎 $
http://www.usafe.af.mil/

Rhein-Main AB, APO AE 09007-5000

Rhein-Main AB
http://www.usafe.af.mil/bases/rhein/base.htm

Schwetzingen, APO AE 09042

  1st Personnel Command (USAREUR)
    http://144.170.217.12

Spangdahlem AB, APO AE 09126-5000

  52nd Fighter Wing (USAFE)
    http://www.spangdahlem.af.mil

Stuttgart, APO AE 09128
  ✉ ecpa@hq.eucom.mil

    ★ U.S. European Command (EUCOM) 🔍 📖
      http://www.eucom.mil/

      See Chapter 6.

      Special Operations Command Europe
        http://www.eucom.mil/hq/soceur/index.htm ✎

  Defense Information Systems Agency European Field Command (DISA)
    http://159.77.8.2

Wiesbaden, APO AE 09096

  NEW 3rd Corps Support Command (V Corps, USAREUR)
    http://www.3coscom.wiesbaden.army.mil

Wuerzburg, APO AE 09036

  1st Infantry Division (V Corps)
    http://www.1id.army.mil

Greenland (Denmark)

Thule AB, APO AA 09704
  NEW http://www.csg.ctisinc.com/arctic/logistic/thule.htm

Guam, Marianas Islands

Andersen AFB, APO AP 96543-4003

  Andersen AFB and 36th Air Base Wing
    http://www.andersen.af.mil/

Thirteenth Air Force (PACAF)/Southwest Pacific Air Defense Region (NORAD)
http://www.andersen.af.mil/13org_new.htm

Naval Station Guam, FPO AP 96536

Commands and tenants include U.S. Naval Forces Marianas/U.S. Naval Activities Guam (PACFLT), and Public Works Center Guam.

NEW Navy Guam Homepage
http://www.guam.navy.mil

SPAWAR Systems Facility Pacific Guam (Finegayan)
http://nisegq.nosc.mil/

Formerly the NRaD Facility Guam (NCCOSC).

Iceland

Keflavik AS, APO AE 09725-2005
✉ keflavik@smtp.mediacen.navy.mil

Base tenants include Iceland Defense Force (ACOM), 85th Group (Eighth Air Force, ACC) and U.S. Naval Forces Iceland.

Iceland Homepage/Naval Computer and Telecommunications Station Iceland
(NCTAMS LANT)
http://www.nctskef.navy.mil

Italy

Aviano AB, APO AE 09824-5000

Aviano AB and 31st Fighter Wing 📖
http://www.aviano.af.mil/

Sixteenth Air Force (USAFE)
http://www.usafe.af.mil/bases/16af/home.htm

NEW 16th Air Expeditionary Wing
http://www.usafe.af.mil/bases/16af/16aew/index.html

Gaeta, FPO AE 09501-6002
✉ 6thfltpao@naples.dla.mil

> Commander Sixth Fleet (USNAVEUR)
> http://www.naples.navy.mil/c6f/
>
>> *Located aboard the flagship USS La Salle (AGF-3).*

La Maddalena, Sardinia, FPO AE 09612

> *The Naval Support Office provides support for the Submarine Refit Training Group and Submarine Squadron 22.*

Camp Darby, Leghorn Depot Activity (Livorno), APO AE 09613

> **NEW** 22nd Area Support Group (SETAF)
> http://www.setaf.army.mil/22asg

Naples, FPO AE 09620

> Naval Support Activity Naples
> http://www.naples.navy.mil/
>
>> *Home to headquarters for Allied Forces Southern Europe (a major NATO command) and various Navy support commands and units.*
>
> **NEW** Service Force Sixth Fleet (CTF 63)
> http://www.naples.navy.mil/ctf63/
>
> Commander Fleet Air Mediterranean (CTF 67)
> http://www.naples.navy.mil/cfm/cfm.html
>
> Naval Computer and Telecommunications Area Master Station Mediterranean (NCTC)
> http://www.naples.navy.mil/nctams/

Naval Air Station Sigonella, FPO AE 09627
✉ sigonella@smtp.mediacen.navy.mil

> Sigonella and Sicily Homepage
> http://www.sicily.navy.mil/

Vicenza (*Caserma Ederle*), APO AE 09630

> **NEW** Southern European Task Force (USAREUR)
> http://www.setaf.army.mil

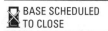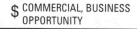 

Japan

Camp Fuji, FPO AP 96387

NEW Camp Fuji
http://www.okr.usmc.mil/mcbases/fuji/fwp1.htm

Camp Smedley D. Butler, Okinawa, FPO AP 96373

Includes Camps Courtney, Foster, Hansen, McTureous, and Schwab.

Marine Corps Bases Japan
http://www.okr.usmc.mil/

III Marine Expeditionary Force (III MEF)
http://www.iiimef.usmc.mil

Includes the 1st Marine Aircraft Wing (1st MAW), 3rd Marine Division (3rd MarDiv), 3rd Force Service Support Group (FSSG), and subordinate units.

NEW 3rd Marine Division (III MEF)
http://www.3mardiv.usmc.mil

Camp Zama, Sagamihara, Honshu, APO AP 96343

Camp Zama
http://www.zama.army.mil/

U.S. Army Japan (USARJ) and 9th Theater Army Area Command (USARPAC) (USFJ/PACOM)
http://www.usarpac.army.mil/docs/USARJ.htm

Kadena AB, Okinawa, APO AP 96368-5141

Kadena AB
http://www.kadena.af.mil/

18th Wing (Fifth Air Force, PACAF)
http://www.kadena.af.mil%20/

353rd Special Operations Group (AFSOC)
http://www.hurlburt.af.mil/hqafsoc/353sog.html

U.S. Fleet Activities Okinawa
http://www.navy.mil/homepages/comnavfor-japan/cfao.htm

Marine Corps Air Station Iwakuni, Honshu, FPO AP 96310

> NEW MCAS Iwakuni
> http://www.iwz.usmc.mil

Misawa AB, APO AP 96319-5009

> Misawa AB
> http://www.misawa.af.mil

> 35th Fighter Wing (Fifth Air Force, PACAF)
> http://www.misawa.af.mil/orgs/35fw/indx.html

> Naval Air Facility Misawa
> http://www.navy.mil/homepages/comnavfor-japan/misawa.htm

> NEW Naval Security Group Activity Misawa (NSGC)
> http://www.misawa.af.mil/orgs/nsga/index.html

Naval Air Facility Atsugi, FPO AP 96306

> *Home of Carrier Air Wing 5 (USS Independence).*

> NEW NAF Atsugi
> http://www.atsugi.navy.mil

Sasebo, Kyushu, FPO AP 96322

> U.S. Fleet Activities Sasebo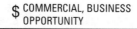
> http://www.cfas.navy.mil

> NEW Amphibious Group One (CTF 76) (Seventh Fleet)
> http://www.ctf76.navy.mil

Yokosuka, Honshu, FPO AP 96601

> U.S. Fleet Activities Yokosuka
> http://metoc.npmof.navy.mil/yoko

>> Public Works Center Yokosuka
>> http://www.pwcyoko.navy.mil/

>> Ship Repair Facility
>> http://www.srfyoko.navy.mil/

> U.S. Naval Forces Japan (PACFLT)
> http://www.navy.mil/homepages/comnavfor-japan/

BASE SCHEDULED TO CLOSE $ COMMERCIAL, BUSINESS OPPORTUNITY   E-MAIL ADDRESS   INTERNAL SEARCH ENGINE

Commander Seventh Fleet (PACFLT)
http://www.c7f.navy.mil/

> *USS Blue Ridge* (*LCC-19*)
> http://www.c7f.navy.mil/ridge/c7fblu.html

> *USS Independence* (CV-62)
> http://www.navy.mil/homepages/comnavfor-japan/indy/indy.htm
>
> *To be replaced forward by the USS Kitty Hawk in mid-1988.*

> Submarine Group 7 (CTF 74)
> http://ctf74.ctf74.navy.mil/csg7.html

Naval Computer and Telecommunications Station Far East (NCTC)
http://www.nctsfe.navy.mil

Yokota AB, Honshu, APO AP 96328-5078

Home also to headquarters Fifth Air Force (PACAF) (PACOM).

Yokota AB and 374th Airlift Wing 📖
http://www.yokota.af.mil/

`NEW` U.S. Forces Japan (USFJ) (PACOM)
http://www.yokota.af.mil/usfj/usfj.htm

Asian Office of Aerospace Research and Development (AFOSR)
http://www.nmjc.org/aoard/

Johnston Atoll

APO AP 96558

U.S. Army Chemical Activity Pacific (USARPAC)
http://www.USARPAC.army.mil/docs/usacap.htm

Chemical weapons storage and disposal activity.

Kuwait

Camp Doha, APO AE 09855

Joint Task Force Kuwait/U.S. Army Kuwait
http://www.kuwait.army.mil

Kwajalein Atoll, Marshall Islands

Kwajalein Missile Range

U.S. Army Kwajalein Atoll (SMDC)
http://www.smdc.army.mil/KMR.html

Panama

Headquarters of the U.S. Southern Command relocated to Miami, FL, in early 1998.

Fort Clayton, APO AA 34004

U.S. Army South (USARSO) and Joint Task Force—Panama (SOUTHCOM)
http://www.army.mil/USARSO/default.htm

Howard AFB, APO AA 34001-5000

24th Wing (Twelfth Air Force, ACC)
http://www.howard.af.mil/

The 24th Wing is also the core of U.S. Southern Air Force Forward.

Naval Station Panama Canal, Rodman, FPO AA 34061

Home to headquarters U.S. Naval Forces Southern Command (SOUTHCOM).

Naval Station Panama Canal 🔍
http://www.ncts.navy.mil/homepages/navsta-panama/default.htm

Marine Forces Atlantic (MarForLant) South (Forward)
http://www.mfs.usmc.mil

Portugal

Lajes Field, Azores, APO AE 09720-5000

65th Air Base Wing (Eighth Air Force, ACC)
http://www.lajes.af.mil

U.S. Forces Azores (ACOM)
http://www.lajes.af.mil/jstaff/jstaff.html

Puerto Rico

Fort Buchanan, APO AA 34040

> NEW Fort Buchanan
> http://www.buchanan.army.mil

Naval Station Roosevelt Roads, FPO AA 34051
✉ roosyrds@smtp.mediacen.navy.mil

> Naval Station Roosevelt Roads
> http://www.nctspr.navy.mil/nsrr/

> Naval Computer and Telecommunications Station Puerto Rico (NCTAMS LANT)
> http://www.nctspr.navy.mil/

> NEW Atlantic Fleet Weapons Training Facility
> http://apollo.netspr.navy.mil/index1.html

Saudi Arabia

Saudi Arabia hosts a variety of Air Force and military units, the Joint Task Force Operation Southern Watch (CENTCOM), the Office of Program Management, the Saudi Arabian National Guard, and the U.S. Military Training Mission.

Eskan Village

> NEW Eskan Village Homepage
> http://www.eskan.swablack.af.mil

Prince Sultan Air Base

> NEW Prince Sultan Air Base
> http://www.psab.aorcentaf.af.mil

South Korea

Camp George

> Area IV/20th Area Support Group
> http://147.242.140.4/

Army Materiel Support Center—Korea
http://143.138.250.38/

Camp Hialeah, Pusan, APO AP 96259

Home to the 19th Theater Army Area Command.

Depot Support Activity—Far East (IOC)
http://www.ddsafe.com

Kunsan AB, APO AP 96264-2090

8th Fighter Wing (Seventh Air Force, PACAF)
http://www.kunsan.af.mil/

Osan AB, APO AP 96267

U.S. Air Forces Korea and Seventh Air Force (PACAF)
http://www.osan.af.mil/

51st Fighter Wing (Seventh Air Force, PACAF)
http://www.osan.af.mil/51fwpgs.htm

Seoul (Yongsan Army Garrison), APO AP 96205
✉ cnfk-pao@emh5.korea.army.mil

★ U.S. Forces Korea (PACOM)/U.S. Army Korea 🔍
http://www.korea.army.mil/

*The commander is also the commander of the ROK-U.S. Combined Forces
Command and the United Nations Command (UNC).*

Office of the Special Adviser to the CINCUNC
http://144.59.76.136/

Prepares a daily media summary of Korean issues for the U.S. command.

Eighth U.S. Army (EUSA) (USFK/PACOM)
http://www.korea.army.mil/usfk/eusa/eusa.htm

U.S. Naval Forces Korea (PACFLT/USFK)
http://144.59.63.170

U.S. Marine Forces Korea (USFK)
http://www.korea.army.mil/usfk/marfork/marfork.htm

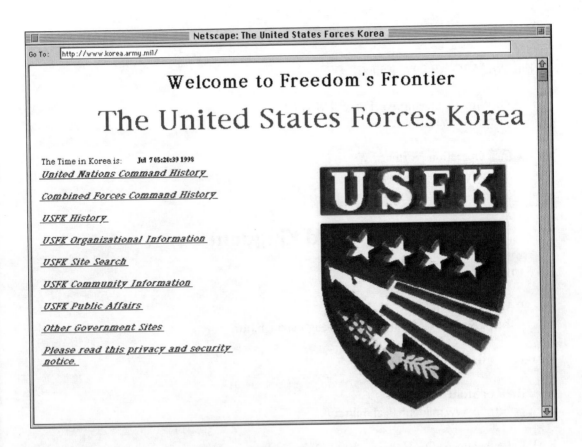

Netscape: The United States Forces Korea
Go To: http://www.korea.army.mil/
Welcome to Freedom's Frontier
The United States Forces Korea
The Time in Korea is: Jul 7 05:20:39 1998
United Nations Command History
Combined Forces Command History
USFK History
USFK Organizational Information
USFK Site Search
USFK Community Information
USFK Public Affairs
Other Government Sites
Please read this privacy and security notice.
USFK

NEW 501st Military Intelligence Brigade
http://www-501mibde.korea.army.mil
http://144.59.245.5/index.htm

Uijongbu, APO AP 09258

2nd Infantry Division (EUSA)
http://www-2id.korea.army.mil/2id.htm

Spain

Rota, FPO AE 09645
✉ paorota@post.ncts1.navy.mil

NEW Naval Station Rota
http://rota.navy.mil

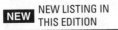

Turkey

Incirlik AB, APO AE 09824-5000

39th Wing (Sixteenth Air Force, USAFE)
http://www.incirlik.af.mil

NEW Operation Northern Watch
http://www.incirlik.af.mil/onw

United Kingdom

RAF Croughton, APO AE 09494

RAF Croughton
http://www.usafe.af.mil/bases/crough/crough.htm

RAF Fairford, APO AE 09456-5000

RAF Fairford
http://www.mildenhall.af.mil/ssu/

RAF Lakenheath, APO AE 09464-5000

48th Fighter Wing (Third Air Force, USAFE)
http://www.lakenheath.af.mil

London, APO AE 09510
✉ cnepao@post.ncts1.navy.mil

NEW U.S. Naval Forces Europe (USNAVEUR) (EUCOM).
http://199.208.201.37

Office of Naval Research Europe (ONR)
http://www.ehis.navy.mil/

*Includes European Office of Aerospace Research and Development (AFOSR);
the Army Research, Development, and Standardization Group—United Kingdom
(AMC); and an extensive collection of ONR Europe Newsletters dealing with
scientific developments of military interest in Europe and the Middle East.*

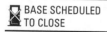 BASE SCHEDULED
TO CLOSE

 $ COMMERCIAL, BUSINESS
OPPORTUNITY

 E-MAIL
ADDRESS

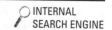 INTERNAL
SEARCH ENGINE

RAF Mildenhall, APO AE 09459-5000
✉ 3afcc@milden.af.mil

RAF Mildenhall
http://www.mildenhall.af.mil

Third Air Force (USAFE)
http://www.mildenhall.af.mil/3af/3af.htm

100th Air Refueling Wing
http://www.mildenhall.af.mil/100arw/100arw.htm

352nd Special Operations Group (AFSOC)
http://hqafsoc.hurlburt.af.mil/352sog.html

RAF Molesworth, APO AE 09470

RAF Molesworth
http://www.molesworth.af.mil/

Acronyms

AAN	Army After Next
AB	Airbase
ACC	Air Combat Command
ACOM	U.S. Atlantic Command
AETC	Air Education and Training Command
AFB	Air Force Base
AFC2N	Air Force Command and Control Network
AFCA	Air Force Communications Agency
AFDD	Air Force Doctrine Document
AFDIR	Air Force directive
AFFTC	Air Force Flight Test Center
AFI	Air Force instruction
AFIS	Armed Forces Information Service
AFIT	Air Force Institute of Technology
AFMC	Air Force Materiel Command
AFMIC	Armed Forces Medical Intelligence Center
AFNS	Air Force News Service
AFOSR	Air Force Office of Scientific Research
AFREC	Air Force Reserve Command
AFRES	Air Force Reserve
AFRL	Air Force Research Laboratory
AFS	Air Force Station
AFSC	Armed Forces Staff College
AFSOC	Air Force Special Operations Command
AFSPC	Air Force Space Command
AIS	automated information system
ALC	Air Logistics Center
ALMAR	All Marines
AMC	Air Mobility Command; Army Materiel Command
AMCOM	Army Aviation and Missile Command
ANG	Air National Guard
APO	Armed Forces Post Office
ARDEC	Army Armament Research, Development and Engineering Center
ARI	Army Research Institute
ARL	Army Research Laboratory
AS	Air Station
ASC	Army Signal Command
ASD	Assistant Secretary of Defense
AU	Air University
BBS	bulletin board system
BMDO	Ballistic Missile Defense Organization
BRAC	base realignment and closure
BUMED	Bureau of Medicine and Surgery (Navy)
BUPERS	Bureau of Personnel (Navy)
C2W	command and control warfare
C3I	command, control, and communications

C4I	command, control, communications, and computers	DCSLOG	Deputy Chief of Staff Logistics
C4ISR	command, control, communications, computers, intelligence, surveillance, and reconnaissance	DCSOPS	Deputy Chief of Staff Operations and Plans
		DCSPER	Deputy Chief of Staff Personnel
		DDN	defense data network
CALL	Center for Army Lessons Learned	DDR&E	Director of Defense Research and Engineering
CBDCOM	Army Chemical and Biological Defense Command	DeCA	Defense Commissary Agency
		DFAS	Defense Finance and Accounting Service
CENTAF	Central Air Forces	DFSC	Defense Fuel Supply Center
CENTCOM	U.S. Central Command	DIA	Defense Intelligence Agency
CHINFO	Chief of Naval Information	DIOR	Directorate of Information Operations and Reports (OSD)
CGSC	Command and General Staff College		
CIDC	Army Criminal Investigation Command	DIS	Defense Investigative Service
		DISA	Defense Information Systems Agency
CIM	Corporate Information Management	DLA	Defense Logistics Agency
CINC	Commander in Chief	DLI	Defense Language Institute
CIO	Central Imagery Office; Chief Information Officer	DLSA	Defense Legal Services Agency
CM	Crystal Mall	DLSC	Defense Logistics Services Center
CNATRA	Chief of Naval Aviation Training	DMA	Defense Mapping Agency
CNET	Chief of Naval Education and Training	DMPA	Defense Medical Program Activity
CNO	Chief of Naval Operations	DMS	defense message system
CS	Crystal Square	DMSO	Defense Modeling and Simulation Office
CSA	Chief of Staff of the Army		
CSAF	Chief of Staff of the Air Force	DMSP	Defense Meteorological Satellite Program
CSS	Central Security Services	DOD	Department of Defense
CTF	Commander Task Force	DODEA	Department of Defense Education Activity
CVW	carrier air wing		
CVX	new aircraft carrier	DODDS	Department of Defense Dependent Schools
DA	Department of the Army	DPSC	Defense Personnel Support Center
DAB	Defense Acquisition Board		
DARPA	Defense Advanced Research Projects Agency	DREN	Defense Research and Engineering Network
DCAA	Defense Contract Audit Agency	DRMS	Defense Reutilization and Marketing Service

DSAA	Defense Security Assistance Agency	JEL	Joint Electronic Library
DSB	Defense Science Board	JIC	Joint Intelligence Center
DSS	Defense Security Service	JP	Joint Publication
DSWA	Defense Special Weapons Agency	JSTARS	Joint Surveillance Target Attack Radar System
DTIC	Defense Technical Information Center	JTF	Joint Task Force
DTSA	Defense Technology Security Administration	LANT	Atlantic
		LANTFLT	U.S. Atlantic Fleet
DUSD	Deputy Under Secretary of Defense	MAG	Marine Aircraft Group
EUCOM	U.S. European Command	MAW	Marine Aircraft Wing
FAC	facility	MCAF	Marine Corps Air Facility
FAQ	frequently asked questions	MCAS	Marine Corps Air Station
FM	Field Manual (Army)	MCB	Marine Corps Base
FMFM	Fleet Marine Force Manual	MCCDC	Marine Corps Combat Development Command
FORSCOM	U.S. Army Forces Command	MDW	Military District of Washington
FPO	Fleet Post Office	MEDCOM	Army Medical Command
FSSG	Force Service Support Group	MICOM	Army Missile Command
Ft.	Fort	MidPac	mid-Pacific
ftp	file transfer protocol	MILSPEC	military specifications and standards
FY	fiscal year	MINEWARCOM	Mine Warfare Command (Navy)
GCCS	global command and control system	MEF	Marine Expeditionary Force
GPS	Global Positioning System	MSC	Military Sealift Command
HQ	Headquarters	MTMC	Military Traffic Management Command
htm, html	hypertext markup (language)	NAD	Naval Aviation Depot
http	hypertext transfer protocol	NAF	Naval Air Facility
IOC	Army Industrial Operations Command	NAS	Naval Air Station
ISC	Army Information Systems Command	NATO	North Atlantic Treaty Organization
ISSC	Army Information Systems Software Center	NAVAIR	Naval Air Systems Command
JAG	Judge Advocate General	NAVFAC	Naval Facilities Engineering Command
JAGNET	Judge Advocates General Network	NAVSEA	Naval Sea Systems Command
JAST	Joint Advanced Strike Technology (Joint Strike Fighter)	NAVSPACECOM	Naval Space Command
		NAVSUP	Naval Supply Systems Command
JBC	Joint C4ISR Center		
JCS	Joint Chiefs of Staff	NAWC	Naval Air Warfare Center

NAWC WD	Naval Air Warfare Center Weapons Division	PAC	Pacific
NCCOSC	Naval Command Control and Ocean Surveillance Center	PACAF	Pacific Air Forces
		PACFLT	U.S. Pacific Fleet
		PACOM	U.S. Pacific Command
NCTAMS	Naval Computer and Telecommunications Area Master Station	PAM	pamphlet
		PEO	Program Executive Office(r)
NCTC	Naval Computer and Telecommunications Command	PERSCOM	Total Army Personnel Command
		PHD	Port Hueneme Division, Naval Surface Warfare Center
NDP	Naval Doctrine Publication		
NDU	National Defense University		
NIMA	National Imagery and Mapping Agency	PM	Program Manager; Project Manager
NISE	NCCOSC In-Service Engineering	RAF	Royal Air Force Base
		RDT&E	research, development, test and evaluation
NORAD	North American Aerospace Defense Command	ROTC	Reserve Officers Training Corps
NPS	Naval Postgraduate School		
NRaD	NCCOSC RDT&E Division	RSIC	Redstone Scientific Information Center
NSA	National Security Agency		
NSGC	Naval Security Group Command	SACEUR	Supreme Allied Commander Europe
		SACLANT	Supreme Allied Commander Atlantic
NSLC	Naval Sea Logistics Center		
NSWC	Naval Surface Warfare Center	SMDC	Army Space and Missile Defense Command
NTTC	Naval Technical Training Center	SPACECOM	U.S. Space Command
		SSC	Space and Naval Warfare Systems Center
NUWC	Naval Undersea Warfare Center		
		SSDC	Army Space and Strategic Defense Command
NWC	National War College; Naval War College		
		SSG	Standard Systems Group (Air Force)
OCHAMPUS	Office for Civilian Health and Medical Program of the Uniformed Services (DOD)		
		STRATCOM	U.S. Strategic Command
		SUBLANT	Naval Submarine Forces Atlantic Fleet
ODISC4	Office of the Director of Information Systems for Command, Control, Communications and Computers (Army)	SUBPAC	Naval Submarine Forces Pacific Fleet
		SURFLANT	Naval Surface Forces Atlantic Fleet
OSD	Office of the Secretary of Defense	SURFPAC	Naval Surface Forces Pacific Fleet
OSIA	On-site Inspection Agency (DOD)	TAACOM	Theater Army Area Command

TACOM	Tank-Automotive and Armaments Command	USARAK	U.S. Army Alaska
		USAREUR	U.S. Army Europe
TECOM	Army Test and Evaluation Command	USARPAC	U.S. Army Pacific
		USD	Under Secretary of Defense
TEXCOM	Army Test and Experimentation Command	USMA	U.S. Military Academy (West Point)
TRADOC	Army Training and Doctrine Command	USNA	U.S. Naval Academy (Annapolis)
TRANSCOM	U.S. Transportation Command	USNAVEUR	U.S. Naval Forces Europe
		USS	United States Navy Ship
UAV	unmanned aerial vehicle	USSOUTHAF	U.S. Southern Air Force
UNC	United Nations Command	WHS	Washington Headquarters Services
USACE	Army Corps of Engineers		
USAFA	U.S. Air Force Academy	WSMR	White Sands Missile Range
USAFE	U.S. Air Forces in Europe	WWW	world wide web

Index

A

Major Numbered Combat Organizations

About the Author

William M. Arkin (**warkin@igc.org**) is a writer and consultant well known for rooting out military information. His reference books on military affairs include *Research Guide to Current Military and Strategic Affairs*, *Encyclopedia of the U.S. Military*, and the *Nuclear Weapons Databook* series. He has written extensively on the Internet, including "The Internet and Strategic Studies" (Center for Strategic Education, Johns Hopkins University School of Advanced International Studies, 1998) and "The Internet and the Bomb: A Research Guide to Policy and Information about Nuclear Weapons" (NRDC, April 1997) (www.nrdc.org/nrdcpro/nuclear).

Arkin is a Visiting Fellow at the National Security Archive, a nonprofit public interest organization in Washington, D.C., that supported the initial research for this book. He also serves as a consultant to the Natural Resources Defense Council (NRDC), the Human Rights Watch Arms Division, *The Washington Post,* and Washington Post Company new media and online subsidiaries. He is also a consultant and news contributor to MSNBC and NBC News. He writes a column for *The Bulletin of the Atomic Scientists*. His articles have also appeared in *The New York Times*, *The Washington Post*, *Los Angeles Times*, the *International Herald Tribune, The Nation, Airpower, Army, Marine Corps Gazette*, and *Washington Quarterly*. He was an Army intelligence analyst from 1974–1978. He lives in South Pomfret, Vermont.